INSIDE THIRD WORLD CITIES

INSIDE THIRD WORLD CITIES

Stella Lowder

CROOM HELM
London & Sydney

© 1986 Stella Lowder
Croom Helm Ltd, Provident House, Burrell Row,
Beckenham, Kent BR3 1AT
Croom Helm Australia Pty Ltd, Suite 4, 6th Floor,
64–76 Kippax Street, Surry Hills, NSW 2010, Australia

British Library Cataloguing in Publication Data

Lowder, Stella
  Inside Third World cities.
  1. Cities and towns——Developing countries
  I. Title
  307. 7'64'091724   HT149.5

ISBN 0–7099–1647–7

Printed and bound in Great Britain
by Billing & Sons Limited, Worcester.

CONTENTS

FIGURES

TABLES

ACKNOWLEDGEMENTS

I wish to thank the following for permission to reproduce figures, or to base figures on material from their publications: the journal *Africa* for Figure 6.1 by Yusuf, which appeared on page 180 of vol. 45; G. Bell and Sons for McGee's model of the South East Asian City used in Figure 7.1, which appeared on page 128 of his book of the same name; *Economic Geography* for Figure 7.4, which is based on Figures 2, 3, 6 and 7 of Sargent's article from pages 360, 362, 366 and 367 in vol. 48; *Geographical Review* for Griffen and Ford's model used in Figure 7.1, which appeared on page 406 in vol. LXX; *GeoJournal* for Davies' model used in Figure 7.5, which appeared on pages 64 and 69 in the second Supplementary Issue; Inter-India Publications for Yadav's model which appears in Figure 7.1: *Journal of Tropical Geography* for Krausse's model in Figure 7.2, which appeared on page 25 in vol. 46; John Wiley and Sons for the map of Bukhara in Figure 2.1 which is based on Giese's which appeared on pages 148–9 in French, R. A. and Hamilton, F. E. I. (eds) (1979) *The Socialist City; L'Espace Géographique* for the map of Tunis in Figure 2.1 which is based on Lowy's which appeared on page 26 of vol. 1; The University of Tokyo for the model by Tanabe in Figure 7.1, which appeared on page 25 of *Proceedings of the Department of Humanities* LXXVIII, Series in Human Geography, vol. 8.

1 PREFACE

When I first came to Britain, I made a note of all the things that differed from my home city of Lima. It was a way of coming to terms with a very different environment but what caught my eye were the contrasts in living standards. I had left a rapidly expanding, primarily commercial city in which just about everything seemed to be made in the USA. A small elite indulged in conspicuous consumption but life for the comparatively modest middle classes revolved around work and family. Education was perceived as the vehicle of both their and the working classes' children's achievements, only the latter had much less access to it. Already there were signs of a subemployed force, whose members spent incredibly long hours not doing very much. Nottingham, where I went to university, was a small city rooted in the coal and lace industries and synonymous with brand names like Raleigh, Player and Boots. Society was far more egalitarian; there was a health service open to all and even slum housing was made of durable materials.

I was reminded of these superficial impressions during a discussion with students about a television programme set in a 'shanty town'. This rapidly led us to consider value systems. As my students struggled to appreciate what sort of shelter is appropriate to a hot and dry environment, I remembered how indifferent I had been to Nottingham's slums *before* I had experienced a British winter. Subconsciously we all interpret reality according to our own value system, which is seldom shared by other cultures and societies. This is why economic and social indicators yield antiseptic formulae, rather than real insight into living standards elsewhere, and why analyses of city-level economic and social structures do not really illuminate the opportunities and constraints that condition daily life. It is difficult to surmount this barrier, even after experience of living within a few Third World Cities. Our historical appreciation, for instance, is biased in favour of the part of the world in which we acquired it; as a result we are uninformed about many regions and hold a different view of events to that of the inhabitants of the others. One cannot spare the time to remedy this ignorance at more than a very general level or for a few places. We are also deterred by language, the sheer volume of new names and incidental facts we must absorb and the range of relevant publications. Perhaps awareness of these limitations is responsible for the mass of material about Third World Cities which appears to have been collected for its inherent interest rather than for a specific purpose.

The study of Third World Cities is daunting for there are few systematic comparative analyses of cities, let alone of those stemming from different regions. Research frequently hints that the structures within them are different to those found in the West but rarely attempts to measure or to develop theory to explain that difference. Does it arise simply from the forms capitalist structures take in much poorer economies, or from the peculiar role played by Third World countries in the world system of trade and finance, as affirmed by Third World economists? To what extent does culture, religion and social organisation contribute to it? How do residents perceive their societies and their own needs and to what extent are their views shared by the state, international companies and institutions? Finally, what tools does one employ in the attempt to answer these questions, for research has tended to proceed through comparison of a Third World context with Western ones by means of the concepts and the methods developed in the latter.

It is necessary to focus such broad questions, for capitalist structures, religion, culture and social ties all transcend city boundaries, while the focus of this book is on life within them. While much research has been concerned with petty enterprise and unauthorised housing, they have been either descriptive or linked to broader economic and social theory, rather than to those of the city as a whole. This book represents an attempt to provide a city-level analysis of the circulation and consumption of goods and services within them. In writing this book I have made certain assumptions: the literature on capitalism in the Third World is very extensive, particularly that concerned with production. I have not allocated much space to reviewing it, as excellent book-length accounts are available. I have also assumed that readers need no instruction in the terms and statistical techniques commonly employed in analyses of Western cities, given their dominance in urban texts. I have tried to strike a balance between referring to a huge number of isolated cities and restricting attention to a few examples which would permit in-depth analysis of their contexts. The cases in each chapter include relevant background material, while the initial chapters concerning indigenous urban traditions and colonial legacies provide regional frameworks for their respective cities.

My personal experience of the Third World is limited to Latin America but I have been fortunate to have much contact with specialists in other regions. Glasgow University has a Centre of Development Studies, as well as an Institute of Latin American Studies. The expertise of my colleagues in the Department of Geography spans the Arab World, China, East Africa and Latin America and two of my research students based their doctorates on Khartoum and Kumasi respectively. Colleagues elsewhere also kindly directed me to references, reacted to arguments and criticised first drafts. I am most indebted to Peg Peil of the Centre of West African Studies at Birmingham University, to Tony O'Connor and Peter Ward at University College, London, to John Soussan at Reading University and David Fox at Manchester University and to the libraries of the Universities at Birmingham, London and Manchester. The book was produced through the efforts of Elisabeth Cousin, who deciphered my writing: Margaret Cape, Każia Kram and Mike Shand drew the illustrations and Ian Gerrard prepared the prints, to all of whom I am most grateful.

Today, Lagos is the most studied and perhaps the most planned urban area in the country. There is an awareness that the multidimensional problems of the metropolis arose because of the unique role it has played in the country's developmental efforts . . . it is evident that success has continuously eluded attempts to solve its problems.

M. A. O. Ayeni, 1981

Almost every development cliché has swept through Lahore. The private efforts have been equally vigorous and persuasive. Even squatter settlements are a proof of peoples' capability to create housing out of nothing. Lahore cannot be described as a city suffering from inaction and neglect . . . All this development has not significantly improved the quality of life in Lahore.

M. A. Qadeer, 1983

This rustification of the urban milieu [of Fez' *medina*] then impels more families of city-stock to leave the city. At the beginning of this demographic movement, the city still offered a very agreeable environment for living; following the change . . . it has become, not uninhabitable — since nearly 250000 people live there — but difficult to live in. In fact its population has trebled in 40 years.

T. Burckhardt, 1980

Behind the relative stability in population was a process of considerable change promoted by the investments of financial institutions and large-scale construction firms . . . The continuous process of urban redevelopment . . . stimulates rapid increase in land and housing prices in the centre [of São Paulo] and the displacement of poorer groups from previous areas of low-income housing.

R. Batley, 1982

An indignant report on the neglect of Beijing put matters more directly: 'Man is a consumer and not merely a producer' and in the city these consumption needs are many and varied — 'electricity, heating, grain, clothing, transport, culture, recreation, health and above all, housing'.

R. J. R. Kirkby, 1985
xii

1 THIRD WORLD CITIES AND THEIR CONTEXTS

Read any newspaper, listen to any broadcast or watch any television news programme in Britain and one cannot escape the impression that cities in the Third World are large, poverty stricken, socially divided and present problems on a scale hitherto unencountered by administrators of their developed counterparts. The events which are considered newsworthy and the manner in which they are presented combine to generate a number of popular misconceptions about Third World cities — that life in them is chaotic and unorganised, that they need help and that institutions which serve cities in Western developed countries may be transferred to them beneficially. These impressions symbolise much of the confusion surrounding these cities in which the ethnocentricity of the viewer plays a part. The media tailor their programmes to their audiences; observations are expressed in terms comprehensible to them, rather than those relevant to the country in which they occur. Of course, Third World cities *do* have substantial populations that are poor by any standards and which lack access to basic utilities but their condition does not arise from rapid population growth and ignorance *per se*; these are symptoms of underlying processes within national economies and societies.

The aim of this book is to counteract some of the superficial impressions about Third World Cities (TWCs). The nature and implications of underlying historical, economic, social and political structures become apparent in the organisation of such facets of city life as housing and provisioning. Research over the last three decades has much improved our understanding of the mechanisms at work in employment, land and housing markets and in structuring retailing. It is becoming evident that the conventional wisdom on how to improve conditions needs to be reconsidered by all concerned. This educative process reiterates two maxims: (a) outward form is not a reliable indicator of the quality or viability of a structure, whether it be physical or administrative; (b) changes that do not touch the underlying factors responsible for generating particular conditions are palliatives beneficial to a few, rather than solutions. These truths need stressing where perceptions are coloured by different cultures and economic systems. It is counterproductive to promote measures based on the principles governing cities in developed contexts and then to attribute their short comings to cultural differences in the Third World setting. Culture is a product of society and what distinguishes TWCs from cities elsewhere is the political and economic constraints within which their societies evolve.

Originally the 'Third World' was a political term applied to those countries which were aligned neither with the Western developed nations of the First World nor with those of the Soviet-dominated Eastern bloc of the Second. Subsequently economic criteria were attached to the term. The Third World consisted of nations with low *per capita* incomes, a high proportion of employment in the rural sector and low ratios of professionals to population. This tendency culminated with the designation of a Fourth World composed of the 40 poorest nations by the World Bank. The wide range in wealth, service provision and employment structure revealed by such economic indicators within the Third World lessen their value as a classificatory device. Furthermore, it is not the type of economic activity so much as the context and its resulting organisation that is distinctive. The Third World consists of those countries whose economies are dominated by the capitalist networks emanating from North America, Western Europe, Australia, New Zealand and Japan. This definition leaves a very few countries in an ambiguous position: Cuba which is now an active member of the Soviet trading bloc and China, which until recently practised autarky. Significantly their cities display features attributable to their different contexts and to the corresponding organisation of society.

The concept of a city also has various connotations. Fundamentally a city is a settlement with certain responsibilities for self-administration; they are usually large, dense and the majority of their residents are occupied in non-rural pursuits. The political criterion alone is not a useful definition for the purposes of a comparative study, as scale is a critical factor in the nature of administrative tasks, while the lack of data precludes the addition of such variables as density and employment. Even the population criterion is difficult to apply worldwide, given the reluctance to publish figures for other than administrative units, the inconsistencies between their boundaries and the functional areas of cities and the periods that lapse between censuses and before their results are published. Nevertheless, population has been considered the most reliable indicator of city status and here a city is considered to be a settlement surpassing 100000 people. There are at least 1051 of these in the Third World, 1234 if one includes China (Table 1.1). These figures understate the situation, as a number of countries have not had censuses for a considerable time. The *Demographic Yearbook* for 1983 contains data for the 1960s for Iraq, Tunis, Libya and Uganda; South Africa and Malaysia's figures are for 1970 while the Lebanon, El Salvador, Colombia and several central American countries report nothing more recent than the early 1970s. If these shortcomings are over-

Table 1.1: Location of Third World Cities (population in millions)

Regions and Countries, sub-regions	.100 .499	.500 .999	1.000 4.999	over 5.000	Total
Africa, sub-Saharan	70	12	5	–	87
Nigeria	25	1	1	–	27
South Africa	12	2	2	–	16
Arab World	76	13	6	1	96
North Africa	42	6	3	1	52
Middle East	34	7	3	–	44
Asia	357	53	32	6	448
India	173	29	9	3	214
Indonesia	24	3	4	1	32
Iran	18	3	2	–	23
Pakistan	18	5	2	1	26
Philippines	22	1	2	–	25
Republic of Korea	28	2	3	1	34
Turkey	20	7	3	–	30
Latin America	366	25	23	6	420
Mexico	47	4	2	1	54
Central America & Carib.	21	3	1	–	25
Brazil	114	4	6	2	126
South America	184	14	14	3	215
Total[a]	869	103	66	13	1051

China	.100 .199	.200 .499	.500 .999	1.000 4.999	over 5.000	Total
municipal estimates[b]	–	128	–	30	7	165
shiqu data 1979[c]	68	72	28	12	3	183

Notes: a. Based on *United Nations Demographic Yearbook* 1983; b. based on *China Map Folio* 1980 and Pannell and Ma 1983, p. 239; c. Kirkby 1985, p. 271.

looked, the accumulated data for regions display remarkably similar patterns; 80 per cent of the cities in sub-Saharan Africa, the Arab World and Asia and 87 per cent of those in Latin America have populations of less than half a million, while 6 to 8 per cent of each have over a million. Three countries, India, Brazil and China dominate the table; they contribute over 40 per cent of the cities while sub-Saharan Africa is the least well represented for even Nigeria contributes only 2 per cent.

The estimation of the population of super cities which exceed five million is complicated. They usually form metropolises which consist of a dominant centre and its subsidiary suburbs or of a conurbation formed when a number of adjoining centres expand and coalesce. However, boundaries may not reflect these formations. Table 1.2 reveals that there is often a considerable difference between the figure for the city 'proper' and its urban agglomeration. In the case of the cities in the United States this reflects extensive urban sprawl: Standard Metropolitan Statistical Areas (SMSAs) are made up of the city and its adjacent counties provided that at least 50000 of their residents are in the core and that two-thirds of their employment is non-agricultural. These rules give rise to SMSAs for Los Angeles, Philadelphia and San Francisco which are over two-thirds the size of their core cities. The cause for the disparity in Chinese cities is their administrative structure. Most publications quote the set of higher figures which represent municipalities; however, these are delimited so as to bind the city to its crucial supply areas of agricultural produce, water and in some cases, even to the mines on which their industries depend. On average over half of their populations are engaged in agriculture. The first set of figures are for the *shiqu* or city district populations of whom 78 per cent are employed in non-agricultural occupations (Kirkby 1985). In other cases an extensive planning region is taken as the urban agglomeration; in Paris' case, this includes 309 communes from adjacent departments, while a whole province of 307572 km^2 is counted for Buenos Aires. The classic conurbation is represented by Greater London which is composed of groups of boroughs corresponding to its Inner and Outer sectors.

The context shared by TWCs is the location of their countries at the periphery of the international capitalist system. The relationship between the expansion of this system and the development of the Third World has been explored by many authors (Brookfield

Table 1.2: The World's Super Cities (populations in millions)

Third World	a	b	First & Second Worlds	a	b
ARAB WORLD			Tokyo 1981	8.335	11.634
			Moscow 1979	7.831	8.011
Cairo 1976	5.074		New York 1980	7.072	16.121
			Chicago 1980	3.005	7.870
ASIA			London 1981	2.498	6.696
			Los Angeles 1980	2.967	11.498
Calcutta 1981	3.291	9.166	Paris 1980	2.176	8.510
Seoul 1980	8.364		Philadelphia 1980	1.688	5.548
Bombay 1981		8.227	San Francisco 1980	.679	5.180
Jakarta 1980	6.503				
Delhi 1981	5.714	6.220	China		
Karachi 1981		5.103			
			Shanghai 1982	6.270	11.810
			Beijing 1982	5.550	9.190
SOUTH AMERICA			Tianjin 1982	5.130	7.780
			Shenyang 1982	4.020	5.140
Mexico City 1979	9.191	14.750	Guangzhou 1982	3.120	5.610
São Paulo 1980	8.493	12.588	Chongquing 1982	2.650	6.510
Rio de Janeiro 1980	5.093	9.014	Changchun 1982	1.740	5.750
Buenos Aires 1980	2.908	9.927			
Lima-Callao 1982	4.410	5.042			

Notes: a. City Proper; b. urban agglomeration.

Sources: *Anuario Estatístico do Brasil* 1983; *Indian Census* 1981; Kirkby 1985; *Census for United Kingdom* 1981; *UN Demographic Yearbook* 1983.

1975; Roberts 1978; Santos 1979). Here only the most obvious characteristics will be outlined. The hallmark of the subordinate role played by the Third World in this system is that their economies are increasingly being structured to respond to its needs. The mechanisms of dependency include the prices of commodities in world markets, the 'favoured nation' status granted by some importers, the activities of transnational companies and their subsidiaries, sources of credit and interest rates. The process was initiated for most countries when they were colonies of European powers. Their rulers increasingly reoriented production to supply imperial markets and siphoned off resources, land and labour from indigenous society in order to do so. Infrastructure generally supported this sector of the economy rather than domestic food production. The dominance of external economic stimuli after independence did not abate. The poverty, lack of natural resources and small populations of some countries made it very difficult to diversify their economies, which were usually based on a single commodity. For them, any downturn in price on the world market or a bad harvest continued to cause a balance-of-payments crisis. Even those producing a range of commodities were not immune to market losses. Such failures rebound on the level of inputs of export-led economies, curtailing their acquisition of essential fuel, transport equipment and machinery. Those with larger and more monied domestic markets tended to industrialise but unless isolated from the international system, such as Latin America during the World Wars, this process has reinforced their subordinate position.

Industrial development fosters new forms of dependence arising from technology which some authors describe as neo-colonialism. Modern industry is dependent on technology introduced by transnational companies or their subsidiaries, who pay the requisite royalty to the holder of the patent. The purchase of such technology entails a higher cost than this, however, as it is designed in contexts in which capital is emphasised at the expense of labour. This is a serious shortcoming for labour-abundant countries. Moreover the lumpiness and sophistication of ready-made technological packages curtail their diffusion to other sectors. The industrial sector is often fragmented as companies become integrated to the networks of rival transnational empires; this structure discourages the development of forward and backward linkages between enterprises within a particular setting. Although many industries are established so as to substitute former imports, their development is conditioned by many factors irrelevant to domestic markets.

A particular form of dependent capitalism consists of offshore manufacturing plants, through which enterprises in the developed countries cut their production costs by substituting the cheaper labour of such countries as South Korea, Taiwan, Hong Kong, Malaysia or Mexico. This activity is generally restricted to those in which a considerable proportion of the costs of production is attributable to labour and which utilise simple or long established technology. As nearly all the raw materials are imported (in bond in the case of Mexico's assembly plants along the border with the United States) and the finished products are exported, the continuity of production depends entirely on the buoyancy of the economies of the developed countries and their willingness to issue permissive trading legislation. There is little the Third World countries can do to influence either factor.

Third World countries are tightly bound to international capitalism and its hard currencies by financial mechanisms. Economic development is financed by soft loans to governments extended by the World Bank, the regional development banks and special aid programmes of the developed countries. These institutions determine the amount, the terms and the purposes to which their credit may be put. This renders borrowers vulnerable to the policies maintained by the operators of the world's most powerful economies. Currently, for example, the United States' practice of deficitory budgeting is bolstered by high interest rates which is reflected in the artificially high value of the dollar. Third World countries see their interest payments on past loans escalate according to these manoeuvres and begin to question the value of the original investments. It is significant that it is the most 'developed' Third World countries like Brazil and Mexico which have the largest outstanding international debts.

These economic characteristics of international capitalism do not occur in a vacuum. Third World societies' principles of organisation are increasingly transformed as social structures are realigned by and along economic interests rather than by kinship, ethnic or religious ties. Social groups defined by such ties may be quite heterogeneous in wealth and poorer or bereft members are integrated through institutionalised reciprocity and patronage. Under capitalism community interests are replaced by class interests which reflect their members' position relative to the factors of production. Classes may be composed of individuals of heterogeneous origin. Societies are continuously adjusting to changes which challenge the established order, whether they arise from population growth, technological innovations or capitalism. In the course of this process groups disintegrate, coalesce and emerge in new forms. Third World societies are complex; capitalist penetration of the economy is uneven so class-based groups can coexist with those based on other interests. Consequently political systems confront pressures generated by very diverse structures and may respond with equally varied and apparently inconsistent policies. It is these internal conflicts and their resolution that underlie many of the observations about life in TWCs.

The impact of the structures discussed is witnessed in the

number and dimensions of the Third World's cities and their growth stimuli (Berry 1976; Friedmann and Wulff 1976). We have noticed the greater proportion of minor cities to super cities and that there are far more of the latter than could be attributed to the dimensions of the urban populations. The seeds of these characteristics were also sown during periods of colonialism, as the forms of development introduced could be managed from comparatively few centres. The scale of capitalist industry also allows domestic markets to be supplied from a single or a very few points. Many cities owe their origins to administrative and service functions rather than the scale of their productive activities. Export-oriented economies emphasise the importance of transport nodes, ports and the capital's political and bureaucratic role. The latter's privileged position is the basis for its attraction for migrants, displaced by the penetration of capitalist structures and increased population in the countryside, while its superior infrastructure and the greater acquisitive power of its population are appreciated by market-oriented industries. These multiplier effects underwrite the primacy of many capitals; rivals only arise when population density and physical distance can support a number of large cities, such as in India, China and Brazil, or where physical barriers ensure the survival of separate sub-systems, as was the case in Colombia up to the 1960s. Otherwise economic structures tend to suck resources from the surrounding region or even the nation to the dominant core, while relatively few benefits trickle back. Even the resulting diseconomies arising from congestion at the centre only seem to encourage decentralisation to adjacent zones which contribute to the metropolitanisation of the capital.

The argument is not that Third World countries have not benefited from the introduction of capitalist structures, nor that the urbanisation that has arisen in response is either good or bad. The focus is on their impact in TWCs which represent the largest concentrations of population affected by them.

A characteristic feature of capitalist enterprises is their reluctance to pay their full costs of production and specifically those of reproducing the labour force. Capitalist interests elude this reponsibility by pressurising the state to invest in urban infrastructure and those types of social overhead capital, such as low cost housing, which are not attractive to private enterprise. The state in turn attempts to recover their expenses by means of taxation and user charges. The conflicts between interests and the social struggles which accompany these processes are particularly poignant in TWCs owing to the fact that capitalist productive systems absorb only a small proportion of the population, while their negative features of pollution, congestion and market domination are suffered by all. Capitalist penetration signifies not only the 'modernisation' of productive systems, or the 'Westernisation' of participants' lifestyles but also a widening gap between the standard of living enjoyed by a minority and that of the majority. Furthermore many measures taken by the state have served to reinforce the advantages of the former and to render life more difficult for the rest.

Observations over the decades within TWCs have caused theoreticians to shift their focus from the outward characteristics of individuals and social groups to those of the constraints under which they operate and finally to the politico-economic framework of the society in which they live. Our understanding of the pro-cesses activating TWCs is based on very fragmented evidence, for research projects are generally confined to single cities or a few in one country and their directors are seldom versed in the literature of more than a single region or continent. Much of the theory developed in Third World contexts is based on Latin American cities and has been only partially tested elsewhere. There are obvious dangers in comparative work of assuming that superficial similarities are indicative of the same processes; this is the challenge of contemporary studies (Abu-Lughod 1975). The literature is studded with concepts which have been jettisoned in favour of more-likely explanations after testing elsewhere; nevertheless research has been mostly confined to the major cities.

After the 1950s, the Third World received much attention. The cold war caused the United States to examine conditions in its 'backyard' of Latin America, while European nations were preoccupied by the changes which led up to the independence of the majority of African and Asian countries. The contrasts in wealth and lifestyle in the capital cities seemed to be a distinctive feature of TWCs and directed research to the plight of the most impoverished residents living in derelict tenements or in makeshift huts erected on any vacant ground, particularly when their number warranted the term 'shanty town'. The initial queries concerned the origins of these people and their lifestyle. An American anthropologist working in Mexico City's tenements examined their survival strategies and formulated the concept of the 'cycle of poverty' (Lewis 1966). He postulated that abject poverty constrained those trapped in it to the extent that it becomes an inherited characteristic of their children. Meanwhile the voluminous research on migration flows to Latin American cities led an Argentinian sociologist to devise the concept of 'marginality', whereby the peripheral location of shanty towns epitomised the isolation of their residents from the city's society (Germani 1980). Both these concepts were utilised to blame the circumstances on the characteristics of the individuals concerned: it was *their* lack of education, improvidence, inability to hold down a job and predisposition for petty crime. To the reactionary, including many states, these were rural hicks who had no place in the city.

Meanwhile a great deal of descriptive data had been and was being collected for TWCs everywhere. This evidence revealed the dualism evident in TWCs employment and housing. Geertz' observations in Indonesia led him to identify 'firm' and 'bazaar' sectors of the economy which differed both in scale and modes of production (Geertz 1963). Hart's analysis of small-scale enterprises in Kumasi was the origin of the 'formal' and 'informal' sectors which were adopted by the ILO in its subsequent analyses of employment in Abidjan (Joshi *et al.* 1976), Calcutta (Lubell 1974), Bogotá (Lubell and McCallum 1978), Jakarta (Sethuraman 1976), São Paulo (Schaefer 1976). Others built on this base, stressing the linkages between the sectors and the presence of intermediaries (Santos 1979; Qadeer 1983). The dualist approach has stimulated considerable research into employment structures, much of which has rejected the utility of such descriptive and classificatory devices. Nevertheless, it is through these critiques that research has come to focus on how capitalist enterprises make use of and tolerate other modes of production operating in the less profitable spheres of the urban economy (Bromley and Gerry 1979). Housing theory has gone through similar stages. Observations in Lima counteracted the negative stereotyped image of shanty towns and their dwellers and were later developed into a theory of urban evolution (Turner 1967, 1968). These arguments were so influential with aid donors that 'site and service' programmes have been widely adopted as a means by which the poor may attain decent housing over time (Payne 1984). Nevertheless the ability of 'self-help' mechanisms to produce sufficient and adequate housing is determined by the capitalist system which structures the 'formal' housing and land markets (Ward 1982; Burgess 1985).

As the research which developed these concepts evolved, greater attention was devoted to the state and its role in society. It was the state that eradicated or tolerated squatter settlements, hounded or acknowledged their inhabitants, replied to neighbourhood demands for services and shaped land and housing markets by planning mechanisms. It was evident that states generally chose to react in favour of particular groups and that its behaviour was tailored to the type of group. It was the state that accepted or rejected the 'cult of development' promoted by international advisors and aid programmes, most of which have introduced Western solutions for transport, housing and utility problems. External finance, technology and planning methods have reinforced the interests of capitalist entrepreneurs trading land, producing building materials or supplying services at the expense of small scale land owners, producers and suppliers. The state condones the mechanisms surrounding economic behaviour in general and decides to what extent they should be allowed to bar the access of the majority to housing, production and finance. Theory arising from these issues reflects the whole spectrum of political ideology; much of this work has focused on the formation of communities, their political behaviour and their relationships with the state (Barnes 1977; van der Linden 1981; Gilbert & Ward 1984).

The implications of the penetration of capitalist structures are vast; the relevant studies concern the macro economics of cities, urbanisation, regional analysis, and sectoral analyses of their employment and housing markets. National level statistics intermingle with survey data collected in a single city among these; it is less common to find syntheses of the structures surrounding several sectors, such as employment and housing, for a city or analyses which assess the generality of the findings to other cities. Furthermore case studies are often confined to particular neighbourhoods like shanty towns, or to a social group defined by ethnicity or poverty. Studies tend to convey either a very general picture or a very detailed glimpse; neither provides an overall view as to what it is like to manage and live in TWCs.

Inside Third World Cities

The emphasis in this book is on the internal structures of TWCs and how they evolve. Large cities do not arise in a vacuum; they are part of a continual process of change generated by external stimuli and internal pressures and moulded by their heritage. Here we are concerned with the mechanisms through which change is expressed, such as legislation and government action, the provision of finance, by whom and for whom, and by daily eating habits. It is difficult to assess the generality of such patterns, as the source material consists mostly of case studies and invariably these are more numerous for a particular region for any aspect. Efforts have been made to provide a general overview of each theme by including a wide range of examples, while the detailed case studies refer to cities representing each of the major regions of the Third World. TWCs as a whole are examined by means of the many models devised to describe and explain their morphology. Thus the chapters form three sections: the first concerns the heritage of TWCs by examining their structure prior to and during the period of European colonisation. For clarity, events occurring before the latter are referred to as 'indigenous' and the term 'colonisation' has been reserved for European domination. The second section is composed of Chapters 4, 5 and 6 which analyse three facets of contemporary TWCs: the structure of their administration, housing, and retailing. The last section evaluates the utility of models applied to and devised for TWCs. Most of the latter have not been tested out of the original context, although the principles on which they were based may have much in common.

The need to examine 'indigenous' and European colonial legacies stems from the series of omissions and emphases current in general literature which cloud our understanding of their contribution to the contemporary TWC. Little attention has been paid to 'indigenous' urban institutions compared to those introduced by Europeans; indeed some authors dismiss them as primitive, scarce and mostly obliterated by subsequent events anyway. The use of tags such as 'pre-industrial', 'partially urban' or 'traditional' implies an unwarranted degree of homogeneity and does not prepare one for the wonderment and admiration expressed by travellers, traders and even *conquistadores*, who often considered the cities they encountered richer and better organised than their European homes. Of course pre-European cities were far from homogeneous or static. The religion, technology and institutions introduced by some earlier conquerors were arguably at least as alien to Third World city populations as any of those imposed by Europeans. The meanest city can reveal a complex genealogy, having been subjugated by neighbouring states or overrun by a more distant military empire or through having received contingents of refugees or immigrants at various periods of its history. City populations fluctuate greatly with the waxing or waning of their political and economic fortunes, sometimes as a result of environmental pressures. Any long standing city's customs reflect the fusion of many traditions acquired from diverse sources. Even empires were seldom able to impose their particular systems in an exact form over great distances, given the quality of communications before the introduction of motorised transport and the logistics involved in changing the habits of daily existence.

A city represents a high level of political, economic and social organisation. Its existence is tangible evidence of the concentration of surplus food which has been either appropriated through coercion (tribute and taxation), or exchanged for other goods and services. This can only happen where elites exist to control production and distribution and where specialisation of activity occurs. They must defend their status and also acquire technical skills to manage their economy and water supplies. A society needs to develop a structure of interlocking roles in order to co-ordinate all these facets of city life. Once developed, the conventions surrounding such fundamentals are not easily displaced by a new authority, although the latter may sack a city, depose individuals, exact new taxes or impose new gods. Moreover innovations frequently undergo subtle adaptations in a different environment; new and old practices co-exist and the emergent dominant form often represents an amalgam of the most useful attributes of both, which in turn undergoes further transformation.

The motives underlying conquest, whether by indigenous chieftain or ambitious European, were power/status and profit but these can be achieved by diverse means and at different scales. For most centuries, power was symbolised by the number of men a ruler could command. Profit consisted of tribute exacted in kind and men which allowed him to maintain his armies and surround himself with the symbols that accorded with his status. Powerful rulers were able to legitimise their position through the institution of religion, the support of large retinues of officials and the patronage of specialists — artisans, the arts and learning. Empires depended on their administrative skills and most developed sophisticated accountancy methods, currency and rules of exchange. Under such political forces, a city's size, functions and importance reflected the military potential of its ruler, as this correlated with the size of his army and area from which he could exact tribute. It was in the interest of foreign traders (as opposed to pirates) to co-operate with rulers. In this manner indigene and European appraised each other's customs initially and adopted those which seemed of practical value in furthering their transactions.

After the fifteenth century such contact was overshadowed by the European technological advantage of firearms. The temptation to seize what could be obtained easily, especially where the peoples encountered could be considered in need of 'civilising' for the sake of their souls, lay behind the conquest of the Americas. Elsewhere European states became involved on a large scale much later, in response to traders' complaints that their interests and property were under threat. This pressure increased when the innovations of the eighteenth and nineteenth centuries allowed trade at a hitherto unimaginable scale and increased the competition between Europeans for both materials and markets. As a result, substantial settlements could arise in response to rationales other than their immediate resource base and a new element was inserted into intergroup transactions: the official appointed directly from Europe and intending to return there, who was generally ignorant and often indifferent to local institutions and yet granted considerable freedom to act, given the distance separating him from his superiors. Such officials might be able, study local institutions and genuinely attempt to promote local welfare; often they found themselves trying to restrain the exploitative tendencies of the trading companies, whose representatives were exerting pressure at home to get them removed. Many officials adopted easier roles; the appointees of every European colonial power included a few despots, many upright but not necessarily enlightened officials and others concerned about not upsetting private vested interests.

The colonial periods represented power struggles between multiple actors with often unclear or conflicting goals. These included the pursuit of Empire by military forces encouraged by European entrepreneurs; the management of a peaceful territory by administrators, whether in liaison with or despite indigenous leaders; the maintenance of status by said leaders, whose behaviour ranged from ethnic solidarity to the exploitation of their subjects; the open pursuit of profit, sometimes by unscrupulous means, on the part of European entrepreneurs. The European colonial phase involved the creation or modification of settlements according to the priorities of exogenous interests wishing to extract profit with the use of minimum financial investment and manpower. The key to their success was control over the land, labour and mineral resources and the methods used to acquire it. The nature of the activity conditioned the type and scale of administrative control exerted, which was reflected not only in the number and character of the settlements but also in the identity of their residents, their rights and the infrastructure deemed appropriate to their needs.

Even if indigenous settlements were not physically destroyed, they could not remain immune to the disruption of the broader economic systems in which they had been embedded. In areas not favoured with attractive resources, the population might be forced to migrate long distances to perform corvée labour or to work so as to pay taxes exacted in cash. In richer agricultural zones, either through sheer ignorance, misunderstanding or deliberate policy, totally new concepts of property were often imposed; these usually resulted in the concentration of rights for a few while those of a major sector of the population were set aside. In either case, the transformation or erosion of previous economic bases detracted from the ruler's former role and further undermined the structure of local society. Settlements catering purely for indigenous needs stagnated, less resources were dedicated to essential communal facilities and existing roads, wells and buildings deteriorated. Neither were conditions in the new cities ideal, given the general unwillingness to invest more than the strictly essential to house expatriates, the military and maintain their workforce. In the few instances where full responsibility for the latter was accepted, such as in Central and East Africa, it was at the expense of the basic freedom of movement of the indigenous population. Such a degree of social control was unusual but the allocation of specific neighbourhoods to those of common origin was common to both indigenous and colonial rulers.

The colonial regimes over a wide area of the Indian subcontinent, South East Asia and Africa south of the Sahara did not attempt to merge their customs with those they encountered: they distanced themselves through the maintenance of separate codes of practice. With the rapid territorial expansion of the contemporary city this has given rise to legal morasses, for different conventions were applicable to the several sectors of a single city, as is evident from the tortuous operations of property markets, inequity in the distribution of utilities and the poor development of support for urban institutions. A major bequest of the colonial experience outside Latin America was the institutionalised inequality of living conditions between a city's districts according to the ethnic identity of its residents.

The key spheres affecting the efficient management of the contemporary city concern the identity and powers vested in city administrations, the amount of the revenues they control, the powers attached to, and the degree of concentration of, urban land and property and the capacity and/or willingness of the residents to pay for housing, utilities and goods. Government is paramount in the definition of the first three parameters, which all tend to embody inherited institutions and customs. Even when new constitutions established an entirely different set of ideals from those current in colonial times, very few countries have found the time and will to revise the legal codes and administrative procedures through which they could be implemented. As a result of such experiences, most contemporary cities in the Third World are trying to operate with a heterogeneous collection of political, legal and administrative practices that are ill-suited to their social and economic realities. In their euphoria over attaining independence, many governments designed idealistic constitutions and rejoiced over the departure of each expatriate. Given the period of their independence, the new fledged Latin American states did not face the same demographic and political pressures. Elsewhere, economic realities soon focused the attention of the states' most able citizens. Concern over national development and the control of natural resources took precedence over that of city administration. The capital cities certainly acquired some flamboyant buildings to house government institutions and to symbolise their new international status, but such 'one-off' projects hardly affected the lifestyle of the typical African or Asian migrant attracted by the razzledazzle surrounding the independence celebrations. Furthermore, the desire to reduce economic dependency stimulated states, including those in Latin America, to encourage the introduction of import-substitution industries. While the objectives of such policies were argued in national terms, the repercussions of consumer-oriented industries included the continuous streams of migrants to the capitals and major cities likely to receive such investment. As a great many studies have shown, few cities anywhere in the world have ever had to face such great absolute and relative population growth rates for such a long period, as those of the Third World in the decades following the Second World War.

The institutions and mechanisms of any system are not easy to change in the second half of the twentieth century. Business transactions must proceed, people must live and one cannot change the basic rules by which they do so overnight. However, when these are not understood, are tortuous, time-consuming, expensive and/or ludicrous, they tend to be ignored and replaced by *de facto* conventions. The authorities have the choice of turning a blind eye, taking a bribe or protesting and prosecuting. The action taken is determined by the scale and social acceptability of the practice. However, this is difficult to ascertain when 'the state' is made up of a small or factionalised elite; here it is easy for an official to become the scapegoat of offended vested interests. Moreover, the rapid expansion of TWCs generates considerable confusion, as the structures of different activities and groups adapt at variable speeds to the changes. There is ample scope for capitalist and non-capitalist systems to dominate different sectors of the markets for utilities, houses and goods. Generally legislation is slow to adjust to these realities. There are very few major cities in the 1980s which claim that the scale of the non-compliance with by-laws and planning ordinances is anything but ubiquitous and commonplace. Commonly *ad hoc* resolutions are passed when hopeless impasses become blatant or politically inconvenient. The result is legislation which is amended by decree and which often displays the retrospective acknowledgement of the *fait accompli*.

Physically the cities continue to evolve primarily according to the accumulation of self-interested actions of individuals. Some states have intervened directly in land and property markets and may have attempted to direct development through taxation and/or planning legislation. Most have recognised the need for state control if not ownership of urban utilities. Nevertheless these measures have generally been insufficient to promote a more equitable distribution of basic resources to all sectors of the population. Elsewhere the initiative has rested primarily with individuals whose wealth and power are reflected in the scale of the impact of their decisions. Moreover, city authorities have come to appreciate that the individually minute investments of the very poor are highly significant when grossed up according to their numbers in the population. High-handed control over their actions is only possible under a repressive regime and in any case only postpones confrontation of the problems. No partial account of diverse aspects of comparatively few Third World cities can hope to offer a solution to these problems. However, greater understanding of the constraints inhibiting changes necessary to expedite political, administrative, financial and legal mechanisms which deal with them is an essential first step. As these mechanisms are an amalgam of various traditions and all individuals' actions are guided by perceived customs, some appreciation of the origins, role and utility of these in the daily life of the contemporary city is also invaluable.

A city embodies more than the structures which organise its activities and groups, for these mechanisms also serve to allocate them to spaces such that the most favoured locations are occupied by the most profitable or highly regarded land uses and the wealthiest or highest status citizens. Space is a medium through which status may be expressed or attained: a given location bestows on its holders a particular bundle of opportunities arising from their accessibility to employment, services and housing. There have been many attempts to model the complex patterns of land uses and distribution of social groups in cities. Most of those devised for Western cities have been applied to TWCs. Application in a mechanical and descriptive manner demonstrates their shortcomings: description is no substitute for explanation and similar forms result from different processes. Western cities are the product of their particular historical contexts which will never be duplicated in the Third World. The application of models based on different societal concepts means that certain aspects of life in TWCs are measured by an inappropriate yardstick. The treatment of unexplained differences as mere cultural 'noise' in the system is intellectually unacceptable but many authors use these devices as a means of pinpointing differences which require explanation. Here models serve as a point of departure, rather than as a tool of synthesis.

A number of models have also been devised to portray the behaviour of migrants, entrepreneurs and the state. Possibilist and liberal ideologies have been uppermost in those analysing intra-city movements and the contribution of private enterprise to urban development. These have been refuted by those focusing on the constraints which condition the search for housing or consider the impact of the state's action on social groups. The value of these approaches is far greater than their static counterparts. Unfortunately they have been tested less widely outside the contexts in which they were devised.

Omissions

Studies must have definable limits and yet cities are not closed systems. The concentration on processes operating within cities in this book is justified by the far greater volume of comparative work analysing the impact of capitalist structures at the national and regional levels published. The two main types of processes omitted which link cities to these broader levels concern migration and employment. Specialist studies in these areas are also split between macro- and micro-scale approaches, being based on either statistics for the largest administrative divisions, or survey data collected in a particular type of neighbourhood, or for a specified group. Both fields suffer from the lack of clear-cut terms which are meaningful and easily handled by respondents. Both are forced to convey a static view of extremely mobile and fluid situations.

Migration studies were very commonplace in the 1960s and 1970s and betrayed states' alarm and academics' fascination over the rate of growth of TWCs. The three main thrusts of this research included:

(a) estimates of permanent as opposed to temporary migrants. All large cities contain a floating population generated by temporary circumstances; their governments may have to provide emergency relief but the solution to these peoples' problems lies elsewhere. However many recent arrivals do not perceive their sojourn as 'permanent' and yet stay for many years, while others alternate between city and country in a permanent pendular pattern (Findlay 1977; Gugler and Flanagan 1977; Cooper 1983).

(b) analyses of migration patterns, including stage, chain and cyclical networks. These studies are popular among regional analysts, as migration is an indicator of the links between members of an urban hierarchy (Todaro 1976; Lowder 1978).

(c) descriptions of the characteristics of new residents. These have practical value for the economic and city planner projecting the demand for employment, housing, school places and so on. Academics have been more interested in how migrants become integrated to city society (Barnes 1979; Lewandowski 1980; Perlman 1976).

Employment studies face fundamental difficulties over concepts, foremost of which is the definition of employment. Official records of employment are the least reliable of any collected in TWCs, as the term is applied to work carried out on terms and in conditions comparable to Western cities. Estimates of the workforce to which this applies range anywhere between 15 and 40 per cent in TWCs. These calculations are based on definitions of the 'formal sector' alluded to earlier. The rest of the population are self-employed or work in small-scale units. Few are insured or receive a prede-termined salary on a regular basis. Even fewer can afford to be idle; one can always collect waste or stand around a market or bus station waiting for a chance to carry goods if all else fails. Often children must also contribute to their maintenance. In these cir-cumstances estimates of employment are hazardous and of the unemployed, ludicrous. Those in need are not aware of registers and would not waste their time on such devices, as employers of casual labour rarely use official channels to obtain it.

It is not the nature of the jobs *per se* that is of importance to the TWC but the rewards accruing to those that perform them. These are also very difficult to assess. Apprentices in African cities often work free or pay their master for the opportunity to learn a trade; they may get their meals and a corner to sleep in. Artisans' incomes vary according to how many items they manage to sell on any particular day and market vendors consume left-over foods and the residue from their takings once the next day's stock has been secured. Members of family enterprises often receive no pay other than a share in the living conditions sustained by it. Even those that do have a salaried occupation often hold a secondary job or supplement their income 'on the side'.

In these circumstances it is also impossible to assess working conditions in a standardised way. A great many people work in the street or on waste ground; they may be prosecuted by the police for occupying public space or selling defective goods but that does not change the fact as to how they gain their livelihood. People 'work' incredibly long hours waiting for purchasers or patiently beating out tin cans to obtain the metal for their products. Children assist well before the legal age for employment and pregnant women and mothers with infants have to carry on regardless of their condition.

One can see why the ILO appreciated the limitation of their standard concepts concerning employment and chose to adopt the 'formal–informal' device as an analytical tool. The fact remains that it is almost impossible to gather reliable sets of comparable data for TWCs. A short account cannot improve on the specialist studies alluded to and a sound appreciation of the data available may be gained by reading the compendium of case studies edited by Sethuraman (ILO 1981) and the critical arguments voiced by Streefland (1977), Bromley and Gerry (1979) and Santos (1979).

2 INDIGENOUS URBAN TRADITIONS

Indigenous urban traditions have endured in many TWCs to this day. Unfortunately this does not apply to the Pre-Columbian societies of Latin America, as their populations were decimated by the diseases which accompanied the *conquistadores*. However, zones with much longer and deeper planted urban traditions, the Islamic heartland and the Indian subcontinent, or in West Africa where the colonial phase was comparatively late and of short duration, have retained many social traits. It is these areas which merit attention, although a short review can provide only a glimpse as to how cities were structured.

Indigenous urban traditions are far from simple; their variety and cultural underpinnings elude generalised descriptions. Superficial comparisions are misleading, as the observations stem from different periods and refer to disparate population bases. It is difficult to define urban qualities which can be applied meaningfully across time. Much of our knowledge of the dwellers of earlier cities was recorded by biased strangers: descriptions were provided by conquerors, proselytisers, merchants and much later by the merely curious. Often they reveal as much about the societies of the viewers as about what they saw. Moreover, the circumstances in which they made their observations were hardly conducive to open or customary behaviour on the part of the residents. Accounts tend to exaggerate military details, emphasise the exotic and the splendid and to omit the commonplace aspects of daily life of the majority of the residents. Nevertheless such accounts serve to provide a salutary reminder that many TWCs have very early origins and that the levels of sophistication achieved within them are worthy of considerable pride.

Many contemporary city officials have cause to regret their dismissal of indigenous traditions. Frequently they have proved to be the explanation for the rejection of an innovation, the lack of co-operation with a project or the transformation of a measure into something quite unsuspected. Furthermore, given the inability of contemporary city administrators to provide all the essential communal facilities, indigenous mechanisms continue to

22

cover the deficit. TWCs cannot afford to ignore the initiatives of their citizens, whatever form they take.

The Islamic Sphere

Islamic influence dominates discussion of the Middle Eastern city but Islamic empires constituted but a comparatively recent phase of the area's lengthy urban history. Although military conquest, spreading from Saudia Arabia in the seventh century, had incorporated a vast territory by the ninth, stretching westwards through North Africa (the *Maghreb*) and Spain and eastwards through the Middle East (the *Mashriq*) and northeastwards to the Balkans, Persia, Afghanistan, Central Asia, and even as far as India, conversion and the adoption of customs other than those imposed by force were much more gradual processes. The Empires were nearly always under attack at the margins by the Byzantines, the Crusaders, the Persians, the Mongols and numerous lesser known groups; within, successive dynasties arose, dominated a greater or lesser territory and were overtaken, in the course of which particular settlements might be greatly favoured or destroyed according to their peoples' affiliations. Take the fates of the cities depicted in Table 2.1, for example. Although the chronology has been grossly simplified, it illustrates the way they all passed through the hands of half a dozen empires and with the exception of Damascus, suffered severe damage during the crusades, or at the hands of nomads, pirates, the Mongols, or other dynastic rulers. The political fulcrum passed from the Abbāsid capital of Baghdād in the eighth century to Cairo, as the Fatimid and Mamlūk capitals of the tenth and twelfth centuries and eventually to Istanbul, as the seat of the Ottomans in the fifteenth. During their apogee, these cities supported populations of half a million or more, which then fell to perhaps half that number when the spatial patterns of commerce and taxation altered. Likewise smaller cities arose when made the lesser capitals of subordinate rulers and fell on their demise.

With such complex histories, it is risky indeed to imply that an 'Islamic' city with common features existed or exists today. The Islamic ruler who planted his capital on a Byzantine base with a history going back a thousand years inherited a heterogeneous collection of traditions and peoples which were totally lacking in his contemporary's military encampment in the *Maghreb*. Then,

Table 2.1: The Fate of Selected Islamic Cities over the Centuries

MAGHREB			MECCA heartland	MASHRIQ		
Rabat-Sale	*Tunis*	*Cairo*	*Time*	*Damascus*	*Baghdad*	*Istanbul*
Phonenians 300 BC AD 690	Tenes 1000 BC Carthage 814/698 BC AD 670/698	Memphis 3000 BC AD 641	**Origins ARAB arrival**	2000 BC AD 635	Built as dynastic capital by Al-Mansur in AD 754	AD 330
	Dynastic functional capital; deposed; stagnated; pirates	Fustat founded; Al-Qatai built; destroyed; plague, famine, earthquake;	**900**	Provincial capital Fatimid dynasty	Mamlūk governors Shi'i dynasty builds on left bank of Tigris	Turkish incursions
1030 Sala founded additions made	control of Normans of Sicily	Fustat burned; new town dominant	**1000**			absorbed into Seljüg empire
		Saladin	**1100**	Seljūg province	Sunnī Seljūgs 1258 Mongols Persian province 1401 sacked by Mongols again	
new dynasty: Rabat built, left, rebuilt. Sala chief port; Rabat abandoned			**1200**	Saladin's dynasty		
	Dynastic capital, thriving new dynasty	Mamlūk caliphate capital; growth; plagues & famines; port spice trade to China; pop. 500 000	**1300** **1400**	Mongols sack city Mamlūk control		1243 outlier of Mongol province 1455 capital of Ottoman empire 1520/35 pop. 400 000
		> tax, < trade	**1500**	1517 Ottoman control	1508 Shi'i 1534 Sunni Ottomans	

	1600	1700	1800	colonial phase
	Rabat refounded Moriscos flee to Sala: piracy institutionalised	1766 piracy suppressed by treaty	1828/31 exports via Casablanca	Spanish Sahara 1884 French colony 1912
	1530 conquered by Ottomans base for piracy			French colony 1881
	Ottomans demote to provincial capital; stagnation, decline	French occupation, effect in planning.	Albanian dynasty reforms & sanitation 1847 pop. 300 000	French colony 1881 French mandate 1917/46
			1800 pop. 100 000	French occupation 1798/1801. Nominally British 1883/1914
	1623/5 Safavids alternates between Ottomans & Safavids		1813 Ottomans plague 1835 pop. 60 000	British 1917/28
	1650s pop. 6–700 000 1750s pop. 700 000		1800 pop. 6–900 000 1900 pop. 1 million	threatened but forstalled by revolution

too, a ruler's armies, or he himself, might come from Anatolia, present-day Syria, Saudia Arabia or the *Maghreb*, each of whom had separate traditions. Some cities, such as Baghdad, became a battleground between different factions of Islam, alternating between Shī'ī and Sunnī control. Nevertheless, while acknowledging these substantial differences, there are a number of generalisations which are applicable to many cities in the area.

Today we perceive the 'city' as the opposite of rural; its far more complex and differentiated roles are co-ordinated by a range of relatively impersonal institutions. A city in the Middle East, while being larger in scale, did not necessarily have those connotations. They housed a number of heterogeneous factions, each organised on highly personalised lines; their religious and commercial institutions included members from suburban and surrounding villages; in some cases key figures of the government and of commerce resided outside the walls, while populations within engaged in farming surrounding land.

> In fact, in many situations, no absolute distinction between urban and rural habitats may be drawn . . . [they being] knit together by elements of social organization; [they] interpenetrate or resemble each other in some geographical and ecological aspects. Larger settlements . . . were not generally distinct entities, but most often composites of lesser units. Settlements of all types . . . were clusters of distinct physical and social units. (Lapidus 1969, p. 60)

Lapidus argues furthermore that city people were attached to persons and institutions, rather than to a place of residence; there was considerable movement between settlements, as long as the state was strong enough to enforce peace and maintain intercommunity relationships.

During the Islamic expansionist phase, the dominant means of travel and trade was by camel and caravan; the focus of their communications was inland, away from the exposed Mediterranean coasts. Moreover throughout the Middle East the harsh environment restricted the choice of site for settlement. The Islamic empires were frequently the product of military castes of slave origin; these garrisons with no local roots kept tight control over subject peoples, extracting taxes on all manner of products and providing little in return. The *caliphs* appointed regional governors who chose their base of operations. Often these were attached to existing cities, as separate suburbs, or set up at a short distance, so as to draw attention to their dominance while paying heed to security and the separation of loyal and conquered peoples. Entirely new settlements were often very rough short- lived encampments. The governor's functions were primarily defence, law and order and financial; his staff consisted of a police superintendent, watchmen and guards, tax collectors and accountants.

The prosperity of the city rested with the state. The state determined the status of the governor and consequently, the size of the retinue which he brought to swell its population and its market. Taxes were imposed on production, both agricultural and artisanal. In many areas tax farmers — those responsible for the collection of rural taxes and recompensed through the retention of a share of the revenue gathered — resided in the cities. This concentration of revenues, especially in the richer, more densely populated regions, attracted even larger numbers of craftsmen and traders. It has been thought these were highly organised by occupational guilds. There is ample evidence that the Ottomans used guilds as an administrative means to control both the population and the economy but such use would appear rare elsewhere and before 1500. Everywhere, however, artisans were taxed according to the nature of their goods, as were the traders in the *sūqs* and the merchants travelling between cities. There is evidence that governors ordered the periodic registration of all residents so as to update the taxation accounts.

After Islam had become consolidated in the core area by the eleventh century, a new urban-based elite emerged, the *ulamā*, the teachers and interpreters of the Koran and the *Sharī'ah*. Ironically, while they became a significant element in urban administration, they also became an additional source of factionalism, for many cities included adherents of more than one of the four recognised schools of interpretation, which at times were bitterly hostile to one another. The principal *ulamā*, the *qāḍī*, were appointed by the *caliph*. They presided over the schools (*madrasahs*) attached to the mosques and their activities included leading prayer, recital and study of the Koran, the reconciliation attempted in civil and personal cases of strife, the welfare of the indigent and those in need of protection and the management of pious foundations. The third element in the cities were the *shaykh* or appointed headmen of each community, who were often held responsible for events in it. Latter additions included the *muftī*, a sort of consultant in jurisprudence and notary public and the *muhtasib*, who acted as a guard of public morality in the spheres of commerce and production. This consumer protection service involved patrolling *sūqs* and public places, checking weights and measures, professional qualifications, the cleanliness of baths and streets, the treatment of school children and apprentices and the safety and aspect of buildings. He could warn, fine, confiscate, administer physical chastisement and even drum the utterly incompetent out of business. Under the Ottomans, the office also became involved in tax collection.

Today *qāḍī* and *muhtasib* can still be found in some cities in North Africa, although their powers are limited to the religious sphere as secular officials have been appointed to manage the cities. However, in view of the dominance of Muslim fundamentalism over state institutions in Iran, Libya and since 1983, in the Sudan, it would seem unwise to write off these traditional religio-political officials as members of irrelevant and archaic institutions in the cities within the Islamic sphere of influence.

The physical forms of the cities betrayed their diverse origins. Only a foundation by a prominent ruler, such as the Abbāsid capital of Baghdād, or the suburban creation of Eṣafahān, could achieve the clear-cut design of a master planner. As was usual in troubled times, cities were walled and their governors resided in citadels erected in commanding positions. But most major settlements had had extensions added for the household and garrison attending a new ruler, while other parts decayed or were destroyed, particularly when their populations fell. Travellers frequently comment on ruins and discontinuities observed within the built-up area. Various parts acquired distinctive identities, which can often be attributed to the incorporation of a large body of newcomers, such as a military unit, a ruler's retinue, a transferred population or Morisco refugees. Fez, Rabat, Cairo, Safià, Eṣafahān and Damascus all acquired a distinctive suburb or two from such events. In the fifteenth century, Jewish districts were often designated so as to facilitate their protection; clustering was fostered by Jewish, Christian and Muslim domestic practices because of their different sacred days and attitudes to women. Spatial concentrations on the basis of religion, kinship, language, place of origin and period spent in the city were common in many cities but segregated homogenous populations were unlikely, given that physical, historical and economic factors also contribute to a district's identity. Explanations for such patterns have been attributed to common occupations, ethnic ties and migrational histories.

The cities were a tangible manifestation of Islamic relationships which whether religious, economic or familial were translated into spatial terms (Figure 2.1). For instance, the lack of any corporate bodies in a society composed of state and subjects obviated the need for public buildings and communal meeting places. Only after the eleventh century did mosques begin to proliferate, the existence of a Friday Mosque often being considered the symbol of city status. The mosque complex performed a variety of functions, being not only a centre of instruction in the broadest religious and juridical sense but also the hub of a range of welfare functions and their administration. As cities spread, so did the number of mosques built to serve suburbs out of earshot of the existing ones. The relative status attached to economic activities was also mirrored in space. Gates controlled access to the city, permitting the scrutiny not only of strangers but also control over the passage of goods and the exaction of taxes from merchants. The major thoroughfares led from these gates to the bazaars or *sūqs*, which often exhibited a degree of specialisation in their wares. Some cities inherited colonnades within which to erect stalls, while in others the roadway was encroached on to such an extent that eventually it became completely roofed over, light and air being admitted through regularly spaced skylights. Within these, clean and highly valued goods, such as books and prayer mats, were located near the central foci, the mosque and its attendant institutions. Cumbersome, dirty and less valuable goods, such as firewood or charcoal, the products of potters and butchers, would be sited nearer the gates. The difficulty of penetrating the narrow streets and the lack of open space reinforced this arrangement.

The arrangement of rights of way and residential zones would appear to be the product of urban accretion, as well as a logical solution to environmental and social needs. Given the intensity of sunlight and resulting high temperatures throughout much of the region, vernacular architecture sought to create shade and devise dust-free draughts. Narrow twisty streets, resulting from the non-alignment of adjacent properties commonly arranged on an

Figure 2.1

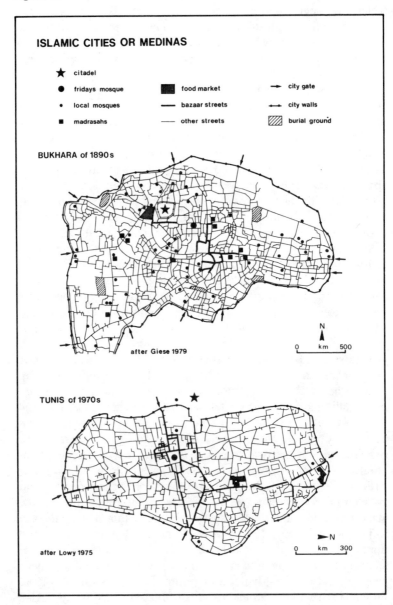

ISLAMIC CITIES OR MEDINAS

★ citadel

● fridays mosque   ■ food market   → city gate

• local mosques   — bazaar streets   ←→ city walls

■ madrasahs   — other streets   ▨ burial ground

BUKHARA of 1890s

after Giese 1979

N

0   km   500

TUNIS of 1970s

after Lowy 1975

N

0   km   300

orthogonal pattern, maximised shade, as did the cellular house in which all the rooms faced inwards on an interior courtyard. Larger properties were made by attaching additional courtyard units, for a larger open space could not achieve the same beneficial thermal properties. Other features particular to specific regions included the use of roof funnels fitted with adjustable shutters which could be operated according to the type and direction of the wind; elsewhere air ducts were fitted under the eaves and sometimes funnels were used to vent dry toilet rooms inoffensively. Islamic society placed great price on privacy, especially for their women, who spent the greater part of their time secluded in the home. The use of culs-de-sac restricted the number of persons needing to approach the home, while twisting entrances prevented intrusive glances; small external windows covered with lattice work provided shade and allowed outward views while concealing the gazer.

Much fascinating detail about daily life comes from Cairo's *Geniza*, a room in which correspondence and documents were cast so as to avoid destroying anything which might contain sacred allusions. Residents of twelfth-century Cairo paid a monthly due for 'protection', the *harasa*, a moderate sum to support the police and watchmen appointed by the governor. As Cairo had been conquered, it belonged by right to the governor. Consequently a ground rent called *hikr*, set at about one-fortieth of the value of the property, was paid for each building but not necessarily by the resident: contracts often stipulated the seller or a third party as the payee and in the next century the community sometimes paid it for the poorer members in their midst. In purely Islamic foundations, neither land nor buildings were ever taxed; taxes were imposed on rent income but rarely on the capital values of property.

The Islamic concept of property distinguished between structures and the land on which they rested. Rights vested in the one did not necessarily include rights in the other. Furthermore while rights may be sold, rented or inherited, these transactions should be binding immediately and involve a defined amount, for the *Sharī'ah* prohibits money lending and in particular, the collection of interest on any transaction. While the right to private property is upheld, it is subordinated to the interests of the state; this enhanced the attractiveness of making mortmain endowments which are inalienable and inviolable. A family's property could be secured both against a rapacious state and spendthrift descendants by this means; however, this did not circumvent the problems created by inheritance laws which granted an equal share to all immediate descendants. The Cairo *Geniza* documents revealed that a house was divided into 24 nominal shares, reflecting the number of parts in the dinar. However the shares transferred by contract or inheritance could be as small as one forty-eighth, an eighteenth, or a sixteenth, clearly equal to less than a single room in a large house. In such circumstances the occupiers of the property were supposed to recompense the rest, but it is not surprising that property fell into ruin when nobody had a commanding share, or when major partners were away for long periods of time.

A great many endowments, however, were pious *waqf* (*ḥubus* in North Africa), which transferred land and property in perpetuity to the community for designated religious or welfare purposes. Houses, mills, baths, libraries and warehouses could also be endowed to supply working or construction capital for mosques, *madrasahs* (which were the origins of universities), hospitals, care of the orphaned or the incompetent, the emoluments of officials or, if the donor so desired, provisions for birds or sick asses (Michon in Serjeant 1980). Given the environment, gifts of water in the form of wells, conduits, public fountains or troughs for animals were considered particularly pious.

Arab influence also extended to the towns in the savanna belt south of the Sahara and along the east coast of Africa (Figure 2.2). The largest and most enduring of these settlements owed their prosperity primarily to long distance caravan trade, for although a whole succession of often overlapping empires (Ghana, Mali and Songhai to mention the most prominent) arose on the savannas between the tenth and eleventh centuries, their survival often depended on the success of relatively mobile leaders and supporting cavalry, which was not conducive to permanent residence. The advantageous location of the trading depots, where forest products from the south were exchanged for those of the desert and the *Maghreb*, allowed them to survive the political upheavals which spelt disaster for settlements attached solely to the success of a particular dynasty. Thus cities such as Tombouctou, Djenne and Gao waxed prosperous as gold dust, gums, cloth, kola nuts, salt blocks, natrium and slaves, the most important item of wealth given the universal dependence on manpower, changed hands.

In a separate sphere of influence, Arabs from Oman and Persia settled in East African states stretching from present-day

Figure 2.2

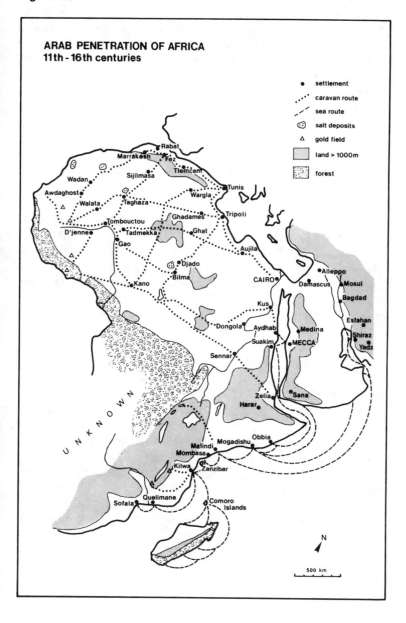

ARAB PENETRATION OF AFRICA
11th - 16th centuries

Mogadishu in the north of Madagasgar, the Comoros Islands and Moçambique in the south. The inland trade here was with the Central African kingdoms, which mined copper, iron, gold and silver, while the coast supplied spices, cloves, salt and imported textiles. The volume of trade carried by human porters through the tsetse-infested scrub could never rival the camel caravans of the desert, although a few staging-post settlements such as Ujiji, Urambo and Tabore did arise. The Arabs integrated with the Bantus, giving rise to an Arab-Swahili culture with a distinctive combination of Islamic institutions adapted to local custom. Whether Saharan or East African, all towns engaged in long distance trade stimulated production in local foodstuffs and developed an important local market and service function.

The old 'Islamic' city, the *medina* is a tangible reality in many parts of North Africa and the Middle East today. Although destroyed in cities such as Baghdād and Beirut, *medinas* elsewhere continue to house large numbers, over 10000 in Rabat-Sale in the 1970s, over 200000 in Tunis and over a million in Cairo. They constitute one of the major problems facing contemporary planners who almost universally view their crumbling and overcrowded fabric with disgust, although they recognise their tourist value. Only the fear of repercussions elsewhere in their cities, if their populations were displaced, has prevented many being razed completely. Their present circumstances can be blamed to a great extent on the survival of Islamic institutions in a context now governed by Western economic principals.

The *medinas* were originally built for a pedestrian society; the tortuous alleyways and multiplicity of dead ends deny access to the motor car, rubbish-disposal van and fire-engine alike. In desperation, city officials of Baghdād, Algiers and Fez, for example, cut modern roads through them in total disregard of their internal arrangements. Most have breached their walls at a number of points and built a major peripheral road at their base. These efforts have not stopped the fabric deteriorating to the point of dereliction, for wealthy residents abandoned these areas when the cities' economic bases shifted elsewhere. The continuity of Islamic inheritance and property tenure structures has resulted in the *medinas* housing a population of poor and relatively recent migrant tenants. The fragmented ownership of the larger buildings, the presence of endowed land to now irrelevant causes and the lack of property registries from which to identify owners, all deter corporate action to improve conditions. As such areas generate a negligible tax base, few city administrations feel any onus to invest in their basic utilities. Only when an exogenous agency takes an interest, such as UNESCO in the case of Tunis, has a city received specialist advice. Moreover, there is no unanimously approved plan as to what should be done to the *medinas*.

At the fringes of the Islamic sphere of influence, the cities did not acquire the full range of institutions or buildings in a pure form. Some Islamic traditions overlaid or accentuated existing urban practices and it would be difficult to disentangle the contribution of each. It is this amalgam, along with subsequent infusions that characterise urban life today in the surviving centres. Walled traditional nuclei are embedded in the contemporary fabric of cities of the sub-Saharan zone. They contain mosques but the residential areas, while equally private, are composed of compounds representing kin groups whose clusters reflect still older traditions. These also impose barriers to innovations, as testified by the failure of decades of efforts to improve their sanitary arrangements. Once again investments tend to be funded internationally; WHO intervened after cholera broke out in the walled city of Kano in 1981, for example. However ancient traditions must continue to satisfy basic needs, given the inability of the majority of the population to afford other building materials or techniques. The state's failure to provide communal infrastructure, or indeed to allow local residents to take part in the planning process, reinforces the customs of self-sufficiency.

South Asia

The Indian subcontinent is another fount of very early urban traditions but most northern cities received an Islamic veneer through the displacement of dynasties such as the Seljūgs and the Safavids from much further west. Only the most deeply entrenched traditions could survive unchanged by the turbulent history of the region, which from the first incursions in the eleventh century to the end of the Mogul Empire in the eighteenth, was one of almost constant warmongering, involving the expansion of indigenous empires, efforts to regain independence and fratricidal struggles for power. Invading armies from the north-west swept across the densely settled and fertile Punjab to the watershed

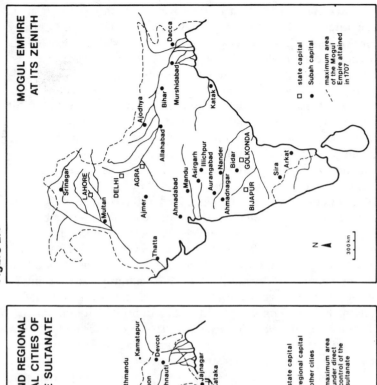

Figure 2.4

MOGUL EMPIRE AT ITS ZENITH

Srinagar
Multan
LAHORE
DELHI
AGRA
Ajmer
Thatta
Ahmadabad
Mandu
Allahabad
Ajodhya
Bihar
Dacca
Murshidabad
Asirgarh
Illichpur
Nander
Aurangabad
Bidar
GOLKONDA
Ahmadnagar
BIJAPUR
Katak
Sira
Arkat

☐ state capital
● Subah capital
--- maximum area of the Mogul Empire attained in 1707

N
300 km

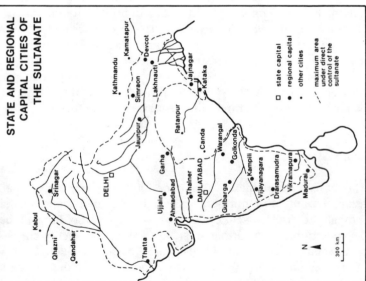

Figure 2.3

STATE AND REGIONAL CAPITAL CITIES OF THE SULTANATE

Kabul
Qhazni
Qandahar
Srinagar
DELHI
Kathmandu
Kamatapur
Simraon
Devcot
Jaunpur
Lakhnauti
Jajnagar
Garha
Ratanpur
Kataka
Ujjain
Ahmadabad
Thalner
DAULATABAD
Canda
Warangal
Golkonda
Gulbarga
Kampili
Vijayanagara
Dvarasamudra
Vikramapura
Madurai
Thatta

☐ state capital
● regional capital
● other cities
--- maximum area under direct control of the sultanate

N
300 km

between the Indus and Ganges systems. Plunderers, such as the Mongols, were then content to withdraw, while imperialists proceeded to expand from this base, first eastwards towards Bengal and then southwards. They usually had to come to terms with the fiercely independent Rajputs and Marathas and both the Delhi sultanate of the fourteenth century and the Moguls of the seventeenth over-extended themselves in their efforts to embrace the Deccan kingdoms. Southern India retained far more Hindu traits; the tip of the subcontinent was never incorporated to either empire and the territory up to the Tungabhadra River formed the 300-year-old Hindu Kingdom of Vijayanagar, which was only finally incorporated by the Moguls in 1565 (Farmer et al. 1977). The empires were organised from their capital cities, for power resided in the emperor. He appointed all officials and designated their place of service within the network of regional capitals. Whenever central power waned, the vast territories broke up into *de facto* autonomous kingdoms and these cities became the seats of scaled down courts (Figures 2.3 and 2.4).

Emperors' nobles won that status through service and in direct proportion to the number of men they could command; aspiring nobles had to maintain large numbers of followers. However, such armies constitute a threat; rulers can diffuse this through frequent campaigns but these have to be financed. Loot from conquest might satisfy short-term demands but does not constitute a reliable means to sustain a state. Both the Sultanate and the Mogul Empires were supported by a complex taxation system based on Islamic ideals, Ottoman and Persian experience and the several customs long entrenched in the many regions of the subcontinent. As elsewhere, the land was considered to belong to the emperor by right of conquest; however, the rights of the cultivator were guaranteed on the payment of *kharaj*, a tax which ranged from a third to half of the estimated crop, considering the area cultivated and the quality of the land. This tax on agricultural produce made a significant contribution to city life, for the Moguls paid for the noblemen's services, whether military or administrative, via the award of a *jagir*, that is the revenue due to the state from a designated number of adjacent villages. In addition, tax contractors, *zamindars*, were granted concessions to collect the taxes in a specific area and were reimbursed for their services through the retention of sums above the amounts demanded by the exchequer. Nobles also used contractors to collect their dues and when not on active duty, they, important *zamindars* and other large-scale revenue subcontractors, all resided at rulers' courts and in cities. Agrarian taxes thus supported a very significant proportion of city dwellers. Indeed the increasing greed of the nobles and the continuing need to co-opt potential foes through the award of more *jagirs* has been considered an important contributory factor to the eventual fall of the Mogul Empire.

The Emperor appointed all key executors, military commanders, city governors, *qadis* and revenue officials so as to prevent collusion between officials. The mechanism of patronage both bestowed status and also granted the means to live up to it; status was displayed through patronage in turn to those less favoured. The court and its appointees were conspicuous consumers; they lived in palaces, maintained harems, dressed in the finest textiles, adorned themselves with jewels and were entertained by musicians, dancers and artists. The multitudes they supported expanded the demand for more mundane articles, giving rise to a close correlation between a settlement's market value and its political status.

Cities were not just the base of elites, however; although their presence undoubtedly stimulated manufacturing, the removal of barriers within the empires also improved trading conditions and allowed regional specialisms to be exchanged and even exported. Certain manufacturers and skills, such as luxury items and those involved in the construction of monumental architecture, could only be supported in the cities. The guild organisation which evolved from pre-Muslim days, was a distinctive urban institution, for occupations in villages were organised through a set of hereditary service relationships. The guild system of Mogul days would seem even more important than in the Islamic heartland, as it was strongly interwoven with the fabric of not just the city economy and society, but in the case of the merchant and finance guilds, the maintenance of the state. Taxes raised on produce were the major source of urban revenue but the guilds performed important roles as financiers and trustees. They banked deposits of public money on which they paid interest; they administered pious endowments and deposits dedicated to specific welfare activities; they maintained local temples and invested in communal facilities such as wells and tanks. They conducted customary courts which dealt with domestic and civil disputes between their members and provided insurance against sickness and the needs of widows and orphans in their community. The *mahajar* of the banker's guild held the most prominent position in their hierarchy: its hereditary head often acted as the city's *de facto* representative, while it is known that the guild's grand head, the *Jagat Sheth*, played the role of imperial treasurer to the Emperor Akbar. It was the *mahajars* who were entrusted to transmit the funds raised at one end of the empire to the armies fighting at the other and to handle the transactions involved in the early negotiation with European merchants. The state was also involved in many types of production, especially spinning and weaving and the manufacture of weapons and ammunition. Prominent officials were put in charge of such workshops and even resorted to the 'capture' of particularly skilful craftsmen to work in them. The few studies of the period reveal that, for example in Ahmadabad and Lucknow, salaried craftsmen existed, work was put out to specialists and a successful individual entrepreneur might own a considerable number of subsidiary workshops. Market and manufacturing towns were stimulated by the Empire's efforts to collect revenue in the form of cash.

Mogul cities housed a plural society divided by place of origin, race, language, religion and even within the Muslim community, between Shī'ī and Sunnī. The Empires tolerated other beliefs, although the fact that Muslims were exonerated certain taxes, a practice common elsewhere, encouraged the conversion of those accorded little status by their Hindu creed. The complexity of city society stemmed not just from the varied origins of the population; Hinduism by the ninth century embodied a stratified hierarchy of a plethora of castes and sub-castes, each identified with particular occupations, duties and lifestyles and each acknowledging a unique set of social relationships with every other one. This became more rigid with Brahmin purists urging social segregation in the eighteenth century, which in turn favoured the clustering of occupations and residences of caste members. Community was fostered through the endowment of temples, wells, tanks and the extension of charity to the pious and the needy by their richer brethren. Muslims also frequently clustered on occupational and ethnic grounds and sometimes specialised in types of production and services spurned by Hindus. A similar tenet of faith encouraged the investment of personal wealth in the support of religious institutions, the unfortunate and the provision of communal facilities. Both communities prized privacy in the home and for their womenfolk, who seldom ventured beyond its immediate vicinity alone.

Nevertheless cities did not favour the strict observance of either Hindu or Muslim ideals. They housed very large heterogeneous populations. Migrants stemmed from diverse regions, each with its own langauges and caste ordering; the number of Muslims was increasing and in some areas the population included Jains, Buddists and Sikhs besides. Neither could Islamic institutions have the same force in a milieu where their jurisdiction was confined to only a part of the population. Consequently the *ulamā* tended to assume a more restricted administrative role and work in conjunction with the bazaar merchants of diverse religions, while the spiritual element of Islam was upheld by *ṣūfī*, who generally held themselves independent of the state. The appointed governor of the city, the *kotwal*, assumed a secular role and was primarily concerned with policing in its widest sense. While law and order were paramount, the office was also responsible for overseeing construction, sanitation and above all, trade and the collection of taxes. His staff maintained roads, cemeteries and slaughter houses, supervised the activities of sweepers and scavengers, collected taxes, dues and tolls and maintained registries to aid the pursuit of all these functions. Community leaders (*mohulladars*) were co-opted to advise and expedite the fulfilment of tasks requiring public participation; many infrastructural elements were acquired through the charity of their leading members.

The physical structure of such cities reflected the fact that their ruler's might was ultimately military and the state's wealth was redistributed via personalist and paternalist mechanisms. The major cities had substantial defences: Hyderabad's stone walls were nine and a half kilometres in circumference and Delhi's nearly five; other cities had imposing stone or brick walls and they were all punctuated with bastions, defended gateways and often surrounded by moats. Generally at some commanding point within the enclosure stood a fort or citadel; Agra's had walls 21 metres high. The main palaces, mosques, temples and mausoleums attained very high standards of workmanship on a grandiose scale, of which the most famous is probably the Taj Mahal. However, the use of white marble, stone filigree screens and the embellishment of walls with precious stones and tiles or metal was common in any city which housed a prominent court for any length of time.

Cities in the populous north and west received the strongest Islamic influences. Account of the layouts of some of them have obvious similarities. Colonial administrators observed that the peculiarity of Ahmadabad was that the houses were

> generally built in blocks or *pols*, varying in size from small courts of from five to ten houses to large quarters containing as many as 10000 inhabitants. Large blocks were generally crossed by one main street with a gate at each end and were subdivided into smaller courts and blocks, each with its separate gate branching off from either side of the chief thoroughfare. (*Imperial Gazette*, 1908)

Long, ribbon-like bazaars threaded through these walled cities, leading from the principal gates to focal temples, mosques or palaces. Suburbs grew up around the gates and along the trade routes leading away from principal cities, while certain activities were nearly always located outside where they would not offend cultural mores. In most, the contrast between the space and gardens surrounding palaces and temples and the narrow, twisting and tortuous lanes, often ending in culs-de-sac was striking. The houses abutting these buildings were often described as handsome; they were built of stone or brick and decorated with wood carving or elaborate stonework, according to region. They could be of several storeys but the poor tended to live in single-roomed huts generally made of mud and wattle.

Utilities in such cities were provided by a combination of charity by high status individuals, household self-sufficiency and caste occupations. Water supplies stemmed from the first two while sanitary arrangements were the preserve of the latter. Water was procured from tanks, wells and natural sources. Houses were built around compounds, the larger of which were equipped with either deep dry wells, called *sandas*, or with *mugli*, a latrine connected by a pipe to a small pit. The latter had a shutter set in the compound's perimeter wall, which permitted an untouchable to empty it without entering the premises. These were inappropriate to dense populations; *sandas* contaminated the water wells sunk in their vicinity and became a prime contributor to disease. The problem associated with the *mugli* was the lack of suitable disposal grounds when the cities expanded. Sweepers would scatter the effluent over the first convenient waste ground encountered and so encourage its use for that purpose by the population not so provided. Inevitably the runoff contaminated surface water sources.

The weakness of the cities lay in the fact that their economic base depended to a great extent on patronage. When cities lost their court, the impact on their physical structure could be devastating, for the poorer houses were easily eroded if not maintained. Lahore in its heyday as Imperial capital had covered some 16 or 17 square miles, but it rapidly decayed into 'a heap of ruins'; a few scattered houses and a couple of Sikh forts lay within its shrunken walls while a wide expanse of broken remains indicated the surrounding swath of once populous suburbs. Delhi provides an even more vivid example of such swings in fortune. As the imperial capital of the Sultanate, it attained an estimated population of 400000. But the Mongol Timur Beg sacked it in 1398 and the early Mogul emperors established their capitals at Lahore, then Fatehpur Sikri and later at Agra. Only the later and less powerful Emperors returned to Delhi and even then not to precisely the same site. Emperor Shah Jahan was responsible for the seventh and most elaborate city in the environs, which we know as Old Delhi, but it only housed about 150000 in the eighteenth century; it had taken thousands of labourers years to construct the Red Fort and the Jami Majid temple. Unfortunately the regained splendour attracted the Persian Nadir Shah, who sacked it in 1739 and then the Afghan, Ahmad Shah, who did so twice over in mid-century. These events signalled the demise of the Moguls and the rise once again of a great many states each with a court-based city, many of whom owed allegiance to larger regional confederations such as that of the Marathas.

The sheer physical scale of the subcontinent, its difficult terrain, comparatively dense population who, however, could still migrate if pressed too hard at a particular location, and its loose tribal societies in which each clan leader made their own decisions, all served to blunt any institutions imposed, even those of the great empires. These facets were utilised by the Europeans to gain local support for their activities and to harass that of their competitors. However, they themselves came up against their complexities in turn. They encountered large cities whose populations fluctuated dramatically with their political fortunes, populations moreover divided by faith, language, origin, caste and allegiance. The regional variety in land tenure procedures and ownership patterns reflected the fact that Islamic tenets concerning commercial transactions and inheritance dominated in some places, while they coexisted with others governing the rest of the population in others, or were unknown elsewhere. Production and trading mechanisms were also affected, as were a great many processes governing daily life in the cities. To this day such complexities face city administrators, particularly within the old walled cities and the much larger areas which have grown up spontaneously outside. Owing to the lack of resources, residents of such areas must still use and devise rudimentary and often very unsatisfactory water supplies and sanitary arrangements. However, the impact of these in a city of many millions is obviously far greater than in one with a population of 100000 or so.

West Africa

Indigenous urban traditions had independent and ancient roots in West Africa; cities were created as politico-religious cores of empires, confederations or at least acted as dynastic capitals. Cities with such ethnic associations include Ife for the Yoruba, Kano for the Hausa, Kumasi for the Ashante, Ibadan for the Egba and the Fulani conquerors deliberately founded Sokoto as a focus for their empire (Figure 2.5). Smaller cities might well owe allegiance to them through the ties engendered with their own creation, or constitute another quasi-independent city state. A large city absorbed the produce from the surrounding hinterland; while land was plentiful, there was every incentive to found new daughter communities when expansion of cultivation was constrained by the distance factor. It was also possible for the disaffected to settle elsewhere. Allegiance patterns reflected the relationships between lineages, status being granted on the basis of period established.

These settlements merit town or city status because of their sophisticated social, political and economic organisation, which gave rise to distinctive institutions, despite being small by contemporary criteria. Their populations fluctuated greatly according to the fortunes of their leaders: sixteenth-century Kano was estimated to have a population of 75000, but only 40000 when hard pressed by the Fulani in 1827. Early population estimates were often based on the number of houses or the area covered by the settlement and their availability is spotty. In 1585 Gao, the capital of the Songai Empire, was reported to house a population of 75000, while Tombouktou, before it became a renowned centre

Figure 2.5

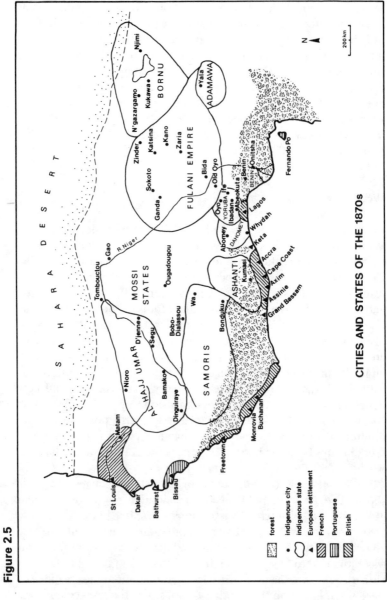

CITIES AND STATES OF THE 1870s

of Islamic learning and acquired its substantial complement of *ulamā* and *madrasahs*, had 25000. In the 1820s Sokoto housed 120000, while estimates for Ibadan range between 75000 and 100000. Abeokuta had an estimated population of 60000 (Gugler and Flanagan 1971).

There is a very wide discrepancy, as much as 50000 people in some instances, between the population estimates made by residents and those of visitors to many of these cities. The cause would appear to lie in the concept of the city. City states expressed political status via physical ties with subordinate settlements. Some societies, such as the Kingdom of Benin, required the headmen of lesser towns to reside, along with a sizeable retinue, in the capital, while others demanded that they should do so for extended periods. Elsewhere rulers, such as of Kumasi, could not maintain all their retinue and younger household members in town; they dispatched them to farm land at the periphery in order to both provision themselves and their superiors in the cities (Hull 1976). These workers continued to regard themselves as city dwellers and indeed spent much time there during the slack agricultural season. Many traders also claimed citizenship although they obviously spent most of their time elsewhere. Thus the African included all those associated with a particular city in his estimate, while the European did not. A conservative estimate of the permanent population of the capitals of city states lies between 20000 and 50000.

The centralised city states had developed by the nineteenth century complex socio-political hierarchical structures, the most common elements being strata of nobles, officials, commoners and slaves. Family structures in polygamous societies are complex and are frequently matched by equally diverse inheritance systems. Positions may be acquired via the male or female line, passed to brothers or sisters, or sons or daughters, or to a brother's or sister's children. The number of descendants ensured that there was a pool of eligible candidates on whatever criteria used from which the most able candidate could be selected for office. Most societies included a specialised group within the nobility charged with the selection, ritual installation and sanction of the actions of the paramount rulers. Other hereditary nobles did not always take an active part in the management of the state, particularly in the nineteenth century; in Dahomey, Maradi and the Kingdom of Benin, their support was ensured through distancing them from any practical role and so rendering them dependent on the largesse of the state and in particular the incumbent ruler. Active roles, such as war raiding and defence, the organisation and control of tax collection, long distance trade and city provisioning were often entrusted to either commoners of proven ability in lesser roles, or as in the Islamic world, to specially trained corps of slaves or eunuchs. The commoners were free born cultivators, artisans and petty traders who made up the bulk of the population. Slavery was common throughout Africa as the condition bestowed on war captives. There is evidence that a few societies used them in ritual sacrifice but this is rare; their productive powers were far too valuable a resource to be disposed of in this manner. The savanna kingdoms used them as soldiers and to cultivate the state plantations; most kingdoms used them as state servants. The Ashanti considered the second generation as freeborn and exacted heavy penalties if allusion was made to their origins.

The rulers' retinues of religious leaders, administrators, nobles and immediate kin, retainers, multiple wives and children and even more numerous servants made up a sizeable complement of the thousands of people who did not provide their own subsistence from the soil. In addition the cities housed specialised craftsmen, experts in bronze casting (Ife and Benin), fine textiles (Kumasi) and terra cotta sculptures, apart from the more usual range of artisans. Such cities were dependent on provisions from the surrounding area. Many kingdoms exacted either an annual tax on production or a tribute from subordinate settlements which was paid in kind. In addition, most taxed trade through the use of roads (by the donkey or camel load), on particular commodities (such as salt, slaves or gold) and on entering or leaving a city or its jurisdiction. Rulers often monopolised particular commodities; gold nuggets were the property of the kings of Ghana and Mali, while the Oba of Abomey owned all the slaves in nineteenth-century Dahomey. Occupational groups were also taxed and commonly officials had to pay the requisite fee on taking office. There are instances when the state claimed a percentage of a man's movable goods as an inheritance fee or death duty. Travellers' observations suggest that tax systems were often organised on a concessions basis such that officials profited from anything raised above the base rate established by the ruler's council. Dishonesty was controlled by such measures as the official's sons being kept at court while the duty was discharged, the employment of a network of spies and by the payees making independent submissions of the amounts involved.

A settlement's ruler derived much of his power through his control over access to land. Throughout much of Africa, land was conceived of as an element vested in all members of a community, including those deceased and those not yet born. As such, it was not a commodity to which possession could be attached. Use of land was acquired through membership, usually at birth, of a particular group and was the right of every adult. As trustee of the original settlers, the head of every settlement allocated lands according to the subsistence needs of the applicant; on his demise, it could be reallocated, usually to his immediate kin. It was forfeit if not used after a certain time. Specific uses, ranging from the right to collect firewood or tap palm trees, to the planting of trees or erection of a compound could also be attached to land. Since tradition also established that a man had the right to reap the fruit of his labours and to pass them on to his kin, the time-scale vested in residential compounds tended to establish individual rights over particular parcels. This became particularly significant for the areas immediately adjacent to cities and could curtail their expansion, thus forcing the creation of daughter settlements further afield.

Similar principles structured the cities. Immigrants were allocated to wards which housed relatively homogeneous groups on such criteria as race, ethnicity, culture and period of residence. Segregation was reinforced by the incorporation of further kinsmen but did not hold the contemporary connotations of a ghetto; the larger cities were made up of a great many wards, each of which was self-governing internally and represented by leaders chosen according to their custom. Cities were composed of conglomerations of such communities loosely arranged around such foci as the royal palaces, or in caravan cities, the market-place. In Yoruba Kingdoms proximity to the *afin*, the palace compound, indicated a lineage's position in the administrative hierarchy, while in more northern cities the institutions promoted by the Islamic faith had greater influence.

Comparatively little attention has been paid to West African city structures owing to their lack of monumental buildings, the absence of written records and because much of their construction was in materials which required constant maintenance. Large public works reflect the ability to generate wealth and mobilise a labour force. Even the centralised states were comparatively small and short-lived; those based on valuable trade and which had the use of either slave or corvée labour had greater opportunity to build. Much of this public effort was expended in massive walls and moats around the cities. Benin's inner wall measured, from the top to the bottom of the moat between 16 and 17 metres high; it formed a circuit of eleven and a half kilometres. An archaeologist has estimated that about 5000 men working ten hours daily throughout the dry season would have been required to complete it. Additional walls of various dates complete the complex cellular structure whose use is not known; the combined length of the entire system exceeds 100 kilometres. Benin was not unique; both Kano and Zaria had circuits of eighteen and a half kilometres and nearly twelve kilometres of walls surrounded Katsina.

The buildings within these cities have tended to be underrated owing to them being predominantly built of lateritic mud, which has a high clay content. On the desert margins there are few alternative materials. However, unfired brick and mud (*swish*) architecture can encompass a great variety of forms (round, square, rectangular) and roofing materials (from thatched cone shapes to flat cemented ones). Such materials need constant maintenance against the ravages of moisture, intensive sunlight, termites and other insects. The speed of renewal allowed innovations introduced by traders to be reflected very quickly. The Muslim preference for square shapes and flat roofs tended to displace round houses in the north, while it has been suggested that the *impluviam* houses built around interior sunken courtyards, which seem totally unpractical given the rainfall regime of the forest zone, had much filtered Roman origins. The Mediterranean probably also inspired the patterned pavements made from potsherds planted edgeways.

The common household unit was the compound, but rooms could be neatly arranged or scattered haphzardly in their interior. Muslim influence is revealed where public rooms are the only ones which breach the perimeter wall while access to the private part inhabited by the women is indirect. Compounds could also be regularly spaced along ceremonial avenues or more informally clustered in groups in each ward with open spaces separating them. One common way for kings to distinguish their dwellings was by increased height which rendered their palaces visible from all parts of the city. Frequently nobody else was permitted to build more than one storey. In addition rank could be indicated through the use of different roof forms and decorative porches at compound entrances. Their walls might be decorated with patterns in high relief or like the Oba's palace in Benin, be reddened by mixing animals' blood with the mud cement. Palace compounds were not only very large, being composed of various courtyards, separate sets of apartments and linked by colonnades, but initially constituted cities within cities. They often housed several hundred people, including nobles, officials and servants, many of whom might be the children of subordinate chiefs. The latters' sojourn served both as training and as a symbol of allegiance (Hull 1976).

The cities also housed a floating population which nevertheless contributed to its economy. Long-distance trade involved caravans of merchants and their assistants which required stables, dormitories and warehouses. These were often situated in a separate ward at the periphery. In Muslim areas, students flocked to learn from the *ulamā*. This seasonal removal of otherwise idle young men assisted survival in the countryside, while the city's prosperity was taxed owing to the Muslim precept of charity which required that such scholars be accommodated and fed. However, they also provided a labour force which frequently became associated with particular seasonal crafts, such as weaving and dyeing and thus served as the means by which urban skills were diffused to the countryside.

External threats constantly assaulted the cities. Many were situated in fragile natural environments, any deterioration of which could spell their demise but enemy attack was more often the cause. Arab contact repeatedly took the form of *jihads*, holy movements designed to impose or reform Islamic institutions. Many kingdoms on the Sahara's margins succumbed to these. The Sultan of Morocco's invasion, staffed by European mercenaries more interested in gold, captured Tombouctou and Djenne, the prominent cities of Songai in 1591. The Fulani Emirate overtook the Hausa states and was pressing the Yoruba by the nineteenth century. Some cities were destroyed, others abandoned and new ones established within the protecting forest cover as a result. In addition, Europeans were establishing trading 'factories' on various parts of the coast. Contact with the foremost of these, in the fifteenth century, proved disastrous for the weaker states, for the Portuguese acted as buccaneers and marauders, physically destroying most of the east coast settlements in quest for booty. The stronger West African states were able to enforce a more respectful trading relationship with the Europeans; they established a whole chain of new settlements stretching from Old Calabar in the east to Grand Bassam and Rufisque/Goree in the west for this purpose.

Some West African kingdoms were capable of withstanding these events through the adoption of many aspects of modern state organisation. By the nineteenth century the demands of peacekeeping and defending a large territory, of implementing complex revenue systems and trading with strangers, who were technologically superior in weaponry and had a dominant interest in gold and slaves, stimulated fundamental changes in social structures. Administration was increasingly undertaken by trained professionals of proven ability embedded in systems which prevented an excessive concentration of powers. They appreciated the need to oversee European activities and frequently restricted them not only to particular settlements but also to designated wards within them. Trade was controlled: the king of Abomey's agents conducted their transactions first, charged customs duties, set the price at which goods could be sold and licensed indigenous traders. Slave trading was the monopoly of the Oba of Benin, so as to maintain the economic power of the elite and present the indiscriminate distribution of firearms and powder. The use of buffer settlements allowed these kingdoms to acquire and appreciate elements of European culture and technology, without being alienated from their own roots, and to protect their populations from the rapaciousness of adventurers. Where these steps were not taken, the challenge to fundamental institutions often led to the indigenous societies' eventual destruction, as described vividly in the case of the Congo (Southall 1971).

Conclusions

The indigenous cities in the regions described were built by complex societies with sophisticated political systems capable of organising extensive territories before the advent of modern communications. They demonstrated the ability of predominantly agrarian societies to accumulate surplus wealth and train specialists who transformed it into extremely fine architecture, sculptures, carvings, textiles and jewellery. Their internal organisation reflected the relationships between groups of subjects and the state, whatever form the latter took. Even early cities housed heterogeneous populations. Although social and economic interactions tended to take place in the context of personal networks shaped by ethnic criteria, indigenous cities do not appear to have been rigidly segregated. Indeed the presence of various peoples enabled cities to circumvent the disadvantages caused by the taboos of specific cultures through their respective choice of specialisation.

Social structures are reflected most clearly in the cities' morphologies. Indigenous cities were often composed of self-contained neighbourhoods each of which evolved as a discrete community. Another common feature was the responsibility accepted by these for their poorer and weaker members. This was expressed tangibly through the provision of utilities by patrons and wealthier members. This sense of community was also embodied in the various cultures' perceptions of property and the rights of individuals over it. The survival of some of these traits alongside colonial and post independence innovations is the cause of some of the greatest problems facing TWCs today.

3 COLONIAL CITY LEGACIES

Colonial rule was imposed on much of the Third World but at and for very different periods of time (Figure 3.1). Occupation started in Latin America in the sixteenth century but independence had been gained by all parts of the mainland by the first quarter of the nineteenth century, before the colonial phase had really got under way elsewhere. Trading posts and refuelling forts were established on the west and south coast of Africa and around the Indian subcontinent at about the same time as the incursions of the Spaniards and Portuguese in America. However, for India the real colonial thrust dates from the mid-nineteenth century and occurred later still, between the 1880s and the turn of the century in Africa. Thus the British were in India for about a century but the colonial phase for most African countries lasted only about 70 years and as few as 50 for some. Elsewhere European presence has been even more transient; in the Middle East it was limited to protectorate status over a limited area for a couple of decades, mostly between the two World Wars. The most enduring colonies have tended to be small and isolated, such as the islands in the Caribbean, the Pacific and the Indian Oceans, or, strategic locations on the principal sea routes, or on the doorstep of powers it was not possible to colonise. Singapore, Hong Kong and Macao continue to play their peculiar economic role, even though the former is now independent and the terms of the lease on Kowloon (mainland Hong Kong) dictate that it should be returned to China by the end of the decade.

The period of colonisation is the key to the identity and objectives of those involved, their ability to carry them out and the sort of cities they established. The Spanish *conquistadores* were the rump of an army unemployed after expelling the Moors from a recently united homeland. The circumstances ensured that the *conquistadores* had a heightened intolerance for anything other than strict Catholic conformity. They were accompanied by a large number of clergy and the church reinforced and was in turn supported by the government throughout the colonial period. Elsewhere the church did not enjoy such a close relationship with

52

Figure 3.1

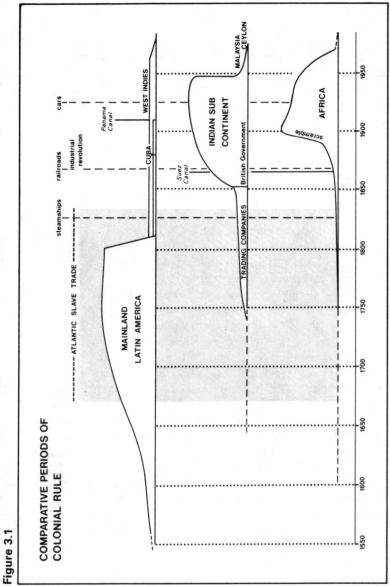

COMPARATIVE PERIODS OF
COLONIAL RULE

the state. Churchmen tended to follow formal colonisation and missionaries were often controlled and viewed with suspicion by secular administrators. Neither did colonisation arise out of an initial military presence with the avowed aim of capturing a large territory in India. Standing armies were introduced to defend established trade against the activities of rival European companies and their allies only after the British Government become involved in 1858. In Africa the major stimulant to colonisation lay in rivalry within Europe; the continent merely contributed a scenario in which to express it.

Colonisation would have been short-lived if the invaders had not perceived a profitable outcome, for neither the Spaniards and the Portuguese in Latin America, nor the British in India, nor the majority of Europeans in Africa in the nineteenth century were interested in establishing themselves as farmers. Thus they had to maintain indigenous production both to feed themselves and to yield a surplus to sustain a colonial administration. The lure for the Spaniards was precious metals; pre-Hispanic institutions of work service and tax in kind generated labour and supplies for mining activities. India's original attractions included high quality textiles, finely wrought metal objects and a wide range of spices. In Africa the Portuguese, Dutch, English and French had founded factory settlements but these were mere fortresses, protecting warehouses, offices and quarters for a few essential workers; they served as dispatch points for products produced and handled by indigenous traders and as refuelling points for the fleets involved. Many were abandoned as trade became concentrated at the most profitable sites. This was particularly evident in West Africa after the British navy upheld a ban on slave exports in 1807; the trade continued from points ensconced within protective sandbars and lagoons. The expansion of trade on African soil was effectively barred by the state monopolies of the densely populated and well-organised kingdoms and in North and East Africa, by Arab rulers and traders. Only in South Africa had Dutch settlers steadily penetrated inland. Elsewhere the interior was little known and provided little tangible evidence of trade potential to the British, compared to that offered by India or America, while the French preferred to invest in Russia and Turkey. The demand for colonisation did not stem from the commercial sectors of Europe, the bulk of whose investments was directed elsewhere.

The evolution and form of colonial economies were related to the technology available at the time. The Spanish sailing caravel of the sixteenth and seventeenth centuries, hindered by the need to transship at the isthmus, meant that a year could pass in a round trip to the west coast of South America. Until the reforms of 1778 gave a much greater degree of autonomy to the Plate area, which allowed it to be supplied regularly by its own port on the Atlantic, mule trains carried goods over the Andes to this far-flung outreach of empire. Such cumbersome, slow and dangerous journeys limited what was transported to the most valuable and essential. Colonial administrators in other contexts had steamships at their disposal; railroads could be built to handle bulk cargoes and mass transport. The Suez canal speeded travel to India and the East Coast of Africa and motor vehicles provided more flexible land mobility. All these innovations were introduced well after the independence of most Latin American countries.

The evolution of the colonial phase was also conditioned by the juxtaposition of peoples from very different environments. The outcome in Latin America was catastrophic, for its indigenous populations had no immunity to Old World diseases (measles, whooping cough, mumps, diphtheria, typhus, smallpox and cholera); they died by the thousands as epidemics raged through the densely settled basins. Large areas became depopulated and their infrastructure fell into ruins. The evidence is spotty and has been the focus of much patient research; the general conclusion is that most of the continent did not regain its pre-Columbian numbers until the 1950s, some 400 years after the arrival of the Spaniards. Resistance to colonial institutions could not be effective in such a context. The disease equation was reversed elsewhere, for it was the Europeans whose initial numbers were few and who were decimated by the great variety of tropical fevers encountered, whether cholera and typhus in India or yellow fever and malaria in the 'white man's grave' of West Africa. Consequently colonial administration had to develop a firm structure and written rules which could function with a constant turnover of staff on relatively short terms of service. Junior officials were generally single and most others left their families at home.

These broad criteria underlie the roles played by cities during the colonial phase. A coastal base provided the first toehold and performed a crucial role as springbroad for occupation inland. Colonial authorities had to establish a presence in indigenous capitals both to control the inmates and to tap their produce.

Being for the most part grossly outnumbered, lines of communication which permitted the arrival of reinforcements were necessary and key junctions and weak points on these had to be defended. The redirection of trade towards the coast and overseas, rather than between interior districts, strengthened settlements on these axes. When regular sea borne trade became a practical proposition, new settlements arose to oversee the dispatch of products either at the points of production or processing. When trade operations involved a sizeable volume of imports, such centres acquired a distributive function as well.

If the number and size of cities reflected the structure of colonial economies, their morphology was often a guide to their governor's attitudes to their milieu. Colonial institutions were concentrated in the cities, where appropriate symbolic structures could display their power. European conventions could be adopted in a pure form on greenfield sites, especially when the indigenous presence was slight. However, where the latter dominated or pre-dated the colonials, peaceful co-existence required the specification and agreement on social conventions on both sides. Early administrators frequently found themselves regulating the behaviour of independent Europeans, as well as curtailing infringements by indigenous residents. Frequently the easiest solution to avoid conflict arising from different cultural backgrounds was residential segregation; indigenous habits of daily life were ignored as long as they took place within their own sphere and did not intrude on the lives of the Europeans.

The scale of the colonial empires required the design of complex mechanisms to implement policies which evolved over space, as the colonial frontier was pushed inland, and over time. These were seldom a case of crude military might and their form varied both with the context and the official. It is necessary to examine some examples in depth in order to appreciate the extent and importance of the structures inherited by contemporary TWCs.

The Indian Subcontinent

This area epitomises perhaps more than any other the complexity of technical, financial and management options facing very large cities housing heterogeneous and mostly very poor populations. As revealed in Chapter 2, these conditions already existed when the East India Company and its other European rivals started trading with Indian princes. When the Company's rights were transferred to the Crown in 1858, nearly two centuries after the original bases had been established in Madras, Bengal and Bombay Island, the cities received a veneer of British administrative institutions, which varied in thickness between regions under direct rule or native control and British supervision. These conditioned what decisions about the cities were taken and by whom. However, the British generally found it easier, as native rulers had before, to tack on zones for themselves, than to transform what they found. Over the long term, the restructuring of the economy and the anchoring of administration and production in space by investments in railroads, roads and canals and government procedures had greater and more pervasive impact than any administrative action within the cities.

The trading companies, including the East India Co., had not interfered with the internal organisation of indigenous cities. Their representatives made use of local traders as intermediaries and agents and business was transacted according to customary codes. Europeans resided in a distinctive zone close to their fort, while migrants were encouraged to create communities according to their own traditions. This was particularly evident in Madras, which was composed of segmented village-type communities associated with particular occupations. The houses, single storey mudbrick and thatched constructions, with wells in the courtyards, were undistinguished but for their alignment along the broad streets laid out by the company. As in any traditional setting, George Town contained a mix of residential, work and commercial functions practised in the same street, if not the same dwelling. Under company regime, urban growth remained at a rate which allowed the traditional mechanisms of piety, charity and the association of status with donations to the public good to provide communal facilities.

The change in British authority increased the scale of operations and enhanced the centralisation of decisions. The concentration on economic goals, large-scale infrastructure and the elimination of local mints, had greater effects on the number and location of cities than any mutiny or rebellion, for city populations were redistributed and restructured throughout the colonial period (Figure 3.2). As the railway network became reality, the cities situated at important nodes and termini attracted the bulk of the trading and broking business. Elsewhere echelons of intermediaries were displaced with the imposition of a national coinage and the erosion of regional submarkets. Export crops and textiles replaced the previous trade in goods destined for a political elite and brought new social groups to prominence. Traditional specialised skills declined while those of textiles were boosted; the focus of trade was no longer the 'great consumer cities' but the railhead or the garrison. In the north, for example, Kanpur, Fyzabad and Delhi received influxes of brokers and buyers, while Kanpur attracted workers to the boot and shoe factory which shod the entire army, and to the mills that clothed it. Furthermore such advantages were fixed by investment; no longer would sites be abandoned on the succession of a new dynasty or to escape pestilence. Meanwhile previous entrepôts, such as Mirzapur, Kalpi, Lucknow and Farrukhabad, declined or diverted investment to new activities, such as aniline dye manufacture, carpet weaving, calico printing and the making of brass vessels, as in the case of the first mentioned (Bayly 1983).

The British, imbued with the concept of *laissez-faire* and anxious to avoid unnecessary expenditure, failed to appreciate the impact of these economic changes on the cities. The curb on the native rulers' power attacked the base of the patronage system. When the British commandeered the agricultural land rent, they denied them a source of income to fuel the traditional cities' economies. State pensions were no substitute, as they did not allow for the continued support of large retinues, nor the sponsorship of community monuments and services, all symbols of status and authority, nor the extension of charity on the previous scale. Members of the supplanted gentry who had managed that economy were often reduced to poverty, which facilitated the transfer of property in the cities to moneylenders, officials of the new regime or to new landlord and merchant families. Meanwhile pressure on the urban fabric increased through the arrival of migrants, displaced by changes in the countryside, natural increase in population or environmental calamity, to work in the mills. These provided no accommodation, so cities such as Bombay and Calcutta became crowded with single males sharing accommodation or throwing up huts on any available ground at the periphery. Even in Madras, not really an industrial city, migration accounted for 70 per cent of the growth in the last decade of the nineteenth

Figure 3.2

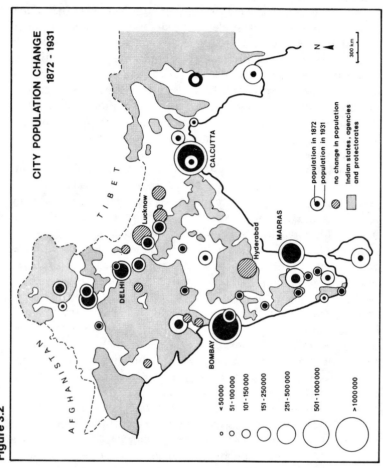

CITY POPULATION CHANGE
1872 - 1931

century. This population was housed by incorporating more and more of the roads into the existing structures, for being a comparatively poor city, few buildings attained more than one storey (Lewandowski 1975). Under such conditions, existing services broke down and it became increasingly difficult to provide new ones. Urban sprawl encapsulated burial grounds and uncontrolled industrial processes polluted water sources. Improvements to urban structure were prompted by epidemics, fire and floods, rather than by traditional mechanisms or any coherent policy.

This failure to consider the needs of the cities arose from the inefficiency of the bodies designed to cater for them and their low priority in the eyes of the Imperial government. Initially municipalities based on their English counterparts had been created but were unable to perform the same functions. Colonial administrators mistrusted systems which outlined policy but left the details of implementation to be devised by provincial governments. What had been conceived as a flexible means to allow for regional variations, became an opportunity to avoid and hamper local participation in city affairs. But there were more fundamental constraints on their operations than these: indigenous conventions outruled the imposition of property taxes, the major source of municipal funds in Britain. As most other sources of revenue were monopolised by the Imperial government, municipalities were chronically underfunded. Furthermore elitist income and property criteria ensured that even when municipal officers were elected, they were mostly expatriates. Not only did they not represent the majority of the population, they could not even perceive their views, as they lived in segregated areas well away from the crowded indigenous city.

Imperial rule bestowed on cities the symbols of its authority in the form of new buildings to serve the administration and commerce but it did not affect the living conditions of more than a small part of their population. In most cities *civil lines* and a *cantonment* housed administrators and garrisons apart from the 'native city' and buffer zones composed of railway lines, industrial premises, physical features or commercial zones underlined the demarcation (Figure 3.3). The new official classes could remove themselves from the sites of enterprise: they copied the British Garden-City movement by building their houses in spacious grounds and ensured that they were adequately served by roads, water and later, drains. The division was entrenched in

Figure 3.3

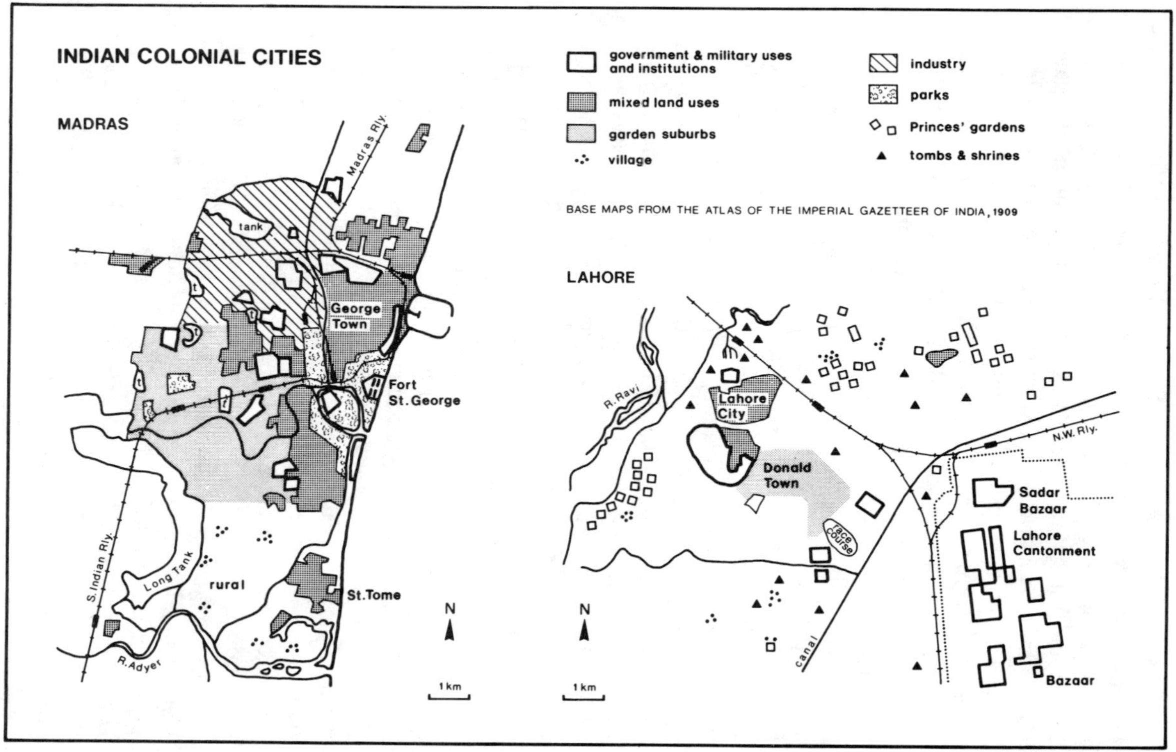

INDIAN COLONIAL CITIES

☐ government & military uses and institutions

▦ mixed land uses

▨ garden suburbs

⋰ village

☐ industry

▩ parks

◻ Princes' gardens

▲ tombs & shrines

BASE MAPS FROM THE ATLAS OF THE IMPERIAL GAZETTEER OF INDIA, 1909

MADRAS

Madras Rly.

Tank

George Town

Fort St. George

St. Indian Rly.

Long Tank

R.Adyel

St. Tome

rural

N

1 km

LAHORE

R. Ravi

N.W. Rly.

Lahore City

Donald Town

TAOB COURAM

Sadar Bazaar

Lahore Cantonment

Bazaar

Canal

N

1 km

administrative structures. The Sanitary Reform Act of 1859 placed European zones under military supervision while Sanitary Commissioners were responsible for the native towns. In Hyderabad, Poona and Bangalore, they even formed separate municipalities. Furthermore the practice of seasonal migration to cooler climates by provincial governments meant that a sizeable proportion of state funds went to build up Poona, Simla and Ootacamund rather than improve the conditions in Bombay, Calcutta or Madras.

Conditions in the indigenous cities deteriorated until massive investment and major technological innovations were essential and often required considerable population displacement. Consider the water and sewage problem: in most cities, traditional latrines were in use and inadequate for the expanded population, who made use of any waste ground. A common source of water satisfied all functions. Sanitary Commissioners devised various types of improved public latrine and attempted to seal polluted wells and control the construction of indigenous models. However, the scale of conservancy operations was already a major undertaking. For instance, a state capital like Allahabad, with a population of 106000, generated some 30000 gallons of sullage and up to a 100 tons of street sweepings a day in 1870/1 (Harrison in Ballhatchet and Harrison 1980). It required 638 sweepers, drivers, assistants and supervisors to cart it all away. The sweepings were dried and used to fuel the water pumping station, while the sullage was buried in trenching grounds at the city's periphery. This land was rented out at a lucrative price to cultivators the following year. These operations absorbed about a half of the municipality's budget.

The expansion of this type of service in the bigger cities was impractical. During the monsoon, unsurfaced roads and alleyways became quagmires, impassable for heavy carts. Richer cities like Calcutta and Kanpur constructed railroads and tramways which provided a commuter service during the day and 'night soil specials' to the trenching grounds at night. But labour was hard to keep when other opportunities arose and because poor districts could not pay higher charges. Further technological innovations became imperative in the introduction of piped water: many cities had been built on low lying, swampy or reclaimed ground and had no proper drainage system. Waste water undermined buildings, became stagnant in pools and transmitted disease. However, before sewers could be constructed, the cities had to be surveyed, straighter and wider streets imposed and the sites of buildings controlled. In the old cities, these procedures were often seen as an unwarranted invasion of privacy, an attack on traditional customs and ancestors, or as directed at particular communities. Indigenous behaviour had to be understood before headway was made: water, for instance, was often wasted to a prodigious extent through the populations' concept of it as a free and natural element as long as it flowed from the tap, rather than as a costed resource that should be turned off when not needed.

The problems caused by neglect and the rapid, haphazard expansion of the cities could not be approached merely through investment in sanitation. A major rethink of their administration was long overdue. Provincial governments treated all their municipalities alike, regardless of their population. The majority permitted little participation as they considered them as an extension of their various departments. This view was challenged in 1880, when the Imperial government designated the municipality as the means of 'educating' the Indian for self-government. Councils were to include far more elected members and to nominate their own mayor. As a consequence, large cities appointed their first full-time paid administrators. Bombay's Municipal Act of 1888 was copied by many cities. Bombay's Municipal Commissioner was a civil servant responsible for administration and answerable to the council's Standing Committee, which held the power of sanction and dismissal. His support team, in accordance with imperial directives, included a Chief Medical Officer, an Accountant General, an Education Officer and an Engineer responsible for public works. They too were answerable to the Standing Committee.

Execution of the reforms fell short of the original aims, which were diluted and delayed by many provincial governments fearing a decline in their efficiency. This relegation of many councils to petty concerns enhanced parochialism and self-interest. In the 1890s it still appeared:

> that the greatest concern of those who controlled municipal government in Madras was in constructing and maintaining bazaars on which they depended; providing sanitary facilities for the areas in which they resided; acquiring land for their own commercial establishments, and developing the port and transportation networks of greatest benefit to them. (Lewandowski 1975)

Ten years later the *Imperial Gazette* was to comment that 'the city cannot boast that it is healthy to Native life, though to Europeans it is salubrious enough' (*Imperial Gazette*, 1908).

In theory the 'new' municipalities could enact by-laws, enforce them and were responsible for an impressive array of obligatory duties. These embraced control measures (the suppression of nuisances, dangerous trades and practices, obstructions, derelict buildings and concerning the disposal of the dead); public services (such as public lighting, cleansing, water supply, sanitation, vaccination, hospitals, primary education and famine relief); and public works (the construction and maintenance of streets, drains, sewers and sewer works, water supply, baths, washing places, markets and slaughter houses). The discretionary duties, only ever attempted by the most flourishing of cities, included the provision of recreational and cultural facilities, post-primary education, private sewage connections, precautionary measures regarding dogs and the collection of statistical data.

In practice, even flourishing cities did not have the means to extend their obligations to the total population. The revenues they collected varied widely, depending on the previous indigenous custom of each region and the history of each particular city (Table 3.1). In the Punjab, Uttar Pradesh and the Central Provinces, the principal source was the octroi, a tax levied on all products consumed within the town, bar those subject to Imperial taxes (salt, opium and mineral oils). In Assam, Burma, Bengal and Madras, the principal tax was levied on houses and land according to their gross rental assessed by the council. Madras and Uttar Pradesh also maintained the pre-colonial tradition of taxing occupations, offices and appointments. The former was discouraged owing to its similarity to income tax which was the preserve of the central authorities, while the latter took the form of flat rates for licences to practice. In addition, most cities collected road tolls and ferry charges, demanded rates to cover such services as piped water, public electricity, latrines and fire protection, and collected fees for education, medication, markets and slaughter houses.

The tax revenue collected could not defray the cost of capital investment inherent in the engineering of pure water supplies, drains and sewers. Most cities depended on loans from central funds for this purpose and by the turn of the century, the interest and repayment of these constituted a major part of municipal expenditure. But the problems were not those of finance alone.

Table 3.1: Principal Sources of Municipal Revenue and Items of Expenditure

Municipality	1901 pop. (thousands)	Revenue 1903/4 Total (thousand R)	Revenue 1903/4 Principal sources %	Expenditure 1903/4 Total (thousand R)	Expenditure 1903/4 % Repayments, loans, interest	% water drainage conservancy
Calcutta[a]	848	8930	55 consolidated rate; 39 loan	8752	39	31
Bombay	776	8470	29 house tax; 28 services	8431	35	23
Lucknow	264	530	68 octroi;	560	14	32
Benares	209	620	48 octroi; 24 loan	640	17	56
Cawnpore	197	1530	65 loan	1130	35	33
Agra	188	530	45 octroi	480	27	30
Lahore	187	640	72 octroi	610	?	25
Ahmadabad	186	1050[b]	? loan; 15 octroi	1102[b]	?	12
Allahabad	175	450	42 octroi; 23 services	450	22	34
Karachi	117	1500[b]	67 octroi	1400[b]	?	15

Notes: a. The revenue and expenditure figures for Calcutta represent the average for the decade terminating in 1903/4; b. the account mentions 'sizeable loans' which are included in the total figure but does not specify amounts in the breakdown under sources.

Source: Based on the *Imperial Gazeteer of India*, new edition 1908, numerous volumes. Figures are in rupees (R).

No changes had been made to grant municipalities decision-making status; procedures were already time-consuming and tortuous and not improved by the addition of yet another tier. A decision to construct a new drain, for example, had to be considered by the provincial sanitation, finance, public works and municipal departments in turn and finally the provincial governor; if the sums exceeded a certain threshold, the whole set of counterparts at national level were also involved. The final decision would wend its way back through the whole stack of officials, some of whom had been replaced in the meantime as the average term of office in one position was only about a year. The official finally charged with building the drain might prefer to implement another project, rather than complete those initiated by someone else and for which he would get no credit (Tinker 1968).

This administrative structure had other traits: solutions to city problems were perceived in engineering terms and based on principles of individualism and land-use alien to Indian societies. Inappropriate measures ensured that planning made little headway in most cities. The institutions concerned, the Improvement Trusts, were guided by the mechanisms promoted by the British Housing Act of 1890, which had been devised for the slums of an industrial and class society. These included the construction of roads through dense city cores and the sale of peripheral land for homes. Later the first Indian Town Planning Act of 1915 drew upon British and German legislation to control land uses. The former had a similar impact as the same measures in Liverpool or Glasgow; the displaced population crowded into adjacent neighbourhoods but in Indian cities there were no equivalent-sized middle-class groups to take up the offer of plots at the periphery and so initiate a housing filtering process. Neither were funds forthcoming from that source to finance further 'improvements'. The mechanisms by which land use controls could be implemented had never been considered. As the planning Act contained no inducements for municipalities and their indigenous councillors had the most to lose by their implementation, it is not surprising that planning officers were supplied with legislation rather than supportive staff.

It was gradually appreciated that town planning could make little headway while it imposed measures directed at the physical fabric with no regard for its inhabitants. Indigenous society was based on spatial communities whose cohesion was maintained by kin and caste ties lubricated by reciprocal services and charitable obligations. They included families of very different wealth; a rich household would be surrounded by the huts of the poor servicing its needs. Families clustered around symbols legitimising their status, such as temples, tombs and rich bazaars; more recent arrivals were relegated to the unconsolidated parts. There were examples where indigenous mechanisms had been utilised in conjunction with planning, as in the Nizam's investments in Hyderabad, two-thirds of which had to be rebuilt after disastrous floods and the contribution to public utilities made by the Pharsee community in Bombay. Patrick Geddes, who spent the last ten years of his life in India, continually stressed the need for planning to interpret problems in terms of the local culture. However, Lutyen used an amalgam of Mogul and class-based symbology to structure the colony's purpose-built capital of New Delhi in 1911. Officials' quarters reflected status by proximity to the Governor's palace and through each building's size and appointments. Thus the houses of carriage-owning expatriates, whose children were ensconced in British boarding schools, were very close to their work and both large and lavish. The house of an indigenous clerk dependent on his feet and with numerous children was both distant and small. The outward arrangement of the entrances, verandas and windows offended Hindu and Muslim mores to the extent that their cows were stabled in the front, while their wives used the back alleys designed to give access to scavengers (King 1979).

City administration was weak owing to its relegation to a lowly position in colonial structures and to the minor powers granted to municipalities. The poor pay, prestige and security of council staff were not attractive to able personnel and council duties were onerous to one having to earn a living. These circumstances did little to discourage councillors' acceptance of 'easements' for attending to matters and most considered the award of junior administrative posts to kin and caste as a proper perk of office, all of which were characteristics of indigenous administration. The repercussions were felt when expatriate personnel were withdrawn during the World Wars and when the municipal reforms of the 1920s made city councils responsible for services. Both voter and representative were woefully inexperienced; incompetent financial management led to short term and *ad hoc* action interspersed with frequent appeals to Central Government. Priorities were selected without proper consideration of their implications, as when ambitious education policies were sustained at the cost of road maintenance and sanitation works. Worse still, councils became the political nursery for the leaders of independence. A few very able managers, such as in Bombay, Allahabad and Kanpur continued to control the tendency to wavering factions and personalist politics, as the Congress Party exerted a modicum of discipline. More often local needs were disregarded as civil disobedience preceded independence.

Latin American Colonial Cities

Although Latin America received the earliest large-scale colonial ventures, these corresponded to a very different technological base and balance of power in Europe; it could be argued that its experience had more in common with the relatively sparsely populated and poorly urbanised areas of Africa south of the Sahara, than with the Indian subcontinent's long urban tradition and established cities. Iberian colonial ventures in Latin America can only be described as openly exploitive; the Spaniards arrived with armies on the mainland in pursuit of gold and Indian workforces. Early investment by the Portuguese was tempered by the profitability of sugar production. The spatial diffusion of both was related to perceived exploitive potential, whether of mineral resources or labour supplies. Their economies were organised so as to generate wealth, primarily in the form of silver in the case of Spanish America, where it was demanded as tribute. But this transformation was abrupt; no period of barter or trade preceded the decision to conquer. Moreover the catastrophic demise of indigenous populations destroyed their empires as effectively as any army. Slave raids on parts of the Caribbean coastlands and in the interior of Brazil also depopulated certain regions. Thus it was a depleted set of indigenous temple towns which survived in the former, while new settlements corresponded to the communications and control roles of the colonial regimes.

The differences between the Iberian powers in rate and style of occupation and consequently in their settlements can be attributed to the very contrasting circumstances encountered. The Spaniards were attracted to the highly developed empires found in Mexico and Peru, their production of precious metals and their dense populations. These could satisfy their principal desires of economic rewards (gold), physical support and power (greed) and religious commendation and incidentally, a moral excuse for conquest (God). These lured them to explore other islands and the mainland in search of more labour from their base on Hispaniola. Tales of legendary empires then led them inland in Mexico and after traversing the isthmus of Panama in 1513, along the coast of South America. Once established, the core of their empires coincided with the concentrated populations in the highlands and apart from Lima, which acted as a pivot of essential communication, the coasts were of minor concern. The Plate estuary, for example, had been discovered and Buenos Aires founded at approximately the same date but little development occurred there until it was necessary to forestall Portuguese penetration. Meanwhile the Portuguese faced a tropical forest environment in north east Brazil, whose sparse populations proved both unsuitable and unwilling to work on their sugar plantations. Portugal had more profitable colonies elsewhere and left Brazil in the hands of private enterprise. Concessions, *capitanias*, consisting of a 50 league-wide strip penetrating the interior, were granted to nobles (*donatarios*) to develop as they could. Settlement here was primarily coastal and consisted of sugar processing and disembarkation points. Even when the Crown provided a skeletal structure centred in Bahia (now Salvador) in 1549, penetration of the interior took place slowly up to the end of the century with cattle ranching developing on the drier lands. It was the accidental discovery of gold at the end of the next which stimulated the drive into the interior in the eighteenth century.

Colonisation over such distances is conditioned by the gradual appreciation of the nature of the new environments and the need to be self-sufficient, even when stimulated by man's cupidity. A great many settlements were founded and abandoned soon afterwards by the Spanish in the fifteenth and early sixteenth centuries. Some were destroyed by earthquakes, others by fire or floods; some lost their founders, who were convinced conditions elsewhere offered more potential, as the frontier was extended. It was not until the second half of the sixteenth century that the urban skeleton became fixed. This process took much longer in Brazil, as the settlement patterns associated with each economic cycle (sugar, cattle, mining, and coffee) consolidated in turn. An important difference is that all of these were associated with pro-

Figure 3.4

IBERIAN SETTLEMENTS IN THE AMERICAS

Settlement Type:

○ Portuguese capital

● Spanish capital

□ Spanish audiencia

· town founded before 1600

○ town founded after 1600

⟋ Spanish convoy route

1000 km

ducts which were to be exported and so despite their location, tended to contribute to the continued importance of long established coastal settlements; the volume of trade increasingly benefited those further south. This was underlined by the transfer of the capital from Bahia to Rio de Janeiro in 1763 (Figure 3.4).

The largest centres of Spanish America were generated by the trade restrictions and monopolies which structured the colonies' economies. Ever fearful of losses to piracy and transgressions by other European powers, the colonies were forbidden to trade with foreigners. Fear of the untrustworthiness of colonial regimes situated so far away resulted in them also being forbidden for much of the era to trade among themselves, or even independently with Spain. The Merchant Guild of Seville had a monopoly over the dispatch and reception of vessels to the Americas, which was only slightly tempered by the admittance of Cadiz, up to the liberalising reforms of 1778. Consignments to the Americas were dispatched in bi-annual convoys. Caribbean trade was centred in Santo Domingo or Hispaniola while most traffic to New Mexico made for Veracruz, for the official *feria*, or sales point, was Mexico City. Those destined for Peru, headed for Panama where a similar official *feria* occurred at Puerto Bello. Thereafter the consignments were in the hands of the equivalent merchants' guild which operated out of Lima. The guilds of Mexico City and Lima held a monopoly which effectively curtailed merchant initiatives elsewhere. Such was their control that cargoes destined for Spain were assembled in these cities, regardless of the origin of the goods. Given the high costs and slowness of land transport, the sea was used whenever possible, but goods still had to pass through Lima, even those destined for Buenos Aires, for much of the sixteenth and seventeenth centuries. This system served to concentrate and perpetuate the wealth of these cities, which stood at the apex of both the colonial administration and the merchant systems and is reflected in their primacy in their respective urban hierarchies, although Lima, established on a virtually green site had only about a quarter of Mexico City's population. Acapulco, on the west coast of Mexico, acquired a minor share of these functions as the dispatch point for the annual convoys servicing Manila, which played the same role for Spain's distant colony of the Philippines. The system discouraged the development for much of the era of regional economies and transport networks to serve them, as each city was obliged to maintain independent contact with the capital and focus its infrastructure to that purpose.

Another set of substantial settlements were the mining centres and those providing essential supplies to them. Silver mining, smelting and later, reduction, required large supplies of wood for supports, construction and charcoal, mercury, salt and copper pyrites. These imports had to be assembled and transported long distances over very difficult terrain. Mule and the less resistant llama trains had to be fed and watered at Andean altitudes where neither was easy. The Mexican mines were rather more accessible, enabling the use of ox carts. Mining towns in their heyday could be very substantial. The most famous of them, San Luis Potosí in present-day Bolivia, attained a population of 160000. More numerous smaller mining towns, such as Zacatecas with a population of 5000, were the base of Mexican silver production. However, the impact on the economy was arguably larger in the latter case: the mines were manned by forced labour levies on the Indian communities in Peru right up to the nineteenth century, while this system had been replaced by waged labour in Mexico in the mid-seventeenth century. Apart from the sites of the silver ores, its conversion into metal stimulated mining for mercury and copper pyrites, the panning of salt and the production of cattle and timber. The populations of the settlements actually engaged in these activities were probably no more than a few thousand but many occupied inhospitable sites and required provisioning by those better endowed.

The chance discovery of gold in Brazil's interior was what attracted exploration inland. However, a much wider social group was involved and the proceedings probably had more in common with a nineteenth-century gold rush in North America than the government controlled exploitation of the Spanish. Certainly Vila Rica, one of the most famous centres attained a population of around 300000 at its zenith and all the urban trappings one could wish. Unfortunately its placer deposits were soon exhausted and its population dwindled to a mere 8000–10000 by the end of the eighteenth century. It was the need to consolidate the settlements and trails developed during the mining boom, to expand the government presence both to control lawlessness and recoup taxes that led to the retrospective administrative and urban presence of the state in the interior and reinforced the future importance of Rio rather than the towns of the north east.

Few Spanish towns, other than those serving the mining industry, had a productive base. Not only did the sparse populations and the poor state of transport curtail markets but also the government was loath to permit any developments which could compete with Spanish imports. The exception concerned textiles, for the coarse cottons and woollens were consumed mostly by the mining populations and the indigenes and so did not compete with the quality clothes destined for the cities. Small factories, *obrajes*, based on Indian labour were important in north west Argentina (present day Cordoba-Tucumán), the high basin of central Ecuador (Otavalo to Riobamba) and in the Mexican basin itself. Latin America also contributed two important natural dyes to Europe: cochineal and indigo. Such restrictions did not apply to Brazil where the government tended to reinforce and raise its taxes from the commercial initiatives of private enterprise. Inter-regional trade beyond that essential to service the mines was viewed with suspicion in the former but could evolve spontaneously in the latter. As a result, the settlement pattern in Spanish America became established (fossilised) early on, while it continued to expand and receive new members in accordance with the continued occupation of the interior in Brazil.

These factors were significant in defining both the role of urban settlements and their relationship with the surrounding countryside. In Spanish America settlements received the title of *villa* and an appropriate coat of arms at the bequest of their founders, provided this consisted of a minimum number of adult Spanish males who were also prepared to build a church, town hall and jail. It cost the crown little to bestow such honours and encouraged settlement, for such 'towns' were the points of departure from which the greater part of the municipality, the rural areas, were incorporated into the empire. Lands were granted as *mercedes*, straight rewards for services rendered, and initially as '*encomiendas*' or lands held in trust. The '*encomenderos*' so favoured were obliged to oversee the diffusion of the doctrine among the indigenous population and to collect the tribute payable to the crown, any excess in the stipulated amount being their reward for the service. Although this system was abandoned in the seventeenth century, the urban command over the rural economy (beyond subsistence), remained. Even in the eighteenth century when many landowners left the 'towns' for their estates, these remained the points through which all excess production had to be channelled, often at prices set by the urban authorities, and from which justice was dispensed. In Portuguese America, however, urban settlement appeared in response to the needs of the productive base. Supply points on trails, especially at junctions or where produce from the coast met produce proceeding there from the interior, market points for the livestock producers or where the merchants from the coast bought the products of the mines, all became small settlements, which only afterwards received formal status and urban trappings. These were dispensed selectively to the most profitable sites and the addition of administrative roles gave them the advantage over others of similar origins.

Certainly few of the Spanish 'towns' deserved that title on the basis of size or the services provided. In 1600 only the foci of the two viceroyalties had populations exceeding 10000. For a long time these two cities exceeded all others many times over and only the most profitable mining centres attained significant numbers (Figure 3.5). Others were based on indigenous concentrations, such as Puebla, Guadalajara, Oaxaca, Cholula and Tlaxcala in Mexico and Quito, Cuenca, Cajamarca and Cuzco in South America. Trujillo and Lima, both coastal sites, had relatively small indigenous bases. They acquired the administrative roles appropriate to their position in the very rigid colonial hierarchy, which was paralleled by the ecclesiastical hierarchy. But the number of new Spanish immigrants were comparatively few and their natural growth rates slow, as one would expect when administrative systems were concerned primarily with tax collection and control, rather than with stimulating the economy or providing services. Few exceeded 5000 inhabitants in 1800. The cities were primarily consumption centres and their relationship to the counryside was predominantly parasitical.

The governing body of the town, capital of the municipality, was the *cabildo*. It was the only institution in which local participation could play a significant role, as all others such as the courts, the *audiencias*, were the preserve of government officials, mostly appointed direct by the colonial office from Spain. The *cabildo*'s remit covered executive, financial and legal functions. Under the first heading, it supervised the police, exercised partial control over the militia, inspected all manner of institutions, fixed market prices and took steps to secure local food supplies. Under the second, it administered minor funds and raised local taxes, such as on property and to cover the periodic cleansing of public places. The council's members also elected from their number those to serve as magistrates of the lowest courts. However, although the quality of transport and comparative isolation undoubtedly gave the *cabildos* considerable autonomy over their day-to-day actions, government officials did arrive from time to time to inspect their books and rule whether their actions were legal. The declining importance of the *cabildo* as an institution towards the end of the

Figure 3.5

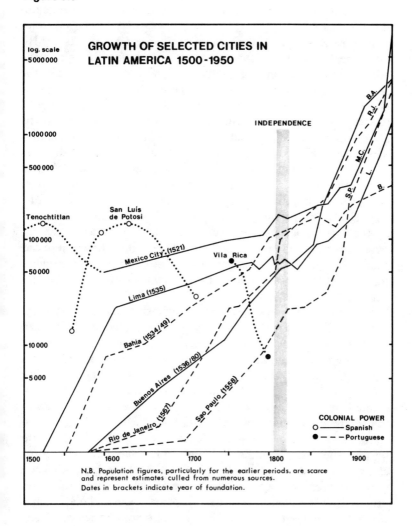

GROWTH OF SELECTED CITIES IN
LATIN AMERICA 1500-1950

N.B. Population figures, particularly for the earlier periods, are scarce and represent estimates culled from numerous sources.
Dates in brackets indicate year of foundation.

colonial period would suggest that such controls, plus the increasing lure of the members' rural estates, rendered participation less attractive. It would seem that one of the most appreciated powers was that over the lands within their vicinity. Technically, these could only be alienated in the name of the crown for the original city charters required lands to be set aside to allow for common needs and future expansion. In many cases these provisos were ignored and certain cities could not expand owing to the usurping of the surrounding lands by the entrenched founding members.

The emergence of municipal structures in Brazil was slower. By Portuguese tradition, town councils were autonomous corporations which could only be established on allodial land. This disqualified most of the earliest settlements which were established on privately owned sugar estates. This situation did not arise with the later developments in the interior. *Vila* status had legal connotations and the settlements had to have a minimum population and their residents, trading wealth, tax income and social status were scrutinised before receiving it. Their residents were obliged to build a church, town hall and prison, as in the Spanish *villas*. The prominent citizens who comprised the *camara*, the council, were elected, appointed or even inherited their position depending on the region in question. Their ability to exercise considerable power over the vicinity was undoubtedly a major attraction to the ambitious. In many areas privately controlled anarchy reigned supreme beyond the scrutiny of the central authorities based in the cities of the littoral.

Greater attention was paid by the Spanish to the outward form of their cities than with the quality of the living conditions within them, despite the widespread powers of their councils. Founders stemming from a military tradition could appreciate the utility of a regular layout and where sites permitted, cities such as Lima were focused on a large central square which occupied a whole block created by the gridiron lattice of streets (Figure 3.6). This was flanked by the most important institutions, such as the church, the state (governor's house and offices) and the town hall. In the biggest cities these would have been handsome buildings and later church façades were liberally decorated with sculptures of the saints, friezes and columns. Adjacent blocks housed the most distinguished residents, mostly of Hispanic origin and major cities would have had a number of convents and monasteries with their associated churches. Blocks further away were subdivided into smaller plots to cater for the poorer and less prestigious occupants, craftsmen, small traders and *mestizos*, those of mixed race. Construction here even in major cities would be in *adobe* (unfired brick) and roof tiles begin to give way to thatch. The regular pattern tended to peter out at the margins of the settlement where frequently a disorganised huddle of huts housed the indians who

Figure 3.6:

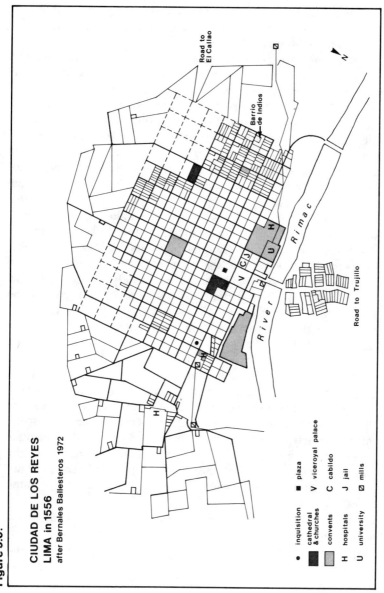

CIUDAD DE LOS REYES
LIMA in 1556
after Bernales Ballesteros 1972

- • inquisition
- ■ cathedral & churches
- ▨ convents
- H hospitals
- U university

- ■ plaza
- V viceroyal palace
- C cabildo
- J jail
- ☑ mills

Road to El Callao

Barrio de Indios

Rimac

River

Road to Trujillo

N

laboured, carried water and fuel and supplied the city with casual labour. Their neighbours were the cemeteries, slaughter houses and other offensive land uses.

Although instructions governing city layout were not published until the Laws of the Indies appeared in 1573, much of the above was established practice and would not have been out of place in peninsular cities of the period. Where limits on space precluded it, such as in the mining town of Guanajuato in Mexico for example, the organising principles if not the forms may still be distinguished. One twisting main road serves this steeply sided bowl in the hills and many lateral ones take the form of stepped paths or even dive beneath the buildings. Several small, certainly not square, open spaces equipped with fountains provide public amenity and the churches and public buildings are spaced out along the spinal road wherever an appropriate site occurs. Here too the smallest houses climb the hillsides and essential but unpleasant services were located downstream and at the periphery.

Race, wealth and social status were closely associated in the Spanish city but their spatial patterns were less obvious at the micro scale. Prosperous merchants and officials had retinues of poorer relatives who assisted in their enterprises, as well as servants and slaves. Master craftsmen employed apprentices and ecclesiastics also employed servants. Master and slave tended to reside together. The ground floor rooms with access to the street of large properties were occupied by shops, storerooms and work-shops; some of these were rented out and their tenants resided at the back of the premises. A prominent doorway gave access to an interior courtyard around which were arranged the residential rooms of the household. Large households frequently required two or more of these; the outer provided private open space for the family and its guests, while the inner catered for the servants and their services.

On the whole towns were unhealthy places with next to no sanitation. Water was often drawn from surface sources for all purposes, or from shallow wells and public fountains. Drainage systems were very underdeveloped and confined to the centre. Filth tended to accumulate in the streets until the *cabildo* ordered its removal. Epidemics frequently ravaged the cities, causing elevated death rates. At such times, all those that could tended to evacuate them and so disease spread to other settlements. High densities facilitated contagion within the towns, particularly within the hovels and makeshift settlements at their peripheries, which often evolved as a means of avoiding the high taxes exacted from traders using the markets within the towns' limits.

Unlike today, however, the overcrowding was not due solely to the exorbitant prices of urban land markets. Sometimes it stemmed from the commandeering of the surrounding lands which prevented expansion but often land was available; *cabildos*, however, were loath to reduce their power through the allocation of the one resource over which they had *de facto* control. The process by which this was eventually done is also instructive for present municipal administrators. Take the case of Caracas, whose *cabildo* had steadfastly resisted the pressure to release *ejido* lands for housing purposes. In 1770 its population of 20000 was bottled up in 115 blocks covering less than two and a half square kilometres. Plots had been subdivided so many times that they averaged no more than just over 15 square metres, while larger houses had been split between several families. The frequency of epidemics finally persuaded the *cabildo* to release land across the river: 700 plots were created over the next 20 years and a further 200 over a similar period thereafter (Waldron 1981). The *cabildo* invited petitions from the needy and its public policy was to give priority to the homeless. Careful perusal of the lists of beneficiaries by Waldron revealed that about 90 per cent of the plots did go to people who met that criteria, while the rest benefited *cabildo* members, government officials and others whose occupations implied comparative wealth, presumably as compensation for services rendered to the city. Titles to these plots were only received once a 'minimum' dwelling had been erected over a period of six months. The destitute received them free but a very low sum and tax was imposed on the rest. The *cabildo*'s minutes revealed a similar range of problems as those encountered today in the administration of such a project. Poor and illiterate beneficiaries often lost or allowed documents to be defaced. In the absence of documents and proper registration of titles by the *cabildo*, plots might be reallocated. Then many wealthy beneficiaries simply refused to pay the tax. Those in arrears, or caught renting their property, or attempting to sell it within the proscribed period, were subject to forfeiture. All this gave rise to multiple claimants to the same plot, including individuals who had bought in good faith. Since between 80 and 90 per cent of the new districts' populations moved over a three-year period, the number of properties sold for profit was high. Part of these sales were undoubtedly to raise capital for individuals with no other source of income but there also seems to have been considerable mobility between settlements during that period. Unfortunately there is no indication as to where the sellers went.

By the late eighteenth century control systems in the colonies were weakening in response to the increased turmoil in Europe and the decreasing power of the Iberian Kingdoms. Supplies failed to arrive and officials did not replace those who had returned after completion of their term of office. For a while inertia allowed procedure to continue but eventually even those occupying key positions in the most entrenched colonial stronghold (Lima) began to question the colonial relationship, particularly as local profits could not but improve if Spanish taxes were abolished. Napoleon's invasion of Iberia and his deposition of their kings was the final excuse which launched mainland Latin America into independence. Between 1808 and 1821 all of mainland Spanish America split up into independent countries, which evolved from the phases of the military campaign and coalesced around the principal administrative foci of the viceroyalties. Brazil, however, was spared fighting for its independence by the arrival of the Imperial Court which ruled in exile from Rio de Janeiro. The vast retinue swelled its population and facilities and the country was elevated in status to equal that of the mother country in gratitude for the haven it provided. Years later, when the Court returned to Lisbon, the heir apparent was left behind as king and it was through him that Brazilian independence was declared in 1822. Independence arising from such circumstances was not designed to undo colonial structures, nor change the role of the cities overnight. Indeed the new nations tended to reinforce the significance of many owing to their role in articulating new economic systems based on the export of raw materials.

Africa's Colonial Cities

Although six nations were involved in Africa, their attitudes towards their colonies, subjects and settlements were little different. Their actions can only be understood in the context of the increasing rivalry between them, which coincided with mounting internal tensions arising from structural changes stemming from industrialisation. Between the Berlin Conference

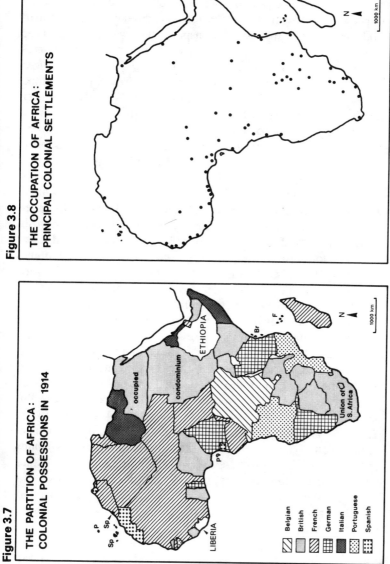

Figure 3.7

THE PARTITION OF AFRICA:
COLONIAL POSSESSIONS IN 1914

occupied

condominium

ETHIOPIA

LIBERIA

Union of
S. Africa

	Belgian
	British
	French
	German
	Italian
	Portuguese
	Spanish

N

1000 km

Figure 3.8

THE OCCUPATION OF AFRICA:
PRINCIPAL COLONIAL SETTLEMENTS

N

1000 km

of 1884/5 and the First World War, the continent was parcelled out in a monstrous game played by rules unrelated to either its peoples or geography (Figure 3.7). The new technologies restructured production and transformed transport; they permitted African colonial systems to be based on the exploitation of raw materials and their trade for manufactured goods. These, even when European settlers were involved, were primarily rural and commercial and required few towns to service them (Figure 3.8). Settlements were bases from which the extraction of minerals, cash crops, or the railroads conveying them, or the ports exporting them could be overseen: they were promoted strictly in relation to their function in expediting production or the administration enhancing it. Elsewhere communities suffered from the withdrawal of land and labour from food production. 'This feature probably did more to dismantle pre-colonial cultures and economies more than most other aspects of colonial experience put together.' (Davidson 1978) The full force of colonial restructuring did not become evident till the inter-war decades of the present century. By then towns and cities formed several distinctive classes (Figure 3.9). Foremost of these, distinguished by their size and far greater growth rates, were the new capitals combining political and economic administrative roles. South of the Sahara, most of these had evolved from the original fortress bases on sites unoccupied by significant indigenous settlement. Although the cores of these cities were laid out according to European patterns, their demand for labour ensured that they had acquired African neighbourhoods evolving spontaneously at the periphery. These accounted for the majority of the population of Casablanca, Dakar, Conakry, Freetown, Abidjan, Accra and Dar es Salaam; one might also include Cape Town and Port Elizabeth of autonomous South Africa. In some cases these roles were grafted on to existing settlements, resulting in a hybrid city with distinctive native and European sectors, such as Tunis, Rabat, Lagos, Douala and Greater Khartoum; even Cairo received distinctive additions in European style.

Colonial economies also required towns located inland at strategic points, generally associated with resources, railway termini or at junctions. Elizabethville, Lusaka and Nairobi originated this way and were designed as white men's towns in which Africans paid off their tax (30 days labour in Lusaka), or were tolerated while employed. Nevertheless here too Africans

Figure 3.9

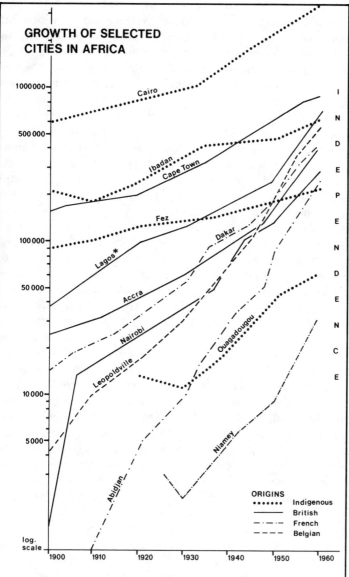

GROWTH OF SELECTED
CITIES IN AFRICA

1000000 —

Cairo

500000 —

Ibadan

Cape Town

Fez

Dakar

Lagos*

100000 —

Accra

50000 —

Nairobi

Ouagadougou

Leopoldville

10000 —

5000 —

Niamey

Abidjan

I N D E P E N D E N C E

ORIGINS

•••••• Indigenous

——— British

—·—·— French

– – – Belgian

log.
scale

1900   1910   1920   1930   1940   1950   1960

N.B. Population figures, particularly for the earlier periods, are scarce
and represent estimates culled from numerous sources.

*Lagos' indigenous base was insignificant in comparison to its
subsequent development under colonial rule.

constituted the majority of the population, although the system
kept these cities artificially small. Governments everywhere concentrated on the symbols of 'their' systems and dismissed the
Africans as local fauna. The French, who never pretended that
their colonies served any other purpose than that of being profitable to France, invested very little beyond the seats of their respective Governor Generals (Dakar and Brazzaville) and major
ports. Consequently their settlements south of the Sahara were
founded late and remained very small. Towns such as Bamako,
Bouake and Niamey, were described as containing the governor's
residence, offices, warehouses, the houses of European settlers
and Lebanese traders and a large African village, whose inhabitants were 'of no consequence . . . uprooted or semipro-
letariate, peasants who had not broken their ties with their
villages, unskilled porters or labourers, "boys", cooks and
domestics' (Suret-Canale 1971).

Finally there were the inland 'Islamic' towns of North Africa
and the Yoruba towns. Most of the former were subjected to
direct military control by the French and acquired resident
garrisons, much as Indian cities acquired *cantonments*. The loss of
transSaharan caravan trade and the declining demand for their
products ensured that Tombouctou and Ouagadougou stagnated
while their coastal counterparts grew in importance. Those south
of the Sahara also reflected these trends, even though those in the
British sphere did not suffer the same degree of political indignity.
The Yoruba towns were better placed, however; given the ill-fame
of the area as the 'white man's grave', no effort was made to form
plantations or displace the African from the production of cash
crops. Thus the towns were able to keep a market function and
those served by the railways (for example, Ibadan) could benefit
from the increased export trade. They also attracted migrants from
the more harshly exploited and less well endowed regions.

Urban policy was very much an adjunct of colonial economies
designed to inhibit African competition with European traders and
with producers in those areas favoured by settlers. Colonial regimes demanded subservience of their African peoples and this was
furthered by impeding their access to property within the cities and
restricting their rights to residence. Everywhere segregation
served to stress their subordinate status. The mechanisms
employed varied according to whether the city predated colonialism or had been founded to service it.

Before colonisation, native rulers had restricted European access to land. In North Africa, for example, no foreigner could own property before 1880 and prior to the Act of Algeciras in 1906, the only way to acquire it had been through the use of an Arab frontman. Thereafter this was unnecessary but in the absence of titles or surveys and in view of the obligations imposed by Muslim Law, new instruments had to be devised to cover land transactions. These circumstances were general everywhere except in South Africa. Most colonies based their system on the Torrens Act of 1902, which had been devised in Australia and was based on the simplified documents used to register the consignments of ships. All owners could register their property but as this exposed them to the jurisdiction of European courts, whose deliberations were conducted solely in foreign languages and used concepts which conflicted with both Islamic and customary laws, few indigenous families bothered. Their neglect exposed them to abuse. Frequently in North African cities, for example, when the French opened *Livres-Foncieres* 'foreigners began to register . . . land that they had not purchased, or purchased from someone who did not actually own it and to register doctored deeds which included larger areas or more rights than they had purchased' (Abu Lughod 1980). By such means significant proportions of *mulk* (privately owned) property changed hands, particularly that of artisans and traders impoverished by the changes in market demands.

Different mechanisms generated much the same results for new towns. Matriculation had also been introduced in French colonies south of the Sahara in 1906. As the state had taken over all 'tribal and feudal' rights, it assumed that of allocating land for native neighbourhoods. However, the *Permis d'Habiter* granted little security to the holder who could not sell the plot and might be removed without compensation. Even when allowed to sell, he was still only compensated for the value of the house if dislodged. This caused serious retardation of property improvements; take for example Abidjan, which only had a population of 17000 before being made the capital of Ivory Coast in 1934. It grew rapidly as a result of migration thereafter but still operated with legislation which prevented occupiers from selling plots unless they had been developed according to the specifications of the French building code — a physical impossibility given the lack of building materials during the war — and granted a title. The justification for such delay was that it granted the native protection, as

Europeans could only acquire fully titled land. However, this did not stop speculation in land, nor the exploitation of migrants; it did ensure that only very rudimentary structures were built owing to the chronic insecurity of the occupiers, many of whom were displaced by redevelopment for 'public purposes' (Haeringer 1969).

The essence of the British policy of dual mandate was to respect customary law, including Islamic law, as far as it pertained to native populations and did not impede colonial institutions. In West Africa this was interpreted such that the native rulers kept the right to allocate land to native applicants but could only do so to strangers on the District Officer's approval. Subsequently the latter took over responsibility for admitting Europeans and other foreigners to Crown land allocated to the Government Reserve Area (GRA). Thus land transactions were conducted by Customary or English law according to the identity of the principals. However, while such a system might have served to protect the African from being cheated out of rural land, it was inconvenient in the growing towns where transactions were more frequent and between the groups. Enlightened governors upheld local customs but not to the extent that they interfered with the evolution of the cities. The Governor of Abeokuta, for example, accepted that the traditional gifts made to chiefs on the allocation of land had become sufficiently substantial and standardised to be the equivalent of its price. Provided safeguards were observed, he concurred that such land should be alienable, as this would encourage investment in property and so land registries were introduced. In another case the Governor of Kano accepted the Emir's recommendation that when the individual shares of an inheritance became valueless, Islamic law should be set aside, the property sold and the proceeds be divided between the descendants (Meek 1949).

Very different strategies were pursued in greenfield sites. In East and Central Africa the Resident Native Ordinances Acts of the 1920s defined the conditions of residence. Only those useful to the enterprise and the expatriate population were admitted to the mining towns of Katanga, the Rhodesias and the administrative centres of East Africa; 'idle' dependants were excluded. The Africans were primarily unaccompanied males who were paid and accommodated as though they were single. A few women were employed as domestics but it was impossible to establish indigenous social institutions with such a distorted population structure. These cities were European settlements sited on Crown land; they were surrounded by 'reserves' which could be occupied by Africans until such time as they were required for more important uses or the Africans completed their work contracts. The earliest grants of Crown land in Nairobi and the first townships of Northern Rhodesia, Livingstone, Broken Hill, Ndola and Fort Jameson, were freeholds. Thereafter plots were auctioned off, as elsewhere in the Empire, as leaseholds not exceeding 99 years. The rates attached to these were very low and only subject to review at 30-year intervals. Subsequent leases on buildings were revalued more frequently. The security granted here contrasted with the annual leases frequently extended to Africans in the reserves. As elsewhere, the Township Ordinances of the 1920s demanded such high standards of building, sanitation, ventilation and low density layouts that the majority of Africans were precluded on cost grounds alone. Large scale employers were responsible for housing their workers but such accommodation was generally limited to bachelor-style dormitories and was insufficient and often squalid. The problem of African residence could be ignored by either grossly underbounding the township or by the use of reserves in which Township Building Ordinances did not apply. Thus Kampala upheld its high standards adjacent to the spontaneous and unserviced developments in Kibuga; Nairobi turned a blind eye to the squalor of the 'African sector' and labourers were restricted to peripheral reserves in Lusaka and Salisbury.

The second major strand of policy concerned segregation. Where cities had been long established, mechanisms had to be applied to European residents as well as to Africans arriving subsequently. The instruments adopted were primarily legal; they were reinforced by the pattern of investment in utilities and justified on the grounds of sanitation. For example, in Morocco, Governor Lyautey wished to preserve the fabric of the traditional city and promote the development of a *ville neuve* for Europeans outside. His solution was to auction off state domain and *hubus* lands for this purpose, arguing that they were destined for the use of the 'community'. The profits were used to finance the necessary site infrastructure and utilities. About half the state lands in Fez, most of the perimeters of Marrakesh and Meknes were disposed of in this way but previous speculation in Casablanca and overspill in

Rabat obstructed such a simple solution. Expropriation and building permits were the tools which overcame these hurdles. The Moroccan expropriation law of 1914 empowered the state to designate any area for 'public purposes' and to compensate those affected, provided they held legitimate (matriculated) titles. Subsequent measures decreed that French settlement *per se* was a 'public purpose' and also granted the state 'emergency powers' to take over and demolish any structure without compensation or right of appeal. Meanwhile the *Règlement de Voire* of 1914 specified in detail the architectural characteristics of every building according to the sector of the city. No alterations out of keeping with 'tradition' were permitted in the *medina*, including modern kitchens and sanitation. The specifications concerning windows and perimeter walls in the *ville neuve* left the dweller so exposed to the public gaze that no self-respecting Muslim could live in one, even if the cost was within their means. Thus Europeans were winkled out of the *medinas*, while Muslims were excluded from the *villes neuves*. Moroccans were bottled up in the former and could not improve their property, while the French-dominated municipality allocated over two-thirds of its funds to utilities and services for the *villes neuves* (Abu Lughod 1980) (Figure 3.10).

Obvious parallels can be drawn with the institutions and mechanisms devised in British colonies. There was a similar split between areas in which the Europeans were disentangled from mixed neighbourhoods and allocated to GRAs and those in which the natives were the ones confined to reserves. Generally the former occurred in West Africa and places where a fair degree of urbanisation antedated European arrival, while the latter was the case in new towns set up to service the export economy. In either case segregation was achieved through manipulation of land grants, the legal procedure attached, and government jurisdiction reinforced by physical coercion. Europeans were discouraged from living outside the township or inside a native one by withholding leases of occupancy; some governors advocated the use of fines and even imprisonment for offenders. The law was another weapon: whereas the Township Ordinances of 1971 had left only the cores under the jurisdiction of native rulers in West Africa, those of the 1940s transferred all neighbourhoods but the GRAs to them.

Governors who promoted segregation used illogical arguments and practices concerning sanitation to justify the measure. By the

Figure 3.10

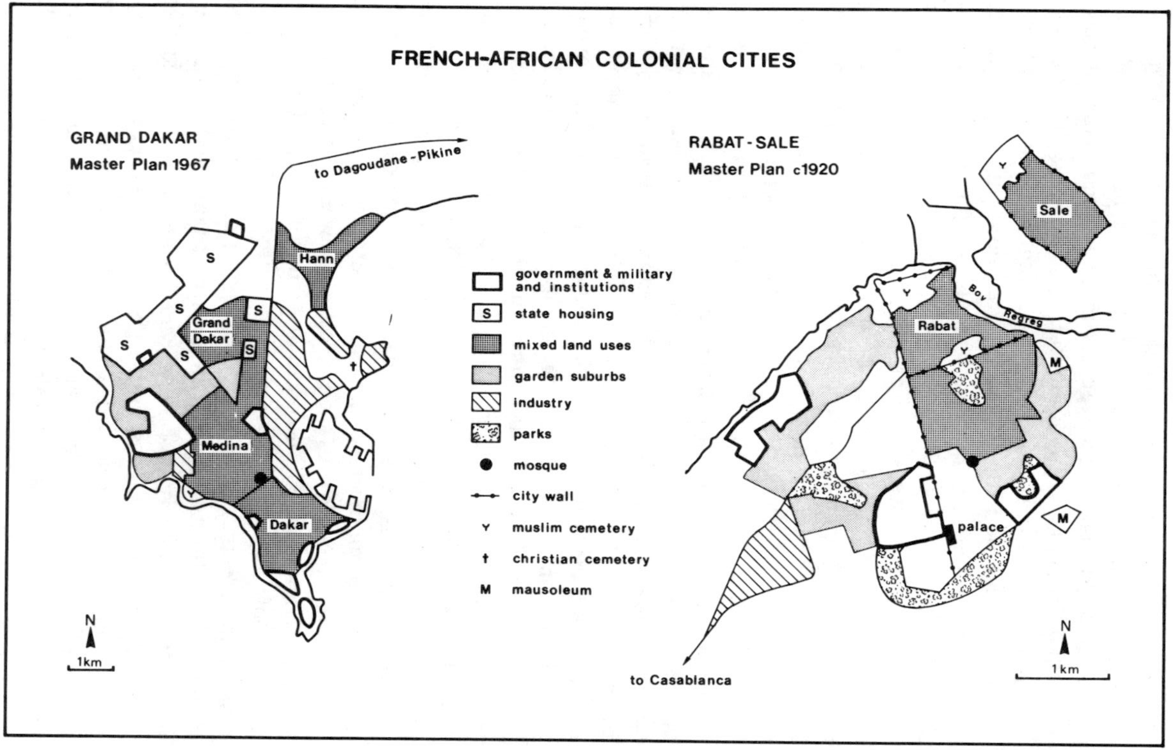

FRENCH-AFRICAN COLONIAL CITIES

GRAND DAKAR
Master Plan 1967

RABAT-SALE
Master Plan c1920

government & military
and institutions

S state housing

mixed land uses

garden suburbs

industry

parks

city wall

Y mosque

● muslim cemetery

† christian cemetery

M mausoleum

to Dagoudane-Pikine

Hann

Grand
Dakar

Medina

Dakar

Sale

Bou Regreg

Rabat

palace

to Casablanca

N 1 km

N 1 km

end of the nineteenth century, sanitary officers had adopted Indian sanitation law and were aware that the mosquito was the prime vector in malaria. Governors in Lagos and Bathurst had shown that if, instead of considering the African as 'a source of contamination', a city-wide policy of swamp draining, land reclamation, sanitation for all and the free distribution of quinine was followed, death from this cause could be eliminated. The two cities only had eight deaths from the disease over a decade between them. Their successors were not so enlightened or vigilant; after outbreaks of plague in Accra and yellow fever in Sekondi, the Colonial Office gave governors a free hand. Like the French in Dakar, they saw the solution in terms of segregation; they proposed to remove thousands of African residents in Kumasi, Sekondi, Tarkwa, Cape Coast, Lagos and many others so as to accommodate a few dozen Europeans in the style that they expected. A subsequent Governor described the scheme drawn up for Calabar as 'illogical, unjust and wantonly destructive . . . incomprehensible to everyone'; the plan banned Africans from maintaining their houses so that 'it will be possible to effect eventual demoliton without paying compensation' (Gale 1981). Everywhere wealthy Africans were turned out of valuable property on prime sites, although every European household of any status continued to include numbers of African servants.

Even though these measures were carried out on the grounds of sanitation, the vast majority of the ever increasing African population seldom received any facilities in return for their taxes. In Governor Lugard's eyes such investments were wasted on them as 'such a community has no desire for municipal improvement. It neither appreciates nor desires clean water, sanitation or good roads and streets.' Thus in 1916 Lagos street-scavenging was limited to the European parts, electricity was installed only in the main street and there were few water connections outside the European sector. It was not until 1928 that the first town planner, fresh from Letchworth and Cape Town, arrived. Since he appeared to consider his brief that of designing garden cities exclusively for the European population, perhaps it is just as well that administrators gave him little power or support. As in India, major services were installed in cities at the instigation of a few outstanding individuals, such as Ibadan's chief engineer who planned and built the water, sewer and electricity network in the 1920s and 1930s (Home 1983).

Although subsequent governors disassociated themselves from the racism of their predecessors, the fact is that they inherited cities structured indelibly by their mechanisms. A major feature was the 440-yards wide building-free zone, the counterpart of the French *cordon sanitaire* and of the German *freie zone*, which supposedly prevented the mosquito or the rat of the native city from reaching the European. Major obstacles, such as railway tracks, industrial sites and commercial zones were also used for this purpose. These attitudes were still evident in an advisory pamphlet concerning township layout for governors issued in 1939 (Figure 7.5, p. 246). Such short-sighted policies initiated processes which are still responsible for major problems today. In North Africa the fabric of the *medinas* deteriorated due to infilling and then overcrowding. New arrivals, squeezed out of the rural economy, could not be accommodated and so resorted to illegal squatting at the periphery where no attention was paid to their needs until conditions became potentially explosive.

The escalating problems of the growing cities were identified too late and the remedies advocated were little heeded by governors, who failed to anticipate the rate of city growth after the Second World War and took few steps to alleviate the overcrowding of African neighbourhoods. Indigenous systems had been constrained for decades and could not be recast to generate investment at a very different scale for new technologies. The first planner appointed to Morocco, Ecochard, recognised these facts in 1946. He advocated the construction of 'minimal' housing on a massive scale, forming satellite suburbs at the peripheries of the cities. This was composed of blocks made up of eight by eight metre cells, each of which consisted of two rooms and a kitchen enclosed in a courtyard, while water taps and latrines were provided in *trames sanitaires* threading each district. No alterations to the shell house were permitted but in some areas the beneficiaries merely received a lot on which they could build. In 1953 he was ousted by business interests, who disapproved of his efforts to control speculation, and his solution was never adopted in full. State housing was built in many cities but it was the middle classes of Dakar, Abidjan and Rabat that benefited, while very few of the poor received a *lotissement* (Figure 3.10). Thus in the decade before independence an economic class mechanism was superimposed on the earlier racist patterns and the policy of urban segregation was perpetuated with the aid of new criteria.

The British Colonial Office remained equally complacent in the face of a problem of 'very large proportions'. The small-scale provision of public housing, most of which was monopolised by civil servants, did virtually nothing to improve conditions for the majority. The problems arising from the cities' constrained sites in West Africa where many consisted of low-lying islands, creeks and lagoons on the coast, increased when development was forced onto the mainland and the cities became physically fragmented. By the late 1930s administrators began to argue that a smaller, permanently resident African labour force would be more efficient, responsible and less threatening than the contingents of single males on short-term contracts. These families could be housed and educated and so become a worthy addition to the cities, most of which gained municipal status in the 1940s. This policy meant in Khartoum, for example, where the colonial regime of 1932 had allocated $50m^2$ plots in the *Deims* to accommodate the male labour force, that $200m^2$ plots, equipped with a latrine for family use, were allocated in 1937. In the transition, some 1000 families were dislodged and access was denied to bachelors; the overspill proceeded to squat or double up with relatives illegally.

Others argued that, as the African was 'not a town dweller', his housing should be provided by the employer or state at a subsidised rent. Employers were awarded Crown land for this purpose and the construction of lodging houses was encouraged. Locations which minimised travel to work were urged. The great African townships of the Northern Rhodesian copper mines were considered as 'models of their kind' and the Colonial Office was proud of planning about 10000 units in which to house the entire African population of all the towns and cities of East and Central Africa over a five-year period. Grants from the Colonial Development and Welfare Fund did allow some of these to be built but their numbers were insignificant except in Nairobi. The Vasey Report of 1950 tacitly recognised the failure of these policies, in that it advocated African home ownership in cities for the first time. It argued that this would stabilise the population, enhance participation in the urban economy and reduce the possibility of ethnic conflict. Neighbourhoods were to be zoned for African employer, public and private housing. Given the costs involved in municipal units, 40 × 50ft plots (12 × 15m), were to be made available on 40-year leases for the Africans to build their own. Public estates could then charge economic rents (Stren 1982). However, despite these measures, the scale of demand, the decades of excessively low wages which in addition to labour law had prevented families from living in the towns and the disregard of the African's need for basic utilities, had reached explosive levels which added fuel to independence movements.

Conclusions

Today, the colonial era is frequently blamed by Third World spokesmen for the narrow range of roles assigned to their cities and for a great many of their ills. Colonialisation, it is claimed, stultified local economies and so inhibited production-based urban growth and later, when it was accompanied by major technological innovations, it was responsible for accentuating city/rural differentials in lifestyle, well-being and the power of institutions in the former over the activities of the populations in the latter. Cities have always been centres of privilege and most areas of the Third World had been subjected to 'foreign' rulers with strange habits before. However, few previous empires had had such strong central institutions not based on simple kinship allegiance and so capable of resisting the fragmentation of authority among the leaders. This undoubtedly permitted more coherent policies to be maintained for longer periods.

It might seem paradoxical after this criticism that colonial authorities in India and Africa have also often been accused of neglecting the cities because of their focus on primary production. It is true that 'national' interests, represented by investment in railways, canals and irrigation, took precedence over city needs in India. Indeed given the distribution of the population this could be justified, if it were not for the very large size already attained by many of the cities and that colonial institutions had undermined the indigenous mechanisms for serving their needs. Although in many parts of Africa today regional planners lament the cities' abilities to corner scarce resources which larger populations spread more thinly over the countryside are desperately in need of, it has also been argued that this comparatively high rate of investment has been necessary to make good deficiencies in basic infrastructure resulting from ignoring the needs of the indigenous populations in colonial days.

Still greater criticisms have been attached to the internal structures of the cities built and to the administrative mechanisms which gave rise to them. Understandably colonial authorities everywhere concentrated on their own needs first; however, these could seldom be satisfied without the presence of a supporting indigenous population. The attitude towards these ranged from simple neglect, much as was meted out to their European counterparts of the sixteenth or seventeenth century in Latin America, to focused discrimination at the turn of the century in Asia or Africa. Most of the criticism is focused on the latter and particularly to the issue of health. Allowances can be made for the fear and ignorance which surrounded the transmission of disease; after all, European cities of the period were pretty disgusting places and also paid the price of high death rates. But it is difficult to forgive the deliberate rejection of recommendations made by knowledgeable medical authorities of the Crown, which are now available for all to see in the official colonial records. Further, natural justice is offended by policies which charged or taxed residents for services which were only supplied to a few, or which reached only designated areas from which the indigenes were excluded. The facts are complex, as has been revealed by the examples cited, but there is evidence to uphold the charge of wilful discrimination on the grounds of ethnic identity, which meant that indigenous populations in most of Africa lived in worse conditions than if more egalitarian policies had been adopted.

A secondary charge arising from the 'convenience' of segregated residence is that colonialism debased the humanity of the indigene through dualist policies, particularly in Africa where they have survived to this day in the institution of apartheid. While these pervaded colonial life far beyond the cities, it was expressed through restricting their admittance to them and residence in them. Apart from the few cases where such controls have only recently been relinquished and in South Africa, the cities suffered from the explosive reaction which accompanied the lifting of such controls on independence. If urbanisation had been allowed to evolve spontaneously in response to the restructuring of economies, the cities would not have been the focus of such voluminous inflows of migrants. No 'developed' city ever had to cope with such sudden and rapid growth, which immediately saddled independent TWCs with a wide range of physical, social and economic problems. No 'developed' city had to cope with these at the same time that national institutions had to be created and as local staffs took over key executive posts for the first time.

The most enduring colonial legacy concerns the set of institutions, which still governed most spheres of action after independence, such as the law and all its ramifications, the structure of the civil service, attitudes to planning and to local participation, the structure and content of educational and health systems. While these have been modified, particularly in the 160 years or so of Latin American independence, few countries have had the courage to face the disruptions which would arise if entirely new systems were devised. Consequently the greatest legacy is intangible and lies in the crucial realm which governs how decisions are made, by whom, for whom and how they are implemented. In TWC terms, these define how a settlement is embedded in the government hierarchy, how much autonomy it enjoys, what resources it commands and what powers it has to implement its solutions.

4 ADMINISTERING THIRD WORLD CITIES

Stable governments rarely emerged immediately on independence in the Third World. Many countries suffered decades of political confusion while charismatic military campaigners learnt new political skills and strove to conciliate rival factions representing regional, ethnic or class interests. Elected governments have rarely completed their term in office; *coups d'état*, political assassinations, military interventions and dictatorships have been the norm. One common result of such events has been the tendency to concentrate power in central government, to enhance that of the chief executive and to develop control mechanisms throughout administration. Independence was also accompanied by new constitutions which introduced changes with significant implications for society. Latin American countries for instance restricted the rights of the church, expropriating their lands and prohibiting their previous financial operations. Slavery was abolished. Partition of India and Pakistan launched the massive interchange of population on religious grounds. Africans could move freely to their cities where they mingled possibly for the first time with co-nationals of very different ethnic origins. Unfortunately, experienced administrators were scarce, following the departure of the expatriates who had dominated executive roles previously. The most able were absorbed by the implications for national goverment rather than by the local impact of such changes. City administration has always been a secondary concern of government.

Nevertheless, large cities play a prominent role in any economy and their citizens are capable of exerting considerable political pressure. Governments cannot afford to ignore them and their intervention usually takes three forms: fiscal structures weld the city to the nation through the tax contributions of the former and the grants allocated by the latter; the state provides, organises or stimulates others to provide and organise the utilities and services that no contemporary city can do without and it arbitrates in the conflicts which arise between local interests within the city. The rapid rate of growth of TWCs since 1960 has generated considerable logistical problems in all these spheres. Large proportions of most cities' populations are impoverished. Despite their efforts to sustain themselves, neither their activities nor their incomes make a significant contribution to state revenues. Any utilities provided for them have to be heavily subsidised. Private enterprise only caters for the relatively affluent and states can afford neither to provide virtually free services on a large scale nor to neglect the needs of those citizens indefinitely. Not only does disaffection give rise to political unrest but makeshift alternatives often prove to be more expensive to all concerned in the long run. Moreover, the independent investments of the state, private enterprise and individuals contribute to the haphazard organisation of cities, which is a problem in itself. It is ironic that while governments stress the need for order and control, most cities have grown and continue to expand according to the proclivities of individuals or through the stimulation of isolated developments by institutions and state dependencies. The explanation for this lies not so much in the growth rates of the cities *per se* as in their administrative structure.

The outstanding feature of most TWC administrative systems is their lack of structure. All too often they are composed of a plethora of central government departments, autonomous state agencies and municipal dependencies, each of which is responsible to a different authority. Jurisdictions often overlap and remits are ill-defined owing to this fragmentation. The consequences for cities are considerable: administrative systems are complex to the extent of incompetence. Conflicts arise when services are split between authorities and deficits occur when not one is reponsible. Entities are often unresponsive as decisions concerning developments are taken elsewhere. As a result the actions proposed may be inappropriate for the particular city in question or are met with indifference by the intended beneficiaries. Moreover government strictures concerning standards tend to foster reliance on the state, which is inadvisable given its limited resources and competition for them.

The plurality of authorities is a reflection of the ambiguities within the state bureaucracy and of its relationship with various sectors of society. Central control is expressed in the very unequal powers granted to the various tiers of government. Local governments are particularly weak, in fact many countries have suspended them for long periods and even where they do exist, they tend to be chronically understaffed, underfinanced and not empowered to undertake development projects. The usual justification for their subjection to authoritarian procedures is on the grounds of efficiency. Municipalities are considered incapable of complex administration owing to the calibre of their staff. The circumstances would appear to promote a self-fulfilling prophecy: meagre pay attracts only poorly qualified personnel, whose financial insecurity and comparatively low social status expose them to the temptation of bribes and the political manoeuvres of their social superiors. As a result, local government acquires a tainted image which reinforces central government's tendency to restrict its powers and to assign pay levels commensurate with the routine tasks it performs. Therefore municipalities maintain registers, collect taxes, issue licences, clear up rubbish and inspect public facilities. They seldom make plans or implement them.

Cities fall under the jurisdiction of both central, regional and local authorities in most countries. The national perspective of the first means that they command their attention only as far as their demands are consistent with the broader development strategies of government. Regional and local authorities have greater freedom to consider specific local problems but their resources are far more limited. State intervention in urban development can take many forms. Its authority is essential in the preparatory stages of projects whose proposals require the expropriation of land or the co-operation of many proprietors. Once this has been done, the options between direct or indirect participation are still wide. An authority may complete all stages of a small project itself, subcontract its construction and subsequent maintenance, or create a dependency to take charge of these operations. If the facility is likely to be self-financing or even profitable, it may be offered to private enterprise as a concession or on a free basis. Where the installations are for a very poor population, or a specific group such as refugees, the state may merely facilitate provision by a charity or through international aid. Where several tiers of government are all instigating projects by these varied means in the same city, the difficulty of co-ordination is manifest. Moreover the spatial outcomes are unpredictable and invariably some neighbourhoods and populations remain unserved, while others benefit several times over. There is considerable need for streamlining administrative systems, improving their internal communications and for reconsidering how resources and responsibilities should be distributed between their various components. However, administration cannot be separated from government and politics; changes which ignore the structure of society and its goals are doomed to failure.

Administrative Structure

Third World City administrative systems appear remarkably similar in performance despite their different forms. Commonly they are subject to the vicissitudes of political events, which are often either in a state of flux or regimented by dictatorial powers. Furthermore, politicians and the military, not content with policy making, often interfere with the internal organisation of administrative departments. As a result administrators can only plan effectively over the short term. The impact on staff is also considerable. Political appointees need to tailor their goals to their support and expected term of office, while regular personnel defend their tenure by unimpeachable adherence to written procedure and inertia. Neither strategy is appropriate for attending to cities' complex needs. Moreover, there is ample scope for improvement in the structure of the systems themselves and their internal organisation, as well as in the procedures they utilise.

Administrative systems may be classified according to the degree of power concentrated at their apex. The most extreme form of centralised system is dominated by national ministries. These are rare, as line officers from such entities seldom cover the menial but essential city services which entail considerable local organisation and daily supervision. It is more common for military and other authoritarian regimes to nominate chief executive officers to manage cities. Other regimes tend to do so when political opponents are elected to head a municipality or when leaders assume too independent a line. They are also imposed when a municipality becomes a political embarrassment because of the financial irresponsibility of its leaders or their corruption. In all of these cases the character of the administration depends directly on the appointee, as supporting staff are expected to follow laid down procedure blindly.

The most usual type of system is based on representatives of the national authorities who leave very little scope for independent action to regional and local levels of government. The principal ministries are represented by departments within the cities and are responsible to them. Although they may collect statistics and report on local circumstances, the decisions resulting from these observations are taken at a higher level of government. Strictly 'city' authorities are relegated to supervising low level functions involving the control of daily transactions, minor services and tax collection. Such authorities employ large numbers of unskilled labourers to sweep and scavenge and teams of inspectors to oversee markets, expend licences, control traffic and read meters. Its clerks record births, deaths and marriages, payments for basic services and taxes for property, land, vehicles and individuals, according to context.

A similar division of authority is often found in more democratic systems. Directly appointed chief executives often co-exist with local councils composed of representative and/or elected members. The latter act as advisors: they may raise proposals and discuss those of the executive but they rarely have the power to enforce the former or to veto the latter. Their impact ranges from being purely symbolic, where their recommendations are almost entirely ignored, to highly significant, where they give rise to policy and changes. On the whole such councils have little effect as they seldom influence budget allocations which are made centrally.

A much less common administrative system vests far greater power in local authorities which are directed by councils composed of elected members. This type of municipality operates on the basis of council decisions and is responsible for a wide range of functions, including planning, urban utilities, education, health and public works. It must employ professional and technical administrators and a much more diversified inspectorate, as well as the usual complement of clerks and labourers. Obviously such a municipality must have a sizeable budget if it is to fulfil its responsibilities. There are many cases of city authorities which fit this description on paper but not in practice, owing to the lack of appropriate financial support.

The implications of these administrative structures for TWCs are considerable: they determine who defines urban policy, the means exerted to implement it and indirectly on its appropriateness. The chance of a policy being fulfilled is enhanced when its sponsor is a central government department but in such cases competing political pressures shape its initial formulation, rather than an analysis of the city's needs. On the other hand a local authority's proposal may be more relevant but is less likely to materialise. The reason for this lies in the structure of government finance. Unless locally raised revenues are sufficient to finance a project, regional and state level support are required, whether the funds are sought from the public or private sectors, or from national or international markets. Frequently cities are not empowered to deal directly with financial authorities other than those of the state.

Centralised decision making and controls affect the efficiency of local administration in a number of ways. First the national scenario imposes constraints of its own, such as the need for some logical means of standardised representation. This entails the definition of a network of territorial jurisdictions and mechanisms for their staffing. However, it is almost impossible to devise schemes which are equally appropriate for disparate social and economic settings, nor are the same procedures as effective in rural, village and city contexts. A standard framework of units devised on just about any criteria usually results in large cities being fragmented, or in the creation of districts composed both of city and adjacent hinterland. If these reflect the way activities are organised (such as in China), they can be efficient but this is not usually the case. Most very large TWCs face considerable problems because they do not have an executive body whose jurisdiction is coterminous with their functional area. Secondly, national level authorities are usually based on sectoral interests which act independently, while the essence of city management lies in the co-ordination of activities within a territory. The means to achieve the latter are very weak in most TWCs. Moreover inter-ministry co-operation is not facilitated by the presence of political appointees in executive positions. Where careers are dependent on the fortunes of political sponsors, officials are more likely to adhere to national policies at the expense of local circumstances. This is particularly common when such incumbents lack the necessary expertise for the posts they hold. Thirdly, the supervisory measures designed to promote good management and rational objectives in city administrations often result in patron-client relationships between the officials of the various tiers. Frequently local circumstances are neglected for the sake of political objectives when this happens. Such relationships also occur between nominated or elected councillors and neighbourhood groups, or between the former and the employees they appoint to the city authority. These networks of personal relationships often direct the allocation of contracts and services. The promotion of vested interests usually ensures that the needs of the underprivileged are ignored.

Personalist politics influences not only the shape of administrative systems but also their internal organisation and performance. Political appointments at whatever level tend to induce frequent changes in policy and rapid staff turnover, given the instability of governments. Both constrain a department's ability to maintain consistency or to plan ahead. When the personnel nominated are unsuited to the posts, even greater damage is done. These circumstances encourage inertia on the part of regular employees and the resignation of those frustrated by the lack of proper direction and career structure. Furthermore departments subjected to such interference are rendered incapable of handling technical matters which must be dealt with by professionals who fully understand their implications. Not only is it costly to place decisions concerning large capital investments in the hands of amateurs but large scale construction projects incorporating foreign contractors or finance stipulate guarantees and define the obligations of the local participants. Governments often decide to create a specialised entity for such objectives, rather than risk its mismanagement at the hands of existing ones or face the difficulty of forcing sectoral authorities to co-operate with each other.

These circumstances explain to a great extent why TWCs tend to contain a plethora of separate authorities. Regional capitals acquired offices representing the arms of central government, in addition to some form of local service administration. As they grow, specialised 'technical' agencies are introduced to manage utilities such as potable water or electricity. These are usually autonomous, or responsible directly to a minister and are empowered to override both the spheres of action and territorial jurisdictions of other authorities. Finally, *ad hoc* agencies may be created to oversee particular short-term needs. They allow construction projects to proceed rapidly, as a single agency has control over all aspects of the scheme; they are associated with metro networks, industrial estates and housing projects for the poor. This strategy is effective in circumventing inter-institutional jealousies and in fulfilling narrowly conceived objectives, such as a construction project. However, it exacerbates the problem of the lack of co-ordination within cities between the actions of separate agencies. The latter arises through the late introduction, weakness and restricted scope of planning in most TWCs.

A spatially oriented activity like planning cannot avoid conflicting with the rest of government agencies which are structured hierarchically and sectorially. At national level, resource and development planning is frequently the preserve of an autonomous agency which reports directly to the chief executive, his deputy or the cabinet. This attachment to a policy arm of government rather than to an administrative one underlines the advisory role of the activity. The same is often true at city level: plans cut across the jurisdictions of other authorities but their designers rarely have the power to enforce their co-operation, especially when they are national agencies. Planning is usually an office of regional governments and many would say, of its capital city. Staff produce Master Plans, which detail their cities' land uses, infrastructure, services and future needs. They list the investments in infrastructure required by specified dates, given the projected population and the norms of construction and services they wish to apply; they seldom detail what procedures need to be devised and by whom to achieve these objectives. This lack of realism is also reflected in their rigidity and in the period taken to prepare them. By the time of publication, interim growth has rendered many of their recommendations impractical or very expensive. Furthermore, the adoption of inappropriate Western norms and the condemnation of indigenous traditions ensures that the costs of even partial implementation are prohibitive. It is not surprising that planning departments do not appear to have contributed much to large TWCs in these circumstances; on the other hand, non-capital cities tend to receive an adapted version of the master devised for one, which may be totally unsuitable, or evolve without any aid.

Although these generalisations are true for most TWCs, it is instructive to assess their validity for specific cases. In 1979/80, Nigeria, India and Brazil had substantial urban populations, although Nigeria had only one 'millionaire' city as opposed to nine in India and eight in Brazil. They also had respectively 27, 148 and 24 cities of more than 100000 people. These countries are federations which confer various degrees of autonomy on their constituent states. Each has created a new centrally located federal capital, although Lagos continues to perform this function for Nigeria, as Abuja is still under construction. Despite their very different societies, histories and economies, their government structure and its repercussion for their cities is not all that dissimilar. This is portrayed in Table 4.1.

Table 4.1: Participation in City Administration by Government Level

	NIGERIA 1979	INDIA 1979	BRAZIL 1980
	Federal Government	*Union Government*	*Federal Government*
National Level			
Creates:	framework for local government structure	framework for local government structure	framework for local government structure
Approves:	statutory financial allocations	public loans	finances; urban planning
Administers:	special urban projects; new federal capital	special urban projects; union capital	National Utility Cos; federal capital
Appoints:	senior civil servants	senior civil servants	senior civil servants
Regional Level	*19 States*	*22 States*	*22 States*
Creates:	Local Governments: Development Boards	Municipal Corporations; Municipalities; Metropolitan Development Authorities	Municipalities Metropolitan Regions
Approves:	budgets, records	budgets; city plans	legality of ordinances
Appoints:	Secretary; senior civil servants; Supervisory Councillors	Chief Executive; Heads Improvement/Development Trusts; senior civil servants	Chief Executive: Deliberative Councillors; mayors of large cities
Administers:	Local Govt. Service Board; Planning & Development Boards; Housing Corp; some services; state grants	Public Services Commission; some utilities & services	Planning: most utilities & services
Local Level	*299 Local Authorities*	*41 Municipal Corporations*	*9 Metropolitan Regions*
Organs:	Secretary; Supervisory Council; Elected council (appointed management committees replaced the elected council after 1979)	Commissionaire; Trusts; Elected council	Deliberative Council; Consultative Council
		1 404 Municipalities Chief Executive; Elected Council	3 972 Municipalities Chief Executive; Elected Council

Their cities are subject to decisions taken at all levels of government. In all three countries the federal government has the dual functions of ensuring that the regional tier does not surpress local level administration altogether and of operating a number of service agencies concerned with planning, urban redevelopment and subsidised housing. In addition, central authorities exert indirect control within cities primarily through financial mechanisms. They approve the budgets for major developments, allocate their shares of nationally collected taxes and award grants to support high order facilities, such as hospitals and universities. Regional authorities also exert control via both legal, political and financial channels. They usually appoint executive staff to local governments and they have created supra-local government authorities to plan and co-ordinate those utilities which cannot be supplied efficiently piecemeal or on a small scale. They usually provide some higher order services directly. City authorities represent the interface between government and citizens through the combination of professional executives with nominated and elected councillors. In all three cases the latter tend to perform an advisory role, while the executives, the supervisory councillors (Nigeria), the trust members (India), and the deliberative councillors (Brazil) formulate policy and are charged with implementing plans.

These hierarchical systems have not gone without criticism. There is no doubt that the intervention of higher authorities in local government is not always politically disinterested, although at times it has served to restrain conflicts between local factions. It has been defended as a measure to attract more able staff and to ensure their political neutrality but the first objective has been easier to attain. For example, the constitutional reforms of 1976–9 granted Nigeria's states considerable latitude as to how councillors should be selected and staff appointed to their local governments. All of them opted for a 'unified service' in which a Local Government Service Commission appoints and posts all staff. This regional level authority handles all promotions and transfers, although local governments may express an opinion and are obliged to report on staff performance. The advantages of such an arrangement were that 'it guaranteed the tenure of qualified staff, it prevented arbitrariness in personnel administration, and made local government service attractive by guaranteeing salaries and pensions'. However, it also permitted the states to control local governments through the appointment of party loyalists and so extend the scope of its patronage at the expense of the party which was supported locally (Gboyega 1983). Partisan politics are rife in Indian cities too and are aired in the municipal corporations' elected councils which are charged with devising policy and legislation. In Calcutta friction constantly arises from the political dominance of the indigenous Bengali community, as the dynamism of the city's economy depends on non-Bengali industrialists, financiers and immigrant labour. When the council's deliberations deteriorate into parochial squabbles with pronounced ethnic overtones, the state government suspends them and administers the city via the commissioner and the Improvement and Development Trusts, whose members it appoints. This has also happened in Kanpur, where wealthy leaders appear to have treated the council as a mechanism by which they can exploit the corporation. However political affiliation can serve to promote discipline. In Ahmadabad, the seat of Mahatma Gandhi and Patel, the corporation has a reputation for efficiency and civic pride. As a result it exercises far greater autonomy than is usual and is reponsible for a far wider range of services (Ashraf 1977).

Political rivalry within cities also arises from their numerous local representatives. Although Nigeria's recent administrative reforms proposed a single entity for most cities, this was not possible for the 3.5 million inhabitants of Greater Lagos, while both Indian and Brazilian metropolises are composed of numbers of independent municipalities (Table 4.2). State governments have devised metropolitan authorities to enforce their co-operation but cities have pointed out that these are often the source of ambiguity. In Brazil they have no statutory role, while in Nigeria and India they are empowered to act independently. In the first case, the corporations advise and draw up plans but have no power to impose their recommendations. Consequently, action can only be taken circuitously via a third party. As the federal government finances major capital investments, it is able to implement projects within cities, either through one of its service agencies or through one created specifically for the task. Here in fact a putative local authority can only achieve its objectives via the mechanisms of federal government. On the other hand friction arises in many Nigerian and Indian cities because the Metropolitan Development Authority acts independently of the Municipal Corporation. The Development Authorities are chaired and staffed primarily by nominees of the state government and are also financed separately. They frequently usurp all but low level functions and have been criticised for adopting an engineering approach and ignoring social and economic realities. The project to develop a 'counter-magnet' for Bombay is an example. The state of Maharashtra created a Development Corporation, CIDCO, to plan the new city but this seldom confers with Bombay Corporation or the other two authorities concerned.

Table 4.2: Characteristics of Principal Metropoli

	population (in millions)	growth (% p.a.)	Area (km²)	Municipalities (no.)
NIGERIA — 1976[a]				
Metropolitan Lagos	3.519 (est.)	15.37 (est.)	271	6
INDIA — 1981[b]				
Calcutta M. Corp.	9.166	3.04	1452	35
Bombay M. Corp.	8.243	2.76	603	2
BRAZIL — 1980[c]				
São Paulo Metrop. R.	12.588	4.46	7951	37
Rio de Janeiro Metrop. R.	9.019	2.4	1172	14

Notes: a. Ayeni 1981; b. *Indian Yearbook* 1984; c. *Anuario Estatístico do Brasil* 1983.

The type of conflicts raised in these examples explain the increasing number of governments that appear to be rejecting administrative systems which concentrate power overwhelmingly at the centre. Nevertheless the forces pressing for decentralisation are tempered by the unwillingness of existing authorities to release control. A common solution to this impasse takes the form of locational deconcentration and the diffusion of authority within the state apparatus. Major cities acquire local offices of central authorities alongside a range of specialist and *ad hoc* agencies. This fragmented structure promotes flexibility, or considerable inconsistency and total confusion, according to viewpoint. It certainly allows authorities to adopt independent policies concerning the division of responsibilities between the state and the private sector, while not denying central government the power to intervene directly or indirectly by means of financial mechanisms.

City Finances

The amount of state investment in TWCs is difficult to assess owing to the large number of dependencies involved. Rarely is it possible to identify the monies corresponding to operations within a specific city from the accounts published by agencies attached to the regional or national tier of government. Many analyses are based on local government statistics for this reason but these units represent only a part of the total investment in cities by the state sector. Furthermore, as the allocation of responsibilites for utilities and services between the various tiers of government varies from country to country, indeed between cities of the same country in the case of federal states, the funds wielded by municipalities are not a fair indicator of their cities' levels of public investment. Nevertheless, as these resources are irrefutably attached to individual cities and are subject to municipal control, it is important to appreciate their sources and how these could be expanded. Frequently options are constrained, as the fiscal revenues generated by many local activities are appropriated by higher tiers of government.

Fiscal structures are extremely centralised in the Third World, judging by the limited evidence. Central government appropriates and spends a far greater share of national revenue than in developed countries. In 1970 local authorities in the Third World spent on average less than a quarter of state revenues, as opposed to the 47 per cent of their industrial counterparts (Linn 1981). In some countries they account for less than 10 per cent of state expenditure. Such financial weakness is both an excuse and a mechanism used by national government to maintain their subservience and to restrict their powers. Unfortunately the few experiments with devolution have not increased the efficiency of city administration nor improved living standards, as local governments have tended to use their powers to achieve short term personal and political ends. Let us reconsider our examples.

Nigeria's reforms were inspired by the Netherlands' Local Finance Fund and Brazil's system of inter-authority relationships. These guided how much public funds were divided between the tiers of government and guaranteed the autonomy of Local Government (LGs) except in cases of financial malpractice. In 1981 all public resources were deposited in a Federation Account from which 30 per cent were allocated to the states and a further 10 per cent were distributed between LGs according to their respective populations and areas. State governments in turn were required to allocate 10 per cent of their total revenues to their LGs on the basis of their population and primary school enrolment (Gboyega

1983). LGs were free to utilise these funds as they wished but their choices were regrettable. Many appeared to consider them as a substitute for local taxes. Northern LGs, such as Kano, abolished the traditional tax on cattle and halved the *haraji*, the community tax paid by all residents. Then a great many LGs voted to double their salaries such that part-time councillors would have been earning more than the full-time executive managers of all but the largest metropoli. Finally the lure of secure funds led to the proliferation of LGs until the Federal Authorities intervened to re-establish the units of 1976. These actions meant that metropolitan revenues did not increase as fast as the urban retail price index and inflation and in Kano's case, they actually fell in *per capita* terms (Frishman 1980).

Brazil updated its municipal ordinances in 1968 and while the principle of autonomy, except in cases of financial misconduct, was upheld, federal support was restructured. Federal authorities destine 5 per cent of the national excise and income taxes to LGs according to their population and *per capita* income. In addition the states and muncipalities share between 10 and 20 per cent of the unified taxes attached to fuels and lubricants, mineral extraction, electricity, sales and industry; the share rises to 40 per cent in the case of vehicle licences. In practice states withheld their LGs' share of these funds and encouraged the formation of more so as to increase revenues from federal sources; the ordinances had decreed that councillors should only be paid for administering units with a population of 100000 or more, so there was no case of personal gain here. Even federal payments were often made in arrears and they were tied to specific priority projects nominated at national level. On the surface, Brazilian municipalities acquired a firm financial base, but as in Nigeria its provision resulted in even greater dependence on national government. National authorities have come to dominate the principal activities which cities normally administer and the *per capita* expenditure levels of Brazilian metropolitan authorities are extremely low even by Third World standards.

A common characteristic of TWCs is the comparatively low proportion of resources which are generated internally. Linn collated the evidence for 17 cities of which eleven were capitals. Of these, Bogotá, Cali, Bombay and Ahmedabad contributed over 40 per cent of total government expenditure within them; Jakarta, Manila and Seoul managed over 30, but Mexico City, Kingston,

Tunis and Managua contributed less than 20 (Linn 1981). This dependence on central government for finance restricts municipal decisions. Neither everyday administration nor development projects can proceed without the security of an established budget but even this is usually only possible on an annual basis. It is common for external monies to be remitted only after considerable delay and unforeseen eventualities at higher levels may preclude them arriving at all or only in part. Payments to state dependencies are notorious for their arrears: officers usually choose to curtail maintenance, services and then salaries, rather than prejudice capital projects for which they could incur penalties. These funds may also arrive earmarked for uses determined by the policies of others.

Strictly municipal resources comprise taxes and service charges. These accounted for between 100 and 30 per cent of the TWC LGs' funds but the ratio between them varies considerably between cities. Statistics relating to 25 cities, dated from the late 1960s to the mid-1970s, revealed that taxes provided over one-half of the resources of ten of them (Linn 1981). This group included three Latin American capitals (Mexico City, La Paz and Rio de Janeiro), four Far Eastern metropolises (Karachi, Calcutta, Madras and Manila) and three much smaller cities in Zaire. Self-financing services made substantial contributions for another third of the sample comprising three Colombian cities, the Far Eastern metropolises of Ahmadabad, Bombay and Seoul and the two small African cities of Kitwe (Zambia) and Francistown (Botswana). The rest raised their local revenues from a more even split between taxes, service charges and unspecified sources. External sources contributed less than a quarter to the sample as a whole but over 50 per cent in the cases of Kingston, Kinshasa and Tehran. Although these data were published in 1981, they reflect conditions over a decade ago. More recent evidence suggests that national level contributions dominate the budgets of smaller cities, while taxes are most significant in the largest and most developed. The budgets published for Brazil's eight metropolises in 1984 indicate that tax income varies between 46 and 53 per cent for the four southernmost (Porto Alegre, Curitiba, São Paulo and Rio de Janeiro) but represents only 31 per cent for Belo Horizonte, a major industrial town, and less than a quarter of the budgets of the three in the impoverished north east, Salvador, Fortaleza and Recife (*Anuario Estatístico do Brasil* 1983). In 1979, tax income contributed 42 per cent to São Paulo's budget; state value added tax made up a third and the remaining 26 per cent stemmed from federal loans and transfers (Barat 1982).

Tax opportunities arise from income, property, sales and leisure; the choice of sector is constrained both by a city's wealth and how it is distributed and by the prerogatives exercised by national government. Income tax, for instance, is usually the concern of national authorities, which accounts for its limited contribution to municipalities. The sample referred to above revealed that apart from Francistown and Mbuji-Mayi (Zaire), where it provided over 60 per cent of their resources, it contributed between a quarter and a fifth to Zambian cities' coffers and much smaller shares to Zairean and South Korean cities. Property and property transactions taxes are far more common. They yielded over half their cities' budgets in such varied regions as Colombia, India (Calcutta, Bombay and Madras), South Korea and Zambia; they are collected in some form in most TWCs. Industrial and commercial taxes on the other hand appear to be restricted to Latin American cities and Manila. They frequently arise from the construction and administration of industrial estates by municipalities. General sales taxes are not popular as they bear most onerously on low incomes which are consumed by the purchase of essentials. They are rare but made very substantial contributions to Rio de Janeiro's and Managua's budgets. More specific sales taxes are far commoner and take different forms according to region. The *octroi* is exacted on all goods entering a city and plays a significant role in Pakistani and nothern Indian cities which inherited Islamic institutions. Beer tax is extremely important in certain African mining towns such as Kinshasa and Bukaru. Tax on motor vehicles, which is often appropriated by national government where they are widespread, generates half of Jakarta's local income and makes much smaller contributions to South Korean and Latin American cities; the latter tax gasolene sales as well. A small levy is often attached to cinema, concert and theatre tickets, football matches, etc. and other spectacles as an entertainment tax in TWCs. Jakarta charges a much higher level for gambling.

The funds generated by all these taxes are not proportional to the needs of TWCs. Municipalities are not responsible for the same range of public utilities and their expenditure levels need to be interpreted with this in mind. Nevertheless the range of *per capita* expenditures revealed in Table 4.3 includes such extremely low values that it is a wonder some municipalities provide any at all. It is not as if they could rely on existing social overhead capital to tide them over a limited period, or as if their populations were stable and ageing. The demand for utilities has never been satisfied and population growth ensures that little headway is made over the backlog. Moreover the poverty of the majority of the residents means that the real costs of development cannot be passed on to the consumer. Furthermore national governments often impose ceilings on service charges, subsidy levels and credit. One of the few options open to municipalities is to increase their efficiency in tax assessment and collection. Another is to introduce measures which will ensure that the gains arising from the expansion process itself are invested in improvements to public services.

Table 4.3: Local Government Expenditure *per capita*

City, Country	Population (millions)	Date	Expenditure ($US)	Date
Tehran, Iran	4.591	1976[a]	26.2	1974[i]
Lahore, Pakistan	3.298	1981[b]	5.0	1979[j]
Ahmadabad, India	1.586	1971[c]	19.7	1971[k]
Calcutta, India	7.031	1971[c]	8.7	1972[l]
Jakarta, Indonesia	4.312	1970[d]	8.3	1973[m]
Daegu, South Korea	1.200	1973[e]	41.0	1976[n]
Gwangju, South Korea	.552	1973[e]	37.8	1976[n]
Daejeon, South Korea	.463	1973[e]	38.4	1976[n]
Bogotá, Colombia	2.870	1973[f]	59.5	1972[i]
Cali, Colombia	.926	1973[f]	51.4	1975[i]
Cartagena, Colombia	.356	1973[f]	20.0	1972[i]
Cuenca, Ecuador	.146	1979[g]	17.4	1979[g]
São Paulo, Brazil	8.493	1980[h]	7.3	1980[h]
Rio de Janeiro, Brazil	5.093	1980[h]	5.1	1980[h]
Belo Horizonte, Brazil	1.781	1980[h]	3.5	1980[h]
Recife, Brazil	1.204	1980[h]	3.3	1980[h]
Porto Alegre, Brazil	1.125	1980[h]	5.1	1980[h]

Notes: a. Quoted by Costello in Pacione 1981; b. estimate; *Pakistan Statistical Yearbook* 1979; c. *Indian Census* 1971; d. United Nations 1972; e. Mills and Song 1979; f. DANE Censo Nacional de Población 1979; g. estimate; Lowder work in progress; h. *Anuario Estatístico do Brasil* 1983; i. Linn in Bahl 1981; j. Qadeer 1983; k. Bahl 1975; l. Ashraf 1977; m. Linn *et al.* 1976; n. Smith and Kim 1979.

Some form of property tax makes the greatest single contribution to most TWCs finances. Property taxes also illustrate the inconsistencies which arise through the fragmentation of authority. Local authorities are responsible for their assessment and collection but usually share the proceeds with other authorities. Revenues are split with higher tiers of government whenever they involve capital gains. Municipalities usually have undisputed right only to those attached to the value of sites and buildings. Other authorities also determine the efficiency of property taxation as an instrument of policy: planning and development are obviously relevant to the assessment of vacant lands, changes in land uses, the urbanisation of land and land improvements but these activities are often appendages of regional or central government. Assessment should take projected developments into account but local authorities may be unaware of such plans, while planners are often ignorant of the functioning of the real estate market and so can be manoeuvred unwittingly by vested interests.

Property taxation occurs in nine common forms. Those concerned with land include taxes attached to vacant land, its site value, transactions, the readjustment or consolidation of land and its development rights. Building taxes concern their value, use, change of use and improvements. Taxes on vacant land are reported most frequently in Asia (South Korea, Taiwan and Pakistan) and in most Latin American metropolises, while East and Central African countries, Iraq and Indonesia prefer levies on site values. The increase in land values, such as occurs when land is urbanised, is taxed most precisely in small, thoroughly administered countries such as Israel and Taiwan but Malaysia, South Korea and Colombia all tax increases arising from public investments. Taxes on transfers have been exacted in Jordan, the Lebanon, Malaysia, Singapore, Taiwan, Mexico and Guatemala (Smith in Bahl 1979). Capital cities have unique taxation structures in most countries; frequently the aforementioned are only applied to cities with at least 100000 or even 500000 residents.

The principles which govern tax assessment are varied. Equitable systems exact a progressive charge according to the value of the property. Many governments prefer to discriminate between broad categories of uses or on the basis of ownership. Commercial and industrial premises are commonly charged on a different scale to that of residences and proprietors pay a lower rate on houses they occupy compared to those they let. Taxes may also be structured to play a functional role, such as when governments wish to encourage the development of waste land or penalise those who contravene the zonation laws. TWCs also forgo much potential revenue through convention. They exonerate a considerable range of properties belonging to foreign embassies, government institutions, religious groups and charities. The first two categories occupy large areas of prime land in capital cities. In addition the principle of social justice results in rebates for peripheral areas to compensate for their inferior services. Calcutta, for example, reduces rates for unsewered districts and where households draw on their own tube wells rather than on the mains. Frequently municipalities exonerate very poor neighbourhoods such as 'shanty towns', as the cost of collection would exceed the monies raised.

Sometimes measures adopted with the best of intentions backfire. One such example is the rent control imposed on old tenements and houses in the city centres. Over the long term some of these have proved disastrous. Landlords have stopped maintaining their property, arguing that the income generated is insufficient; they often increased the occupancy rate so as to inflate it. Consequently earthquakes (in Latin America) and the Monsoon (in India) are frequently accompanied by the collapse of derelict buildings. Moreover these premises occupy valuable sites but generate insignificant taxes. Unfortunately the lifting of such measures is a political matter beyond municipal control. When Ahmedabad's local authority tried to introduce more realistic rates based on the market value of the property, as its annual evaluation system inherited from the British requires, it was taken to court and lost. Furthermore, where tenants have enjoyed security of tenure which allows the inheritance of rights, the occupants of central buildings are no longer the very poor, as is often the case in many Latin American metropolises, which was the original justification for the controls. The comparatively wealthy benefit at the expense of poorer rentees even more in Abidjan, Karachi and Bangkok where owner-occupiers are exonerated from paying property tax.

Regardless of the principle governing assessment, however, property taxation in TWCs is generally deficient because of lack of enforcement. Criticisms of the structure or impact of a particular charge are infrequent, if only because they are difficult to assess from partial implementation. TWCs often report that a substantial proportion of assessed tax is never received or only considerably in arrears. The circumstances create many opportunities for evasion. Rapid growth and unplanned morphology exacerbate the problems arising from the lack of land and property registers and cadastral plans. Taxes, whatever their form, must be attached to a specific property in a unique location and are levied on its owner. Local authorities rarely have sufficient personnel to inspect property and commonly restrict their visits to the most tax-worthy commercial and industrial premises. Evaluations elsewhere are commonly based on an average derived from the assessment of a small number of properties within a neighbourhood, or from the average of published prices for a few recent sales. Even this process is lengthy and reassessments are infrequent. Although legislation usually stipulates a five- or six-year interval between reassessments, over double that period is more characteristic of TWCs. This is often the case in developed cities too but they are not growing at the same rates. Consequently TWC property taxes are extremely low in real terms; the World Bank's Urban Public Finances Project estimates that the average ratio of property tax to income was less than 1 per cent (Bahl 1979). Even so proprietors are very skilled at evasion. Residential tenants often cannot or are afraid to identify their landlord; they report lower rents than those actually paid or do not reveal the hefty 'key' money exacted before gaining admittance. Whenever transfers incur charges, purchasers understate the price paid. Owners who cannot evade identification suspend payment during tortuous appeal procedures. Others simply do not pay or use unofficial means to avoid doing so. Given the ubiquity of such practices, advisors have suggested changing procedures such that taxes have to be paid before appeals can be lodged, transactions cannot be legalised until tax arrears are cleared and that governments should be able to acquire property at the value declared for tax purposes. Unfortunately none of these can overcome bribery, nepotism and surreptitious transactions because they do not touch on the social and political relationships that give rise to them.

Municipal finances may also be raised by taxing the windfall gains reaped by proprietors whose lands are revalued through the market mechanisms stimulated by urbanisation, rather than by their own investments in improvements. This is the sphere in which speculation is most ubiquitous and yet few cities have managed to commandeer a share of the profits. Indeed the process has been perceived as a planning problem rather than as an income-generating opportunity. Consequently a few LGs have bought up and expropriated vacant lands at their peripheries with the intention of releasing them in orderly stages as required. These land banking measures are directed primarily at increasing accessibility to land resources. Authorities often auction off some large lots so as to raise the capital for public housing schemes or to cover the development costs of lots for low income groups. As such, land banking is part of housing policy and it is re-examined in that context in the next chapter.

Another strategy which promotes orderly development concerns land consolidation. The holdings at a city's periphery are often fragmented, unequal in size and of irregular shapes; farm buildings are scattered over them according to the internal logic of each parcel. Unco-ordinated development renders their subsequent servicing more difficult and expensive; it may even entail the demolition of property before installation can take place. Taiwan and South Korea have practised voluntary land reorganisation to avoid those problems: neighbours pool their land and receive in exchange a regular serviced plot proportional to the area they contributed. Here the expenses are borne by the proprietor and paid in kind. About 40 per cent of the land is sold to raise the capital and for public uses. After reorganisation the smaller plot is far more valuable: values increased between 500 and 1000 per cent in Kaohsiung city, for example. Taiwan can operate such schemes comparatively easily as all land on the cities' outskirts has been surveyed and registered, while the Equalisation of Land Rights Act of 1977 incorporates the procedures which penalise vacant lots and ensure regular and accurate assessments on which to base a progressive land tax. The proceeds have financed the construction of low income housing and schools (Lee in Cullen and Woolery 1982).

A similar strategy, which does not involve the reorganisation of property occurs in redevelopment schemes. Here municipal expenses are also defrayed by allocating a proportional share of the costs to each beneficiary and through valorisation charges. The schemes usually entail road building, water and sewer installations. In Bogotá the value of each plot was based on its frontage, area, shape, topography, the owner's income, the changes in use likely from the use of the road, the owner's contribution and its distance from the main road. The proprietors contributed the land necessary for the roads and were supposed to pay a third of the rest of the costs within six months. In fact it took twelve years to collect 96 per cent of the charges. Although such schemes are undoubtedly beneficial to the city, they cannot be entirely equitable to those involved. They invariably include some small lots which are rendered unviable if further reduced and the increased land values of the serviced plots cannot benefit those forced to sell them in order to raise their share of the expenses. At city level this is a regrettable but acceptable cost of development; after all some public institutions were also unable to pay and had to donate land elsewhere in lieu (Doebele *et al.* 1979).

Utilities and Services

Factual data on the provision of utilities and services in TWCs are scarce and need to be interpreted with caution. Needs vary with the physical and social environment and moreover are satisfied very unequitably within cities. For this reason the patterns of their provision — quantitative, qualitative and spatial — are excellent indications of the factors shaping society. The absolute and relative levels of supply are determined by economic criteria attenuated by government policy, which may place a greater or lesser relative priority on a particular utility. Government decides on the division of responsibility for supply between the public and private sector, establishes the qualitative norms the utility or service should meet and erects the administrative structure to provide and supervise its provision by others. However, its spatial distribution throughout a city and its accessibility to particular social groups within its population arise from mechanisms built into the delivery systems.

Utilities and services are a particular kind of goods, for demand and supply factors are tempered by the state's political and moral responsibility to ensure that they reach a certain standard and that they are available on an equitable basis. These goals represent an ideal rather than an achievement in most cities but the gap is more marked in TWCs where demand has always outstripped supply. moreover migration and natural increase have stimulated densification and territorial expansion well past the thresholds at which traditional practices of, for example, water collection and waste disposal, are practical let alone safe. Residents cannot collect firewood and open flame lamps endanger closely built-up neighbourhoods. All residents appreciate utilities which save time, promote health and enhance the employment chances of their children.

Unfortunately most African and Asian cities have always been poorly equipped. Governments and societies have been accustomed to the fact that services are concentrated in particular neighbourhoods and vary greatly in quality; their poorest members have always gone without. Latin American capital cities prior to the 1950s were comparatively better served. Subsequent rapid growth has meant that those levels of provision have been hard to maintain. Peripheral neighbourhoods acquire services slowly and belatedly; greater numbers of people are unserviced even if the proportions have not increased.

Groups are affected differently by the deficits. Individuals do not necessarily change their personal habits as quickly as the city grows, particularly when the utilities which would facilitate this are absent. Economic and social advantages allow some to adopt a completely different lifestyle. These contrasts become visible when a city's expansion has taken the form of discrete neighbourhoods distinguished by wealth and they become entrenched by the pattern of utility networks. Clearly when demand exceeds supply, the distribution of any service entails the selection of beneficiaries. This process is highly sensitive when it is conducted by the state and when the consequences are far greater than the satisfaction of the needs of an individual, as is always the case with urban infrastructure. The mechanisms commonly observed in TWCs have often been considered biased and criticised in political terms (for example, Jacolin *et al.* 1976; Michaelson 1979; Perlmann 1976).

The principles governing the distribution of services by state or private enterprise are partly economic and partly self-interest. They are accentuated by the greater importance attained by those controlling a scarce resource. Citizens are classified as rival consumers, whose personal attributes grant them a greater or lesser advantage in particular markets. The availability of public utilities is limited by purely economic criteria; unless the state is able and prepared to subsidise others, urban infrastructure is distributed to those capable of paying for it. Political criteria intervene when officials are faced with the choice between neighbourhoods of equal merit or ability to pay. Personal characteristics come to the fore when services are consumed for specific periods, such as when admission is sought to a school or hospital; selection may be determined by kinship, ethnicity, caste or religious affiliation, rather than by need, merit or ability to pay.

Although private entrepreneurs are also influenced by political and personal criteria, it is of greater consequence when they motivate politicians and government employees. Patron-client relationships pervade much of TWCs' administrative systems. At their meanest, no transaction can be activated without a recommendation from a patron, unless it is oiled by a bribe. At the other extreme, faithful supportees are rewarded with jobs and lots in public housing schemes, while patrons are supported with votes. Although such relationships undoubtedly organise the weaker members of societies to serve the interests of the more powerful, they are also a mechanism by which the former are integrated and gain access to resources. Efforts to acquire useful patrons fuel the system as much as client-seeking manoeuvres. Nevertheless these relationships affect more than the choice of recipients for favours: ascriptive criteria are difficult to accommodate in standardised procedures. If every government official operates through a micro web of personal connections, administrative structure becomes an impenetrable labyrinth. This is restrained by staff turnover or changes of government and efforts to combat nepotism and corruption. Unfortunately the latter tend to give rise to yet more supervisory checks which increase bureaucracy at the expense of services. Moreover, distrust tends to transform every transaction with a state dependency into a major operation requiring personal attention. Domestic service bills, for example, have to be paid at a central office, as it is assumed meter-readers will collude with the householder; cheques may have to be certified by the bank before the recipient will accept them and personal identification must be ascertained at each stage. A commonplace act, such as registering a child for school, involves the parent in standing in endless queues at different addresses in order to obtain its birth certificate, proof of residence and application forms. One can appreciate why people attempt to circumvent the system and even why it is possible to gain a livelihood in some cities standing in queues for others. Meanwhile wealthier individuals resort to private facilities whenever possible.

Private enterprises are under no constraint to offer their services on an equitable basis. They rarely have the capital to provide utilities which entail city-wide operations, unless these are self-financing, or they are given assurances about the security of the investment and the level of charges. In some cities telephones are provided by a private company on strictly economic criteria. Mass transit systems may be operated by a concessionaire and a private electrical company may distribute power. However, it is rare to find a private enterprise responsible for a city's potable water and sewers except on contract to the government. The private sector tends to concentrate on personal services, particularly in the creation of institutions which serve elites. The majority of secondary schools and specialist colleges, surgeries and clinics are in the private sector in most TWCs. Entrepreneurs also complement the public provision of primary schools and usually dominate the transport sector. These operations make up for some of the deficit in state provision and their smaller scale and more flexible operations can be more responsive to local needs than those devised by bureaucracies. But most are motivated by profit; their charges restrict admission which increases the divisions between social groups. Moreover their presence allows the state to reduce its concern over the extent and quality of its own facilities. As elsewhere in the world, high ranking politicians and officials rarely send their own children to municipal schools, nor attend state hospitals. It would seem that in the state sector greater accessibility to services is often achieved at the cost of quality; resources are distributed in a different form, rather than increased.

TWCs have not evolved in isolation. Nearly every major city has been the subject of studies and recommendations by external consultants and few metropolises have constructed a motorway, a new sewage system or a low-income housing estate without the benefit of finance from one of the international development agencies. The examples cited indicate the form these contributions take and reflect the administrative compartmentalism discussed earlier. Consultants are contracted by a sectoral authority to devise a sewage system, a metro network or a master plan. Such technical proposals are invariably sound but their implementation is often thwarted by institutional and social factors which have been ignored. The repercussions arising from the unenlightened transfer of planning conventions from dissimilar societies are greater still. Frequently dormitory estates serving primarily government employees and middle-class groups have been located at great distances from services or work places. The cost of their utilities is considerable and their residents are dependent on transport for every need. Moreover the highways and utility networks built to serve them direct future patterns of developments.

Seven cities have been selected to illustrate the aspects discussed. They include two national capitals (Lagos and Bogotá), three regional capitals in federal states (Ahmadabad, Calcutta and São Paulo) and two regional capitals of centralised countries (Lahore and Cuenca). In population terms two are in the superleague class, one is in the mini-city group while the rest are substantial cities of two to three million. Their governments have ranged from liberals to military dictatorships. Most aspects of service provision in TWCs can be discerned from their experiences.

The most essential utilities and services concern basic needs (water, sanitation, waste disposal and electricity), transport (roads, rail or metro and their respective vehicles), education and health. State participation varies in all these sectors. Table 4.4 indicates the level of government directly responsible for each in a very simplified manner. Indirect participation by agencies responsible for finance, policy, quality control or inspection have been ignored. Autonomous agencies have been assigned to the level which appoints their executive head and audits their accounts. Where several levels are indicated for a particular service, they provide separate facilities. The table cannot reveal the extent of the service nor its quality. What it does reveal is that there is no obvious correlation between the size and status of the cities and the level of authority responsible for its services. The municipality provides the basic needs in a national capital and two regional capitals of both a federal and a highly centralised state. Regional authorities dominate in Calcutta and all levels are present in Lagos, Lahore and São Paulo. Municipal authorities are nearly always responsible for waste disposal. The transport sector consists of the construction and maintenance of roads and railways as well as the vehicles associated with each. National authorities dominate rail and metro services and in general municipal participation is restricted to the maintenance of local roads. The exception is Bogotá, where the municipality is unusually active; this arises from the special status enjoyed by the capital which places its municipality on a par with regional authorities rather than with those of other Colombian cities. State participation is weakest where bus services are concerned. Education and health are often two-tiered services, with municipal participation being restricted to the lower, the primary schools and the dispensaries and maternity clinics. Hospitals are often responsible to the regional or national Ministry of Health.

Table 4.4: Level of Government Directly Responsible for Utilities and Services[a]

	Lagos Nigeria	Calcutta India	Ahmadabad India	Lahore Pakistan	São Paulo Brazil	Bogotá Colombia	Cuenca Ecuador
Infrastructure							
Potable Water	NM	R	M	R	R	M	M
Drainage and Sewers	R	R	M	R	R	M	M
Waste Disposal	R	M	M	M	M	M	M
Electricity	N	R	M	N	N	M	M
Transport							
Highways	N	R	R	R	N	M	R
Local Roads	Rm	Rm	M	Rm	N	M	M
Rail/Metro	N	NR	N	—	N	—	—
Bus Service	r	R	M	R	N	m	b
Education & Health							
Primary Schools	NRm	R	M	M	R	NM	R
Secondary Schools	NR	R	R	Rm	R	NM	R
Dispensaries	Rm	R	M	M	M	rm	R
Hospitals	N	R	M	R	N	N	N

Notes: a. Key for Table 4.4 is as follows: Nn — National Government; Rr — Regional Government; Mm — Municipal Government; — — No service; b. Private enterprise. The size of the letter indicates the scale of responsibility.

Infrastructure

Man's most basic need is water; it is greatest in tropical environments. All governments give high priority to water supplies and the seven cities examined have city-wide authorities whose remit also embraces sanitation. They probably overestimate the proportion of households they serve, as government dependencies tend to ignore unofficial neighbourhoods. They report that over 90 per cent of the houses in the consolidated part of Lagos and Cuenca are connected to the mains, while the corresponding figures for Bogotá and Lahore are 74 and 60 per cent. Those without rely on public standpipes, private wells (in Indian cities and Lahore) and surface sources. The latter are certainly contaminated. The average daily *per capita* consumption in litres (lcd) reported are very similar, being 95, 85 and 82 lcd for Calcutta, Lagos and Cuenca. There is far greater variation within cities; the rich of Lahore and Lagos consume 447 lcd and 336 lcd compared to the 151 lcd and 40 lcd of their fellow citizens with access to a single tap. It is estimated that those dependent on a public standpipe utilise only about 20 lcd and in fact current World Bank projects for the very poor are designed to provide between 15 and 25 lcd.

Despite their considerable concern over water supplies governments' actions are often ambiguous. Considerable resources and energy have been devoted to planning and expanding networks and capital projects have absorbed most of the international assistance to this sector. However, little attention has been directed at conservancy and at increasing the efficiency of the existing services. City growth increases pressure on water resources which become vulnerable when withdrawal rates allow seepage from contaminated sources, such as adjacent water courses or pit latrines. Calcutta's parallel hydrant system provides unfiltered water from the Hooghly for washing purposes. São Paulo has to import water from a considerable distance, as more accessible sources are used to generate power and for sewage disposal. Lagos depends on six bore holes while Lahore's water comes from aquifers 82–119 metres deep which are tapped by tube wells; it has no reservoirs. Only a small city like Cuenca can get away with minor purification works on a local stream. The expense of rendering most cities' water fit to drink is not recovered by the charges. Although they all charge specific water rates, these are often absurdly low and insufficient to discourage waste. Only

Ahmadabad has a realistic charge which progressively penalises heavy users. Bogotá also applies differential service charges such that richer neighbourhoods subsidise poorer ones. Nevertheless the residents have to raise 30 per cent of the installation costs before the authority will initiate work. Sometimes action in this sphere is hindered by obsolete legislation. Only in 1976 was Calcutta's authority able to repeal measures which prevented them from taxing *bustees* which had been provided with water and bathing platforms. Cities also neglect maintenance and the replacement of the derelict portions of their networks. It was estimated that half of Lahore's supply seeps away through cracks and broken joints. Their repair would be cheaper than sinking new wells and extending the mains.

Improved water supplies increase the need for drainage and sewers, especially where cities occupy low-lying and swampy sites. Lagos, Calcutta and Lahore are in constant danger of floods; sewage surfaces in the streets whenever storm drains become blocked or the water level rises above the outfalls of the sewers in adjacent rivers and lagoons. The problem is exacerbated by the cavalier disposal of solid wastes and in India and Pakistan by the cows that are kept within the cities. Storm drains and sewers are rarely designed to cope with large volumes of cattle droppings which cannot be dried for fuel during the rains. Sanitation is the most poorly developed utility in most TWCs. Although over 80 per cent of households were reported as served by sewers in Cuenca and Bogotá (the latter's figure is probably an overestimate in population terms), only 39 per cent of those in Lagos, 33 in São Paulo and about a quarter in Lahore enjoy this service. Moreover parts of the networks are ancient and require extensive repairs or replacement and many authorities have inherited fragmented systems. All six municipalities in Lagos LG had separate systems and even a city as small as Cuenca has three. Unserviced households make use of traditional pit latrines, open drains, waste ground and night soil services. Half of Lagos' population rely on the latter and they are widespread in Lahore and the Indian examples. Much of the effluent collected is still used to irrigate vegetable gardens at Lahore's periphery and most of the cities' sewers deposit their contents untreated into the nearest water body.

Sewer networks entail lumpy investments and are most expensive to insert where building is very dense, as in traditional city cores, or very scattered, as on accidented topography or patchy developments at their peripheries. Householders are usually expected to pay for the costs of connection to the mains, but these are beyond the means of even middle income groups in most African and Indian cities, unless provided as part of a subsidised housing scheme. Authorities have tried to overcome this problem by providing communal sanitary blocks but they have not been very successful. Users dislike public facilities and rarely maintain them; as the areas so provided generate little tax income for the city, neither do the authorities and they degenerate into health hazards. To avoid this, more recent schemes in Nigerian cities and in Ahmadabad's Flood Victim Resettlement Project provided smaller blocks shared between only four or six adjacent households; these have proved far more successful for societies which prize personal privacy. The high costs of conventional water closets have also prompted research into alternatives based on composting principles and the acceptance of more realistic standards: Calcutta's Slum Improvement Programme provided a latrine, tap and bathing platform. As there are no indigenous traditions of pit latrines or night soil services in Latin American cities, it is fortunate that their comparatively higher average incomes render conventional facilities more accessible and that peripheral settlements have access to waste ground before these aspirations are satisfied. Latin American authorities do not seem to have considered communal facilities and it is doubtful whether they would be acceptable to residents.

Other types of waste disposal are also deficient in TWCs. It is true that poverty generates less waste: a greater proportion of purchases consist of fresh foods sold in markets and packaging is limited, except for high order goods and the luxury market. Nevertheless Lagos' Solid Waste Disposal Board estimated that the city generated 4.5 million m^3 of domestic refuse a month in 1975. Scavenging is one of the principal services organised by municipalities. It is provided very unevenly: doorstep collection is restricted to neighbourhoods with paved roads to admit vehicles. No service is provided for the densely populated cores or for unpaved peripheral zones. The residents of the former are often expected to take their rubbish to designated tips. These are nearly always unsavoury and attract flies and vermin. Rubbish accumulates on waste ground and along the routes leading to them, as the task of disposal is often given to children; they either cannot be bothered to go that far, or are afraid of the stray dogs and rats found there. Residents periodically set fire to piles of rubbish on waste ground but it is questionable whether the malodorous bonfires are an improvement.

Authorities attribute dumping practices to popular ignorance of the connection between rubbish, pollution and disease. Clean-up campaigns have limited success and most countries try to increase awareness through the schools. However, one could also criticise the actions of the authorities, few of which have long-term plans concerning disposal. The rubbish collected is dumped in convenient sites at the city limits: major Latin American cities use abandoned quarries and designated infill sites. When these are full, they are covered over with a layer of top soil. None of this refuse is processed officially, although the most desperate members of most cities survive by picking over garbage and extracting glass, rags, paper and metal; in Latin America they may even raise pigs alongside, if not actually on the tips. Here dire necessity prompts groups to complement a public service and are tolerated by it. Opportunities for organising a more hygienic means of processing garbage are ignored and few cities have attempted to tap the methane gas generated in the dumps. Generally officials' thinking has concentrated on capital investments, such as the acquisition of more vehicles and compactors, rather than in improving the efficiency of what remains basically a manual operation. Undoubtedly the spatial segregation of residential areas, with their very different levels of service, permits indifference to conditions which would not be tolerated if everybody was subjected to them.

The pattern of costs is very different for electricity. The major expenses are those of generation; once this is achieved the costs of distribution are relatively minor. Moreover the service can be expanded easily and cheaply regardless of the structure of the city, although it is inadvisable to supply flimsy and inflammable buildings. Electricity generation tends to be the concern of a national or regional corporation which maintains the grid; where it chooses not to distribute it personally, this may be allocated to the municipality or a concessionaire. Sometimes these arrangements involve payments in kind, such as when Cuenca municipality is reimbursed for the collection of charges by means of free public lighting. The low distribution costs of domestic electricity ensure that it is the most widespread utility. Moreover authorities usually prefer to supply neighbourhoods, regardless of their legal status, rather than risk accidents and losses through the illegal tapping.

Transport

Nobody can ignore the transport problems in TWCs, as movement over any distance is a major operation. Transport needs have risen disproportionately to city growth owing to changes in the way activities are arranged within them. The indigenous patterns of multiple uses have been replaced by the organising principles inherent to modern industry and by the increasing impact of public institutions on private life. The greatest single change has been the separation of the home from work and frequently from services. Although dormitory estates have been the product of planners, they have rarely included shops, schools or health services, while commercial and productive activities are banned. Employment and services remain concentrated in the city centres, a few industrial estates and in certain high income neighbourhoods. As the first inhabitants of such estates were usually government employees and upper income groups, they provided their own transport. As a result, car traffic has increased faster than any other medium and governments responded with investments in motorways, interchanges, bypasses and street widening schemes. Thus the skewed income distribution which allowed the rich to acquire cars was compounded by the public investments which accommodated them. However, unofficial neighbourhoods and low income housing schemes are also in need of transport. Private enterprise responded to their needs with an odd assortment of vehicles, but many residents walk or cycle long distances each day.

Road transport in many TWCs is breaking down, with traffic jams, long tail-backs at intersections, frequent accidents and badly maintained roads. The conditions reflect not just traffic levels but its composition and characteristics and the indiscipline of drivers. Most roads in African and Asian cities bear a very mixed traffic in which motorised vehicles jostle with bicycles, animal-drawn vehicles and in commerical zones, with human porters and hand-drawn carts. The different speeds, dimensions and stopping frequencies of these users cannot be accommodated efficiently on the same road. The relief provided by motorways, on which animals are banned, is limited when they empty into such a morass. Traffic flow is also constrained by indiscriminate parking, breakdowns and accidents; many of the latter could be avoided by proper vehicle maintenance. Accidents also arise from sheer frustration, the disregard of traffic lights and signals, the poor state of roads and the fact that many users acquire their skills at the wheel, rather than in a driving school.

Government reactions to these conditions include measures to curtail the volume of traffic, to organise public transport services and to regulate and discipline users.

(a) Most authorities are anxious to curtail the wasteful consumption of road space by private vehicles conveying only one or two people. In fact Singapore taxes all cars not occupied by four persons on entry to the city. Lagos tried restricting cars to alternate days according to whether the number of their licence plates terminated in an odd or even digit but this did not curtail the activities of two-car families. Indirect measures have also failed: high taxes on the importation of cars tend to stimulate local industry rather than greater use of public transport and gasolene taxes are passed on to the poorer citizens by the increase in fares.

(b) Private transport will not diminish while public facilities are inadequate. State bus companies are rarely profitable or responsible for more than a small fraction of journeys. The characteristics most often reported include overmanning, poor vehicle maintenance, the sacrifice of vehicles to obtain spares and general poor administration. This occurs through interference, inconsistent policies and the political desire to maintain low fares at the cost of efficiency. Very large Far Eastern and Latin American cities have constructed metros. These are usually heavily subsidised — only a token fee is charged in Mexico City — and reflect the desperate measures cities take to relieve congestion. Private transport enterprises are very varied but frequently involve loose co-operatives formed by the owners of a single vehicle, or drivers who either lease or buy the vehicle by means of a proportion of the daily takings. Minibuses are popular everywhere. 'Collective' cars are common in Latin American cities; they ply set routes, can be flagged down or left at any point and charge a flat rate regardless of the distance travelled. In Asian cities scooter *rickshaws*, *pedicabs*, motorbike 'taxis', on which the fare rides pillion, still carry a sizeable share of the market, particularly over shorter distances such as incurred on shopping trips or in ferrying children to school. Governments strive to control private enterprise through licences, established fare structures and agreement on routes.

(c) Most cities have tried to increase traffic flow by the separation of types of user. Central streets may be pedestrianised at peak periods, service vehicles are banned until nightfall, pedal vehicles have been banned (Bangkok), excluded from the central area (Lahore and Jakarta) or confined to specific streets (Kuala Lumpur). Authorities have tried to change driving habits by imposing heavier fines for infractions but these depend on the police's integrity and ability to enforce them. Vehicle licences and threats of confiscation appear more effective than penalties for misuse. On the whole transport is another sector in which authorities have invested in capital intensive solutions and disregarded indigenous and private resources which carry most passengers. The vast majority of TWC residents cannot afford realistic metro or bus fares and these can only be subsidised at the expense of some other equally desirable utility. The need for transport could be much reduced if services were more equally distributed throughout the city and if these operated within a framework of local catchment areas.

Education and Health

Primary education is far more widely available than basic health care. Literacy and numeracy are given a high priority by all governments but the structures supporting health services restrict general access. The distinction is partly a question of cost: doctors' training, their subsequent salaries and status and their support system of hospitals, ancillary staff and pharmaceutical products are far more expensive than those of teachers and schools. Education is recognised as essential for all but medical treatment is desirable and inaccessible to many. Private participation in both sectors is primarily profit oriented but some facilities are organised by communities and charities are particularly active in the health sector. The quality of services is very varied regardless of who provides them.

Education is supervised by the state but direct participation is limited other than for primary schools. Municipal resources are inadequate for the expanding school-age population in nearly all cities. As a consequence classes are very large, buildings may be used by two or even three schools in consecutive shifts, children lack desks and paper and teachers are not supplied with books. In Lahore, admittedly not a good example of efficient and honest administration (Qadeer 1983), some schools only existed on paper and no teachers had been assigned to others. However, these conditions can be found in poorer districts of all TWCs. Private schools have no shortage of pupils and while some offer a poor education, at least they are situated near their clientele. Secondary school facilities are more restricted. The lack of places in state schools justifies their allocation on the basis of merit, but this is determined by the quality of the candidates' primary school as much as by ability. Attendance also depends on a family's ability to dispense with the child's labour or assistance with domestic chores and to pay for uniforms, books and transport. Drop-out rates are high, as families cannot justify the expense unless the child is obviously making progress. A far greater number of schools are provided by the private sector but their costs debar the majority. They are preferred to most state schools, as they offer smaller classes, greater facilities and social exclusivity but the education received varies from the excellent to the indifferent.

Health facilities take more varied forms. The most efficient state provision concerns the periodic immunisation campaigns against infectious diseases. These are often sponsored by the World Health Organisation and the eradication of smallpox after decades of continuous vaccination is proof of their success. Authorities react promptly whenever diseases like typhoid or cholera are reported and their actions are thorough and efficient. This cannot be said for other health measures: the best public facilities are provided by national social security organisations but these restrict their facilities to insured workers and their families. This leaves the self-employed and the unemployed, in fact the majority of the population, dependent on private, charitable or alternative public facilities. The resources of the entire sector are not numerous. Lagos had 1.7 hospital beds per 1000 residents and the corresponding figures for Lahore are 2.3 and 2.9 for Bogotá — or 1.7 if only charity and free beds are considered.

Governments' policies in the medical sector are increasingly criticised for the capital-intensive approaches adopted in the past. Most metropolises can provide sophisticated treatment for rare diseases while children die from commonplace infections. Services could be made much more accessible if greater emphasis was placed on the training of nurses and paramedicals, rather than that of specialists and in providing buildings. Another source of waste is on drugs. Investigative journalism has revealed the savings that can be achieved if, as in Bangladesh, prescription is limited to generic drugs rather than patented medicines. More use could be made of the indigenous pharmacopoeia. A more disturbing facet concerns the unscrupulous actions of drug companies in association with ignorance. TWC populations often save on doctors' expenses by seeking advice from drug retailers; however, many of these have no pharmaceutical knowledge. Not only do patients suffer from inappropriate treatment but viruses are becoming immune to conventional drugs owing to their blanket use for trivial symptoms.

Conclusions

Administrative systems in TWCs are complex and centralised. Local authorities are given few powers or resources on the pretext that they lack administrative expertise but undoubtedly these restrictions are reinforced by the fear of the increased political leverage which would accompany a more prominent role. Certainly there are many examples of municipal incompetence and individuals have used their office as a source of graft but less attention is paid to more successful cases. Similarly the personal mechanisms which often underpin transactions are striking to the Westerner but do not appear untoward to those embedded in them. They are certainly different but it would be difficult to prove that they were more systematically discriminating than the capitalist mechanisms in developed countries' cities.

A recurrent criticism of government policy, regardless of the level concerned, is that it has concentrated on capital intensive solutions. This has often arisen because funds are more easily found for construction projects and they are easier to supervise than if the same monies were invested in maintenance and personnel. However, these projects are expensive and inefficient without adequate underpinning: a hospital is useless without staff. Furthermore such investments have systematically benefited the more wealthy population: privately educated, medically insured, car owners living in the nicer residential districts of TWCs enjoy a very pleasant lifestyle but they are hardly typical. A relatively small increase in public utilities would make a very considerable difference to the hardships of the majority.

5 HOUSING MARKETS

The shortage of housing in TWCs is notorious. The inability of supply systems to meet demand is usually attributed to the cities' high growth rates which undoubtedly make the task more difficult. House production reflects how social groups control resources with the acquiescence of the state and their disparity in acquisitive power becomes more poignant when financial structures reduce the ability of the weaker to compete. Since the 1950s both demand and supply in TWC housing markets have been affected by two factors: first, increased investment in the sector by the state and commercial interests has not increased the accessibility of housing to all groups, owing to its cost and the mechanisms adopted to establish credit worthiness. Secondly, technical innovations in the construction industry have given rise to high quality but very expensive houses, while dwellings built by traditional methods are cheaper but often do not reach the standards demanded by the municipal by-laws. State action has tended to enhance the impact of these processes through the use of planning instruments encouraging particular forms of housing and channelling these to specific locations. The beneficiaries of these schemes have also gained from the allocation of scarce communally-funded utilities.

These processes have resulted in a distribution of housing which is manifestly inequitable; the poorest groups who comprise the majority of the population remain unhoused. According to the perspective of the analyst, the problem is primarily as follows:

1. Economics; modern houses are too expensive and so research must establish technology capable of building units of an acceptable standard at a reasonable price.
2. Administration; high house prices reflect inefficiency and bottlenecks throughout the delivery system. Reforms are required to simplify legislation, co-ordinate the activities of all those involved and to reduce bureaucracy.
3. Policy; state housing policies have been inadequate or biased and made little attempt to supply all sectors. Unless these are reformulated, or states are prepared to tolerate alternative

forms of provision, they will have to direct increasing funds to policing. This wasteful use of resources carries attendant political risks.

These elements are not independent nor is the housing sector an autonomous system; exogenous events frequently distort both demand and supply. The type of solutions suggested above are only capable of ameliorating certain aspects of the housing shortage. Let us consider why.

There is universal agreement among analysts that the high price of modern houses places them beyond the reach of the majority of TWC populations. Substituting cheaper materials alone seems unlikely to provide a solution; the price reflects the market for all the factors of production and not just that for completed buildings. Shortages invariably push up prices. More building would reduce the scarcity value of housing, but this is dependent on the availability of land, materials, utilities and labour and on the competition for all of these. Cheaper construction methods cannot offset costs arising from the speculative use of land, the transport of materials or the time taken to train labour. Moreover, it is not just the absolute cost of producing a house that makes it expensive and inaccessible but how this is passed on to the consumer, plus the costs which are associated with its location within the city. The size of downpayments and the scheduling of repayments play a significant role in restricting the market, particularly if stringent guarantees are required of the occupants. If the house forms part of a dormitory neighbourhood distant from workplaces, schools and markets, the addition of transport expenses will reduce the demand for them still more. The economic problem arises from insistence on a type of product for which there is only a restricted market. It cannot be widened significantly just by cheapening one or two factors of production.

The restricted demand for modern housing is not solely due to its cost; it is often inappropriate for the mass of the population. There are elites that opine that the needs of the very poor are unworthy of attention because they are incapable of appreciating 'proper' housing. More credible arguments have been put forward by anthropologists; they have shown that some groups endure worse conditions than they need because housing represents a lower priority than other commitments, or because their occupational strategies entail mobility. Still other groups use housing as a vehicle of social mobility; it represents the consolidation of a base within the city. However, this symbol of success is achieved after many years of slow and unpredictable saving. They cannot provide the guarantees demanded by conventional delivery systems.

The arguments attached to the role of housing cannot be separated from the complex debate surrounding the volume, characteristics and role of migrants within TWCs. Very low living standards are prevalent outside the cities and rural migrants tend to be comparatively poor. Few would disagree that high quality modern housing is irrelevant to their immediate needs but the decision to ignore their presence altogether is political as much as economic. Expensive owner-occupied housing is also inappropriate for migrants who reside in cities temporarily and invest their earnings elsewhere. A prime example are the construction workers from all over the Middle East who occupy camps outside Saudia Arabia's cities and who use their wages to acquire property in their home towns. Other migrants may be exceptionally mobile and also travel without their families, as is common in West African cities. The survival strategies of still others require them to be mobile within cities, so as to be on hand wherever work opportunities arise. Such populations require accommodation, but houses designed for nuclear families, to which admittance is gained only after a prolonged period on a waiting list, or after the provision of guarantees from employers or in the form of other property, are inappropriate. Those conditions are only meaningful to groups capable of earning an acceptable living in one place, although the delivery systems usually deny even them admittance. Consequently successful individuals have created neighbourhoods, entirely from their own resources, which, during periods of prosperity, have attained acceptable standards of construction and servicing over the long term. The link with migration in these becomes more fuzzy; considerable proportions of the city born cannot acquire modern housing and may also adopt this solution.

Would improved management of existing resources open up the market? The advocates of institutional reforms are usually speaking from the experience of a particular case. Unfortunately, while it is possible to streamline the operations of a particular agency or to improve the distribution of a specific commodity, it is far harder to visualise the reform of an entire sector. To start with,

the various factors of production involved in housing are composed of separate entities, each with its own internal logic and
responsive to different stimuli. Land is utilised according to the
strategies of its owners and the degree of effective control exerted
by the state. The modes of production for materials differ in kind
and scale of operations. Materials may be manufactured by the
state, private or peasant undertakings, or be imported by transnational companies, the state or private enterprises, or be recycled
from demolition sites by firms or individuals. A similar diversity in
modes of production occurs in the construction of housing and in
the provision of services.

The welding of all these different elements into a single system is
unlikely without a considerable degree of state coercion. One
suspects that control would be achieved at the expense of production and that it would involve an expensive and unproductive
bureaucracy; evidence suggests both are probable. Attempts to
stimulate the production of materials through the suppression of
customs duties on imported machinery, or tax exemptions for new
enterprises, do not appear to result in lower unit prices, although
certain entrepreneurs have been enriched. Efforts to manage the
distribution of materials and to impose price controls have often
resulted in profitable black markets. Moreover, Western management principles are often irrelevant to systems where actions
are shaped by an individual's web of contacts and coloured by
whether the relationship with each is one of patronage, clientage
or has implications in social or political arenas. Outright
corruption is clearly not in a society's interest, but if this is set
aside, the structure of the delivery system is irrelevant as long as it
achieves the desired results — that of providing adequate housing
at the rate required. The highly competitive nature of all the
markets concerned with housing may well yield the most efficient
combination of resources in profit terms. If the outcome is unacceptable to society, the solution would seem to lie in political
rather than administrative instruments.

The key to all states' policies is whether they view housing as a
social right or as a commodity. In the former case, a state accepts
responsibility for housing its population and allocates resources
according to need, which is defined as the size and composition of
the household rather than as a social or economic criterion. In the
latter, provision is left to private enterprise guided by market
mechanisms. Housing is a vehicle of personal wealth and those

unable to afford it must seek the patronage or charity of others. The majority of TWCs are situated in states which concur with this view, judging by their past actions and stated policies.

Since the 1960s state policies would appear to have gone through several phases which reflect their changing reactions to the housing shortages. The most common perceptions evident from these are, in order of appearance, that:

(a) the shortages are temporary; they arise from unique events and are caused by a mobile population which will either leave the city or incorporate themselves over time;

(b) the state must exercise proper control over illegal housing as this represents a challenge to their authority and is detrimental to the proper functioning of the city;

(c) it is beyond the means of the state to solve the housing problem in the way it would like, therefore it is politically expedient to experiment with alternative housing solutions.

There is no doubt that many TWCs have experienced sudden spurts of growth associated with particular events. African capital cities were the recipients of thousands of migrants when restrictions on movement were lifted and job opportunities expanded after independence. The separation of Pakistan and the foundation of Bangladesh flooded Indian cities with refugees. Opportunities also attracted migrants to Latin American cities following the concentration of investment arising from Kennedy's Alliance for Progress programme. But these cities have continued to grow considerably in absolute terms afterwards, even if the rate has slackened. Rapid growth is not a temporary phenomenon, as migration is stimulated by events outside the city as well as within them and a greater proportion of city growth stems from natural increase. Moreover the mobility of individuals would seem a doubtful argument for not attending to the needs of a group. The membership of a neighbourhood may be very fluid, but the fact it continues to expand demonstrates that this is a different type of demand which cannot be ignored.

States have a considerable range of instruments by which they exercise control. The legal framework defines house property, the rights attached to it and how it may be transacted. Planning authorities determine where houses may be located, what uses may be associated with them and what forms they may take. Local authorities tax property, co-ordinate and sometimes provide utilities. State agencies have built houses, financed those built by others and ordered third parties to do so. All these devices are designed to produce a city with a high quality physical structure. The police and even the army have been used to 'eradicate' development that is unauthorised or does not conform to these standards.

The desire to accept only high quality housing as part of the city has long been totally unrealistic. It may still be cathartic to bulldoze a prominent collection of hovels, but the scale of unauthorised housing and its varied quality makes that 'solution' childish. States have always tended to use their instruments with discretion. There is much scope for choice as when to enact legislation, on whom to apply it and how transgressions are dealt with. The most vulnerable groups are the poor and recent migrants, but whether through deliberate policy, inefficiency or despair, officials have often turned blind eyes on their housing strategies, or condoned them through subsequent regularisation, service installation, and political recognition. Most states are now participating in schemes which allocate small plots and permit the use of cheap materials in the construction of very basic dwellings. They acknowledge at last that these reflect the economic realities of a significant part of their housing markets.

Most research has focused on the unauthorised and illegal housing built by those unable to afford units constructed out of permanent materials, provided with water, drains and electricity and finished before occupancy. This type of housing shelters a very substantial population which is hard to quantify: estimates for 50 cities, mostly for the 1960s, ranged from 14 per cent in Amman to 70 or more for Casablanca, Lomé, Ouagadougou, Mogadishu, Douala and Addis Ababa. These are comparatively small cities; the lower proportions reported in Latin American and Indian cities represent far more people than all of them put together (Grimes 1976).

For the most part data stem from empirical studies of specific neighbourhoods over short periods. At first concern with their physical fabric dominated and culminated in some very detailed observations about how dwellings are adapted, extended and upgraded over time, such as the study of George, Lusaka (Schlyter and Schlyter 1980). Then interest turned to the behaviour of the occupants, both as individuals and as a group. Personal histories revealed how housing strategies related to occupation and family structure and contributed to neighbourhood formation (Turner 1968; Payne 1977, 1984). As areas consolidated, residents began making demands for services and recognition to external authorities (Ray 1969; Perlman 1976; Dietz 1980; van der Linden 1981).

An excellent overview of the issues posed by these areas to their cities is provided in 'The Residential Circumstances of the Urban Poor in Developing Countries' (UN 1981). Nearly everywhere a relatively small proportion of the population lives in good quality housing, monopolises access to high order services and occupies an area disproportionate to their numbers. Unauthorised housing takes varied forms, but low standards predominate. These stem not just from the poverty of the occupants, but to their insecurity and because they have been allocated undesirable sites and locations in the city. Growing state concern about them is often an indicator of the changing political and economic balances within cities where numbers are beginning to cancel out the lack of individual power of the poor. Since housing shortages have existed for as long as most cities, it is reasonable to enquire whether these forms have evolved in response to circumstances that are peculiar to TWCs.

Housing Delivery Systems

Four systems are common in TWCs; they differ in their accessibility to finance and land, their blend of the various factors in production, the price of their product and their share of the market (Table 5.1). Three involve legally constituted corporate bodies; the state, whose composite agencies are either responsible ultimately to a Ministry of Housing, or are autonomous agencies created for a specific project; private institutions, such as pension funds, charities and employers and commercial companies. The fourth is the unauthorised, quasi-legal sector composed of large numbers of petty entrepreneurs, artisans and individual householders.

The main distinction between these systems is how they finance their operations. State housing can only be built if funds are allocated from a budget, or from the proceeds of an earmarked tax, or acquired through negotiation from an international

Table 5.1: Characteristics of Housing Delivery Systems in TWCs

System	Producers	Finance	Land	Scale of Scheme: Type of Unit	Users
State	Ministry of Housing Autonomous Agency Welfare Department Planning Department *Ad hoc* Agency	Budget allocations earmarked funds soft loans	Inherited expropriated purchased	Large: multifamily, standard design, core housing	Civil Servants supporters displaced populations
Private Institutions	Employers Pension Funds churches charities	tax relief savings endowments donations	purchased endowed gifted	varied: single & multifamily, standard design	employees depositors selected beneficiaries
Private Commercial	Commercial Banks Savings Banks Pension Funds Land Developers Construction companies Real Estate Agencies Rich individuals	commercial loans mortgages	purchased	varied: mostly single family units, varied styles, exotic	those able to raise cash or obtain a mortgage
Illegal	Small landowners or Developers Artisan Builders Poorer individuals	personal savings self-help	inherited purchased seized	varied: single family units, form evolves with time	self-selected usually poor

creditor. In contrast many institutions are self-financing, as housing provision is their *raison d'être* or the law permits them to divert tax expenditure to that end. Commercial entrepreneurs are self-financing to the extent that part of their capital arises from the deposits of future clientele, but like any other type of venture, much of their operations depend on credit obtained from the finance market. The unauthorised sector depends on small individual investments staggered over long periods; as payments are made immediately in cash, interest charges are avoided.

All systems face increasing competition over land. The state may have inherited lands set aside for native reserves, or for future expansion, or simply considered useless by previous generations. Where these are non-existent or insufficient, it must expropriate or acquire land on the open market. Some institutions, such as the Catholic church in parts of Latin America, have received endowments of land, but most participate in the market. This is shaped by the increased demands for land for all uses and frequently for speculation. The combination of high prices and the relative low ceiling bearable by residential uses encourages an increase in housing densities and a decrease in the allocations of land for communal purposes. Even so the majority of home seekers could never afford the price of surveyed and serviced land. For them, the next best solution is land with some basis of legality, even if the purchase does not yield a title, such as when it is acquired through customary procedures or has not been zoned for residential purposes. If that option is not available, the last alternative is to squat on unused land or land with characteristics which deter more affluent claimants.

The total number of schemes produced by the corporate systems tends to be small, even though each involves many units. The houses are usually built to a standard plan, although a few estates cater for a very selective and individualistic clientele. The unauthorised sector concentrates on very basic shelter which may be extended or upgraded subsequently. This process reflects the economic fortunes of individual owners and their perception of the security of the investment.

These criteria determine the clientele of each system. Both the state and private institutions have selection criteria which have usually reflected occupation or affiliation rather than need. The commercial sector selects residents purely on their capacity to pay. The initiative rests more with the individual in the unauthorised sector, as the possibility of squatting on waste land may exist. However, the element of real choice is very circumscribed for all but the affluent.

State Housing

The state has participated in housing markets most actively where it is guided by socialist principles, such as in China or Cuba, where physical space is at a premium, such as in Hong Kong or Singapore and where it inherited an active policy from its recent colonial past, such as in parts of Africa. Elsewhere the proportion of housing produced by the state has been negligible. It has tended to fall between the responsibilities of the regional and local tiers of government and so has seldom been financed consistently or sufficiently by either to make much impact on the market. Indeed the hallmark of state housing has been the *ad hoc* project which is completed amidst controversy and criticism levelled at the management of the funds or the allocation of the houses. This is unavoidable when numerous bodies are involved and hold overlapping briefs with no hierarchy of authority to structure them. It is made worse when political criteria govern the selection and operations of their staffs, rather than the technical or financial specifications of the scheme. Apart from these considerations, states are uncertain as to whom they should be housing and at what standard. Most often the state has housed key or valued workers, while the needs of those incapable of providing for themselves, or at least not in the form acceptable to the city fathers, have been ignored. This is consistent with the state's low level of participation in the sector.

The low priority accorded to urban housing has been evident even in socialist societies. Prior to 1972, China's housing stock deteriorated while resources were directed to national industrial and infrastructural goals. It was grossly overcrowded, badly maintained and poorly serviced. Government control over the stock did permit it to express its egalitarian policy of allocating space according to the need defined by household composition. Much greater investment has been made subsequently, but this principle has been maintained. New housing estates are planned as self-contained neighbourhoods including employment and service outlets; usually they are composed of four- or five-storey buildings, made up of similar walk-up apartments. A family of five are entitled to 50 square metres in Beijing's new blocks; this is composed of two rooms, a kitchen and bathroom. Previous living space allocations were estimated to range between six and 17 square metres per adult (Buck 1984; Ma 1979).

Low rates of state participation in the sector are common in status-motivated societies for the meagre investments are monopolised by the elites of the community. In colonial regimes housing was a mechanism by which social groups could be distinguished and separated. Expatriate officials were housed not just because their mobility precluded them acquiring it for themselves but so as to control their interaction with the indigenous populations and portray their elevated status. This tradition has lingered on where such nuclei of up-market dwellings were inherited, along with building and planning codes modelled on those of the mother country, who however, had never applied them to the locals. National pride prevented administrators of new states from seeming to value themselves lower than their predecessors; they were also the principal beneficiaries of the policy. This status mechanism is still evident: for example, Bangladesh divides its public housing into seven ranks. Eligibility for these is defined by salary and priority is given to those with the highest pay and greatest seniority on the waiting list for each class. A more extreme case is Lagos, where high rank civil servants inhabit highly subsidised good quality housing, even though many own property elsewhere in the city and they would all qualify for mortgages from commercial sources. It is common throughout Africa and India for institutions, such as universities and hospitals, to accommodate senior staff, while lower grade staff receive little if any assistance. Such provision may reflect demand but does not respond to need.

A more justifiable reason for such state provision is when it is used as an inducement to lure staff and workers to locations which they would otherwise not consider. It has been difficult for states to overcome the reluctance of civil servants to leave primate cities for new capitals, such as Brasilia, Islamabad, Lilongwe and Belmopan; the construction plans for Dodoma and Abuja include housing for officials. It is even harder to attract technicians and labour to remote or harsh environments. Even China encouraged migration to Dukow, the centre of Sichwan's iron coal fields via promises of good housing and it is doubtful whether the iron and steel industry would have developed so rapidly or at such a scale in the lower Orinoco without the Venezuelan government's promotion of Ciudad Guayana.

State housing has also been used to create or service a stable workforce in long established cities with large deficits. The Indian State Housing Boards subsidise basic units for industrial workers employed in mines, the docks or in factories. SOGESA, the Peruvian Steel Corporation, provided housing at its plant in Chimbote in the late 1960s for at that time, the city had the reputation of being one of the least salubrious in the country. This type of housing can have negative connotations; it symbolises the containment of African workers in designated areas for the duration of their contract with mine or factory in South Africa. There it conjures up images of the monotonous rows of identical two room units of the underprivileged inhabitants of Soweto. Such housing is a projection of the state's racially biased status system foremost and only secondly a response to need in terms of the essential workers required by a city.

The needs of those unable to house themselves have been reassessed over the last decade. Previously states constructed multistorey blocks of apartments with shared services. They have been severely criticised: not only did their cost preclude the construction of a reasonable number, but insufficient attention was paid to the size and lifestyle of the households they were presumed to serve. Despite heavy subsidy, poor beneficiaries could not afford to stay in them. They could not take in tenants and the environment precluded their previous urban subsistence economy, which included, for example, planting a banana tree or keeping a few chickens. They often faced the added expense of travel, given the peripheral location of most schemes. As a result many re-settlement schemes reported, as in Rio de Janeiro, that the beneficiaries had sublet the flat to a middle-class household, while they moved back to far worse accommodation located more appropriately (Valladares 1978).

Nor have states who have constructed on a massive scale escaped criticism. Hong Kong's authorities faced the dual problem of appalling poverty and restricted space. Their response took both into account: The first five-storey blocks of the 1950s were extremely basic: long corridors of single rooms allowed 2.2 square metres per adult and half as much for a child; minimal services were shared. Densities of estates made up these 'H' blocks surpassed 4800 persons per hectare and provided no space for markets. Since then pressures for housing have been inflated by illegal immigrants from China and Vietnam. Families squat wherever possible and crowd into rented cocklofts and even bed cubicles. Many viewers admire the state's achievement. In 1981 it was building flats at a rate of 35000 per annum, its space standards had increased to 4.6 square metres per adult and it had contributed 42 per cent to the total stock (Pryor 1983). Others interpret the massive land reclamation, new town creation and planning interventions of the last decade as strategies to reproduce land and stabilise dissent at the cost of the very poor unlikely to benefit from either. For example, upgrading H blocks and clearing ground for new ones involved the decanting of surplus populations to 'temporary' camps at the outskirts; the average time on the waiting list, even for those with adequate income is seven years (Keung 1985). Most state schemes have enhanced segregation on social and income criteria and the less privileged have been forced to relinquish terrible housing in advantageous locations for better in disadvantageous ones.

By the 1970s most states appreciated the inadequacy of their previous housing programmes. Prodded by international consultants and fear of the sheer magnitude of the housing deficit, most are now considering how the poor's own resources may be channelled to best effect. Governments of varied persuasion have experimented with upgrading illegal housing and with site-and-service schemes. Both require a radical change in the way the state interacts with the poor and the streamlining of their institutional structures, if management costs are not to cancel the gains derived from the simplification of land registration procedures and the relaxation of building codes.

Upgrading generally entails the provision of infrastructure beyond the capacity of individual effort to a neighbourhood. Water, drainage and sewers cannot usually be installed without some realignment of buildings and contributions of territory for public access. Active participation by the residents is crucial both to acquire these without hindrance and to ensure the upkeep of the improvements (Payne 1984). Site-and-service schemes are designed for the landless. They usually offer only plots, communal water taps and sanitary blocks; a few provide a sanitary 'core' or a water connection on plot. In the best, technical advice and bulk purchased building materials are available to speed and improve construction. The standards demanded are realistic considering the budgets of participants. For example, Bombay's Huts Renovation Scheme of 1976 involved hut pitches measuring 4.60 ×

3.05 square metres (the average size of the *bustees* they replaced) in rows of ten; services were provided at a rate of one latrine seat for 20 to 50 persons, one water tap per 125 persons and one street light per 100 families (Patwardhan in Dakhil *et al.* 1978).

State housing is the product of policy and has been used for political ends. The allocation of housing has often been a means of acquiring, maintaining or rewarding supporters and affiliates receive dwellings compatible with their status. The ensuing patterns reflect the wider socio-economic structures of the city which contribute to the inadequate accommodation of the poor. Site-and-service schemes would seem to denote a policy of despair, governments are loath to condone the construction of 'slums' but fear the repercussions if blatant need is continually ignored. The schemes are cheap and credit the state with taking action on the poor's behalf; they do not pose a threat to the vested interests operating in other sectors of the housing market. Most low income schemes are grossly oversubscribed; however, nearly all are designated for permanent owner-occupation. There is much demand for rented accommodation, particularly in African cities and whenever mobility is high; it has been estimated that 42 per cent of the populations in TWCs are tenants (UN 1979). Most of them are housed by private entrepreneurs.

Private Legal Housing

Both private institutions and commercial enterprises provide housing, but as the institutional market is minute, the following discussion will focus on the latter. Supply chains of varied length produce commercial housing. Large-scale developers in capital cities may command all operations from land acquisition through to final house sale, while at the other extreme, chains can be found in which each link represents a separate specialised operator. These differences obviously reflect in part the financial reserves of the entrepreneurs but they also arise from local circumstances, such as the pattern of land tenure, the technology employed and the clientele available.

Land tenure reflects both wealth and custom. Land is valued for the role it plays in society, as well as by its utility and the pressures exerted on it. We have already mentioned instances where land is considered as an unalienable right of a people; as such it is useless to the private legal sector. Commercial developers view land as a commodity whose ownership carries all the rights vested in law.

This restricts their interest to registered land, or at least land which can be easily registered. Previous plantations and commercial farms are attractive owing to their legal titles. Smallholders seldom have titles and often can only establish their rights through occupation of the land and the testimony of neighbours. Large-scale entrepreneurs would rather not engage in the time-consuming task of assembling areas large enough to permit scale economies in development from such sources. This gives rise to middlemen who specialise in buying up small plots for urban development, sometimes through trickery. Commercial land is therefore expensive; it is legal and either had a previous commercial use or carries the costs of assembly by third parties. A further price escalator is speculation. The way these factors shape a land market is best illustrated by a specific case.

The objectives and operations of 530 land owning agents in Bangkok were established in 1981 (Durand-Lasserre in Angel *et al.* 1983). Owners of small building plots used them for their own housing, as a means of inflation proofing their savings and for micro-scale speculation. Purchasers of land over the last two decades had dedicated them to houses for sale or to serviced plots. But companies used land as a vehicle of their wider business interests; it served to diversify assets, provide collateral for credit and constituted a speculative aim in itself. Moreover these agents were exerting greater control of the land market. The registry revealed that 50 were involved in 21 per cent of the transactions which represented 61 per cent of the land involved. Most of the other agents were involved in a single transaction. The increasing prominence of large-scale operators is a common observation in TWCs.

Price data are scarce and difficult to interpret; analysts often have to rely on the prices quoted in newspaper adverts in default of official sources. Cross-national comparisons are virtually impossible, especially over time, owing to differences in inflation rates and purchase power. The most meaningful criterion is what proportion of a given city's population can afford to buy land for housing. The answer would appear to be very small and that it will be even smaller in the future. In Tapei, for example, it was estimated an average household would have to devote its entire income over 3.6 years in order to acquire land. The registry revealed that land prices had shot up by an average of 577.8 per cent per annum between 1953 and 1976. The corresponding annual increases in the cost of living index and in family incomes were 12.2 and 51 per cent respectively (Lee in Dakhil *et al.* 1978). In Metro Manila 'it is evident that acquisition of a reasonable piece of land and adequate housing is beyond the reach of the low and middle income groups' (Mendiola in Angel *et al.* 1983). This conclusion was reached after inspection of the average rates of increase in price between low and high cost land between 1974 and 1979, in combination with the range of construction costs per sq m and the average family income levels for these groups. In Bogotá it was 'strongly suspected that more and more people are being excluded from the housing market' (Gilbert and Ward 1984). Evidence showed that land prices had risen in real terms between 1955 and 1978 and dramatic fluctuations over shorter periods indicated the speculative building cycles in particular neighbourhoods.

The materials used in legal housing also push up its price. The building codes in most TWCs demand that only durable materials — burnt brick, cement, concrete, steel, etc. be used. However, these are but fledgling industries in many countries owing to their small market and its dispersed nature. Major construction projects usually import their requirements as it is easier than transporting such heavy materials across the country. Nigeria still imported 70 per cent of its cement in 1978. Moreover, the large investments bound up in industrial, public and commercial buildings allow their builders to commandeer resources whenever these are scarce, thus starving the residential sector. Nearly everywhere building materials are insufficient and the shortages are exacerbated by legislation condemning the use of indigenous alternatives. This scorn for the local is a heritage from colonial days which becomes more entrenched every time a major project is awarded to a foreign contractor. It is doubly unfortunate because Western technology stresses capital at the expense of labour and involves the costs of imports and royalty payments but officials continue to spurn cheaper intermediate techniques. Building codes also specify the use of a wide range of hardware and fixtures which may be imported, or assembled from imported components. Consequently building materials are expensive; they represent between 60 and 65 per cent of non-land construction costs in Indian cities, for example. High costs and bottlenecks in supplies occasionally encourage backward linkages from large-scale construction firms into materials. However, this remains a most complex and fragmented industry, so that legal house supply chains include contractors specialised in the assembly of imported, recycled and locally produced goods.

These problems arise even when finance is not scarce. Saudi Arabia's government has placed a high priority on urban and infrastructural development and the construction industry is the second largest sector in the economy (al-Turki and McCullogh in Dakhil *et al.* 1978). Most private housing is built on credit acquired from the state Real Estate Development Fund, which insists on the use of modern designs and materials. Consequently 66 per cent of the permits granted in 1976 employed concrete, as opposed to about half that number six years earlier. However, Saudi Arabia's cement industry only established its first plant in 1959 and it could not cope with this intensification in demand; nearly 80 per cent of cement is imported. Supplies are uncertain and a flourishing black market reflects the accumulative effect of common circumstances: price controls set regardless of the costs of production, risks attached to imports, difficulties of transport and distribution within the country and the fact the state appropriates what it wants for its own programmes.

Houses are constructed both by modern firms and conventional indigenous ones. Access to finance determines both the scale and the technology an entrepreneur can employ but specifications usually make it impossible for the small family firm to compete for multiple unit or high rise projects with large-scale contractors. Although it is common for labour to move freely between enterprises, these retain their distinctive characteristics and markets. Mass production is the preserve of the modern sector, but by far the greater part of housing is produced piecemeal by conventional builders. Take the case of Greater Manila, for example (Stretton in Rimmer *et al.* 1978). The International Monetary Fund's Conference stimulated the construction of luxury hotels and apartment blocks to house the participants in 1976. These were built by large firms employing Western technology and with access to commercial credit; they also construct public buildings and office blocks. Other large firms employ less complex but modern technology to create luxury housing. These are headed by architects who oversee all aspects of the job; the client merely pays the bill. But the greatest share, in terms of floor area if not by value, is produced 'conventionally'. Seventy per cent is built by independent foremen working directly with the owner. The latter acquires a plan from an architect or engineer and manages the finance, while the foreman assembles the materials, the labour force and oversees the construction. A few small firms do operate in this sector but only 5 per cent of non luxury legal housing is produced *en masse* by large firms.

The fragmented construction sector contributes to its separation from the provision of infrastructure. It may not be clear who is responsible, as basic services are often provided by private enterprises. Large schemes include the layout of mains and sewers in their original plan, but these may not materialise in small and piecemeal development, which are frequently underfinanced. It is a common observation in Latin American cities that enterprises raise the capital for such investment from their prospective clients. But frequently owners have to badger the developer and acquire the support of the municipality before the installations are completed.

Fully serviced modern houses are an expensive commodity. The commercial sector has to be self-financing and compete for capital when other activities are being actively promoted by governments. While property is an obvious destination for domestic savings, speculation in land and property limits access to the rich. High quality dwellings generate the most profit and are sought by those whose credit-worthiness is not in doubt. However, if the market is to be expanded, other occupiers must be financed. Independent building societies are comparatively rare; frequently credit schemes are run by the same enterprises that construct or fund the constructors. As the profits from the repayments contribute to their working capital directly, the criteria on which loans are granted are very stringent. Only applicants with salaried employment need apply and the amount of the loan is related both in absolute and relative terms to their monthly income. Guarantors, generally their employers, are required and interest rates are commonly geared to exchange rates. Additional conditions are often exacted: large downpayments, prepayment for the land or even for the foundations may be required and the loan must be paid off within a stipulated time or before the mortgagee reaches a specified age. The most generous interpretation of the eligibility criteria in Ibadan rendered only 12.7 per cent of the households acceptable; in fact only 1.6 per cent were being funded (Onibokum 1971). In Lima, between 9.5 and 19.3 per cent of the households could meet the conditions established by the state controlled mortgage bank and the commercial banks which would enable them to acquire the cheapest housing within the legal sector (Lowder 1982). Less than 20 per cent of Mexico City's households could rent or acquire with the aid of a mortgage any type of legal dwelling (Connolly in Ward 1982). Legal housing still is elite housing.

Unauthorised Housing

The mass demand is for cheap housing that may be extended during occupation and whose tenure is not dependent on constant outlays. Investment is encouraged by security of tenure. Sites which are accessible to both work places and public services are highly prized. Neighbourhoods congenial to family life are preferred, especially if upgrading is possible over time. The only way most households can acquire such housing is through initiative and not strictly legal means. Unauthorised housing takes a great many forms. Its illegality may arise from tenure of the land, the quality of the dwelling, the layout of the district or because of the location. The subsequent fate of such housing depends on these factors, the circumstances under which it was built and above all on the political climate of the particular city.

Seizure of land without the owner's permission is an illegal act associated with three main types of sites. Conveniently located abandoned land is a prime target but most sites are available because their characteristics deter competitors: they are either highly constrained or physically bad, consisting of bare rock, derelict land, steep slopes and being badly drained or waterless. The severity of these constraints and the scale of the site determines the chances of such a site being occupied permanently.

Every TWC has sites whose characteristics ensure that they are shunned by all but the desperate, such as the narrow strips of land on the banks of Kuala Lumpur's many streams, along the railway lines in many Indian cities, the abandoned 'borrow' pits of the brickmakers in West African cities or the rubbish dumps of Cairo and Lima. These sites may be a key factor in the survival strategies of floating populations, recent arrivals and the very poor, either because they are located near to job opportunities or even because of their characteristics: Cairo's Zabaline population live among the waste they collect, extracting recyclable products and feeding the organic matter to pigs, while Lima's garbage pickers reside on or near the municipal tips. Such sites could never be condoned on safety grounds and indeed most display a constant turnover in population and are forcibly cleared from time to time. Their durability is a sign of the continual presence of the desperately poor.

Another type of site attractive to squatters is the derelict or unused plot within the built-up area of the city. These are generally privately owned: they may be enmeshed in the legal machinery concerning inheritance, which can take years to be resolved in most contexts, or be kept idle for speculative purposes. In the former case squatters may go unnoticed for some time, but if the plot is small, the owner usually will experience no difficulty in acquiring police aid to dislodge them. Frequently it is not necessary; owners may even charge squatters a small rent until such time as they are ready to build. Owners of large plots are usually more sensitive to invasions, however, especially where 'squatters rights' are recognised and governments are sympathetic to their needs. State governments in India have been known to expropriate such land, for example in Calcutta to house Bangladeshi refugees and at times Latin American authorities have ruled in favour of long-term squatters.

Permanent settlement is most likely to evolve from the seizure of peripheral waste land belonging to the state. The lack of competitors for such land and the greater space available often permits settlement on more acceptable patterns, which makes subsequent improvement and servicing feasible without costly realignment. The neighbourhoods can arise from gradual accretion, which is common where much site preparation is required, or mass invasion. Both require forethought and some experience: 'professional squatters' cleared the mangroves, saved the poles and planted them to form the foundations of the houses and catwalks over Guayaquil's swamps (Moser in Ward 1982) and 'professional invaders' became adept at organising the mass delivery of hundreds of potential settlers with their poles and rush matting to the dry embayments between Lima's foothills. By morning the whole area would be pegged out in regular lots, each occupied by rudimentary huts complete with Peruvian flag. The residents of such peripheral areas cannot utilise the services of the established city and must organise water distribution and waste disposal. These conditions ensure that they have some resources and are committed to city life. In such circumstances, no conflict of interest arose. The authorities' reactions are politically motivated rather than in defence of property. The organisers have been considered as 'agitators' and a threat to the state, rather than as petty entrepreneurs providing a service for a fee. However, this is understandable as both the state and politicans have used such mechanisms to generate popular support. This is then maintained through the promise of services and eventual regularisation (Sánchez and Calderón 1980).

Squatting can only arise on unoccupied land which is scarce in most TWCs. It is far more common for settlement to arise from agreement with owners in exchange for modest fees on land protected from the full force of the market. This is the case of land under customary tenure which still occurs in parts of the Middle East, West Africa, Malaysia, Indonesia and Papua, New Guinea. The new 'owners' cannot easily acquire titles which colours subsequent developments. An example of the more traditional case is Ayija, Kumasi, where a plot could still be obtained from the *stool chief* in exchange for a few chickens and a keg of palm wine in 1976 (Stanley 1980). Most houses were built of mud and thatch and were aligned only very roughly with each other. Long-term residents who had rebuilt in more permanent materials found it almost impossible to register their property, given the number of documents required and events quite beyond their control: the planning department, who had to survey the property, were years in arrears with their work and water and sewer connections were stipulated as a prerequisite even though no mains existed in that sector of the city. Transactions were far more commercial in Mushin, a suburb of Lagos (Barnes 1979). However, the Yoruba vest tenure in the entire ethnic group, thus exposing the purchaser to continual claims from persons saying they had not been consulted. Settlers found it expedient to be active in their neighbourhood landowners' association, the *de facto* authorities who could testify on their behalf, so as to control this source of exploitation. In Ibadan counterclaims often arose from intra-clan rivalry (Aronson 1978).

Land is also cheaper when wealthier investors are deterred by the fact it has not been zoned for housing. Many cities' authorities have commissioned detailed physical plans which are often out of date by the time of publication, so that large parts of their periphery may fall in this category. Such master plans have been criticised as the origin of delays, needless expenses and unrealistic standards of legal development. Their designers ignore the existence of areas which do not meet with approval and disregard how much property is created. In the case of Arafat, an urban ward of Dakar, landowners wished to sell land to developers and house-builders, but the planners, the Board for Low Cost Housing and the civil servants upheld the allocation of the land to non-existent industry as dictated by the static Master Plan (Jacolin *et al.* 1976). The executive authorities and regional politicians displayed the conflicting interests common to such situations: they wanted a modern city with controlled building and the protection of 'collective interests' but not at the expense of widespread confrontation with proprietors and electors. The vested interests of leading citizens and local politicians were expressed more overtly, for although they appealed to the executive to uphold their property 'rights' which might be devalued by the presence of the poor, they were nevertheless keen to recruit the latter to further their own ambitions by the formation of a client ward. The constant demand for space ensures that landowners engage in small-scale development in ignorance or defiance of city plans. Indeed where authorities repress invasions and are unwilling to provide alternative housing, they have no option but to condone illegal subdivisions as long as they do not intrude on immediate public needs.

Planning criteria also confirm illegal status because of substandard construction and the lack of infrastructure. Very poor building is a consequence of poverty but it is never likely to be other without a degree of security. Legislation in many instances has prevented the occupants of unauthorised housing from improving it. The lack of services is a logical consequence of the above. Utility companies are unwilling to make investments which will not be profitable or secure while residents are unlikely to co-operate with necessary re-alignments of property unless they are guaranteed to benefit from the changes. But planning authorities are often a comparatively weak component of city government which makes them liable to being used as a scapegoat and a tool by more powerful groups. Speculative builders may use unauthorised land, particularly if they are well connected with the state and prominent in public life. They gamble on the fact the project will not be 'discovered' before it is completed and that authorities would find it difficult to justify the demolition of perfectly good housing on a technicality. Many an estate has arisen from such *post facto* arrangements but this ruse only succeeds where the quality of construction is high and the scheme is serviced.

More sophisticated manipulations may even employ legal

instruments and state functionaries, as was the case in which *ejidos*, communal agricultural land, was transformed into privatised urban holdings in Mexico City (Varley 1985). According to the constitution, such land is alienable only to promote the communal good; then it may be expropriated on payment of compensation, or exchanged for comparable agricultural land. In practice four-fifths of the land expropriated or exchanged has been privatised for middle or luxury class housing, their infrastructure and for industry. The legal procedures were followed by the state and by the companies but somehow the land was diverted to these uses through subsequent operations. Poor individuals exploited the legal loophole which permits *ejidos* to satisfy their urban needs and those of their *avecinados* who are employed in or are otherwise useful to the community. Much of *ejido* land involved is poor quality and the *ejidatarios* engage in urban pursuits, including that of developing their lands. State concern over the proliferation of the *colonias proletarias* of the poor by these means highlights their weakness within society; the other types of development accounted for just over half the area transformed between 1940 and 1976 but they have received little attention.

Attitudes towards unauthorised housing are changing. Currently debate centres on the ability of self-help processes to provide viable housing over the long term. The arguments in favour are that the costs of building are lowered through the mobilisation of otherwise unused resources, that the city economy is stimulated through the demand for materials and labour and that the stabilisation of the occupants' location enables the city to tax them while they may tap its health and educational services. These have been stressed since pioneers such as Mangin and Turner observed how established migrants in an expanding economy could achieve upward social and economic mobility over time. Control over the resources invested in the home was an essential ingredient of the process. Their link highlighted the real achievements of successful residents and the lack of expense to the state. They urged that such ventures should be promoted rather than hindered for the benefit of all concerned. That advice eventually led to state sponsorship of site-and-service schemes. While nobody wishes to curtail these overtures, many analysts feel that the initial assumptions require more critical inspection.

Self-help housing is undeniably cheaper, if only because it does not involve management overheads or interest payments. The occupant manages operations and payments are made in cash. However, it is difficult to ascertain the real costs when payments are staggered over time and these are undoubtably reduced because the building is occupied before it is completed. Cheapness is usually estimated by comparison with state schemes for low income groups. Self-help neighbourhoods have often been considered more successful because the final housing is more appropriate, of adequate quality and the delivery system is tailored to the occupants' lifestyles. Regular payments, no matter how small, are feared by those with irregular earnings and no secure means of saving money. Contrasts in the occupants' investment in their respective neighbourhoods have also been noted. Self-help housing tends to appreciate over time and services are gradually acquired as the community consolidates, while state schemes, if inhabited by the truly poor, have often depreciated through overcrowding and the breakdown of services.

According to some authorities, housing building is the most profitable use for excess labour and savings. The assumptions made about both are often fallacious. Housing represents an element of consumption rather than production for the occupant, unless most of it is intended for rental. Its existence cannot absolve the owner from the need to produce an income on which to live. In scenarios where wages are very low and intermittent employment is common, labour can be contributed only at the expense of productive activities or domestic needs. This is evident from the very slow rates of improvement. Research has shown that certain income thresholds are essential before any investment in housing can take place.

The misunderstanding probably stems from another popular misconception: self-help housing does not necessarily mean self-built. Apart from temporary huts, the modes of production reported are quite varied. Specialists, whether they be traditional thatchers or foundation layers, modern pourers of concrete or structural steel erectors, or plumbers and electricians, are nearly always contracted. The owner may recruit additional labour from neighbours or kin and usually assists himself but unless they happen to be construction workers, these merely substitute for unskilled labour.

The home is a popular destination for savings. Assuming the owner has some security, it is inflation-proof and the results are tangible and long lasting compared to most forms of consumption.

They may yield an income if extensions are rented. However, it is absurd to suggest that poor people do not have other equally valid uses for their money. Remittances to relatives and expenditure on medical treatment, on apprenticeships, or on a festival which will heighten the individual's status, are not wasteful. It is the basic right of any individual to spend their income according to their own priorities.

Does unauthorised housing widen the demand for construction materials and labour within the city? As the houses are not produced by a closed system, it must but the multiplier effects are probably not those wished or visualised by the state. Job opportunities arise from unauthorised housing because the most commonly used materials are vernacular or recycled and both stem from far more labour-intensive modes of production than their modern equivalents. Unfired bricks, soilcrete or landcrete blocks, rush mats and thatching materials usually arise from artisan and peasant modes. Petty entrepreneurs specialise in salvaged materials: conventional houses are often dismantled brick by brick, packing cases are taken apart and even used nails and bolts are carefully straightened. These operations add little value and reflect the cheapness of labour but they provide many with a livelihood. The ability of the sector to generate job opportunities is obviously tied to buoyancy of the city economy for the construction sector is usually the first to reflect downturns and to recover.

Nearly everybody prefers a secure base from which to build up contacts and investments. The demolition of even simple shacks squanders the limited resources of the poor and those of the city and adds to its absolute housing deficit. The maximisation of private investments in housing and services cannot but be to a city's advantage and these are more valuable to all concerned than possible tax revenue or promises of future services. Most cities exempt such areas from taxation as the cost of collection exceeds the yields. Moreover the first medical posts and schools usually arise from the residents' pooled resources supplemented by charitable donations and are operated by volunteers. The state is more likely to intervene once they have acquired a large clientele of established residents.

Detailed studies exist of unauthorised housing forms in many TWCs. They indicate what combination of circumstances and individual characteristics result in the creation of adequate housing.

They reveal that while illegal delivery systems have allowed many to achieve this goal over the long term, intervention by the state may damage the mechanisms which contribute to its success. Illegal delivery systems serve low income groups because of characteristics which shield them from the pressures operating in the legal housing market. Regularised, titled land becomes legal land and its price escalates beyond the reach of the poor forthwith. For this reason *basti* dwellers in Karachi desired security but were not interested in titles which would have exposed them to property dealers. Similarly while utilities are desired, their introduction may result in the expulsion of the original residents. Mexico City's ¯ederal District regularisation programme involved such lumpy payments that many occupants were forced to sell (Makin 1984). Invariably serviced districts become more attractive and some residents are tempted to sell out to middle income groups. This may aid recovery of the state's investment and ensure future upgrading of the neighbourhood but at the expense of the poor. The question as to whether illegal delivery systems can be moulded so as to produce housing which is accessible to the poor and acceptable to city authorities is best answered by the examination of specific cases.

The Tale of Three Cities

Nairobi and Lima are primate cities and Delhi is a federal capital with an autonomous district. All three metropoli have vast territories composed of units previously under separate jurisdictions (Table 5.2). Not all of this is urban. Up until Kenyan independence in 1963, Nairobi was underbounded but its new boundaries encircle a national park, sisal and coffee plantations and large areas of small holdings. Delhi Union Territory consists of the old municipalities of Delhi, New Delhi and the Cantonment as well as an extensive peri-urban area. The metropolitan area of Lima corresponds to the provinces of Lima and its port of Callao, which contain over 30 districts. About 140000 persons in Nairobi and over 450000 in Delhi may be classified as rural; the number is insignificant in Lima as over two-thirds of the territory is unpopulated desert or mountain. The metropolitan context therefore consists of a large territory containing multiple jurisdictions.

Table 5.2: Characteristics of Three Metropoli

	Nairobi (1978)	Delhi (1981)	Lima (1980)
Area in square kilometres	689[a]	1485[h]	3850[p]
Population:			
Total in millions	.96[b]	6.22[h]	4.96[m]
Growth rate per annum	7.5[c]	4.3[i]	4.8[n]
Average size of household	4.1[d]	5.6[j]	5.53[m]
Housing:			
'Unacceptable' units (000s)	100[e]	480[k]	386[m]
Annual increase of this stock	12%[f]	10.8%[l]	9.5%[m]
Population housed by it	40%[e]	36%[j]	43%[m]
Population unable to afford new legal housing	50[c]–70%[g]	70%[k]	>80%[n]

Sources: a. Temple and Temple 1980; b. Kenyan Govt. quoted in Hardoy and Satterthwaite 1981; c. Chana in Payne 1984; d. Peil & Sada 1984; e. Amis 1984; f. Memon 1982; g. Kabagambe and Moughton 1983; h. *Census of India* 1981; i. *Times of India, Directory and Yearbook* 1984; j. figure for cities of over 1 million in 1976; Kurian 1982; k. Sousson 1982; l. Squatters only 1970s; Majumdar, T. K. in de Souza 1978; m. Ministerio de Trabajo, Lima 1980; n. Strassman 1980; p. *Anuario Estadístico del Perú*.

All three metropoli have very substantial populations, whose growth rates exceed all others in their respective countries in the case of Nairobi and Lima and is one of the highest, in the case of Delhi (Table 5.2). They have a considerable housing stock classified as 'unacceptable', either because it is unauthorised and unplanned, or, in Lima's case, it is considered as 'temporary' or as a 'slum'. Unfortunately, estimates indicate that this sector of the housing market is increasing at double the rate of that of the acceptable stock in these cities and that it houses well over a third of their populations. Around two million people in both Delhi and Lima and about 400000 in Nairobi live in buildings which their governors would like to eradicate. Worse still, analysts estimate that at least half the households in these cities are too poor to acquire the cheapest legal house on the market. This state of affairs has arisen not just from the low level of investment in the housing sector but also from the way these funds have been used.

A simplified diagram of the agencies involved in funding housing in the three metropoli is depicted in Figure 5.1. These form a hierarchy whose top rung of international institutions has supplied cheap loans and grants. It includes the World Bank and

Figure 5.1 Institutional Financial Structure in Kenya, India and Peru, 1980

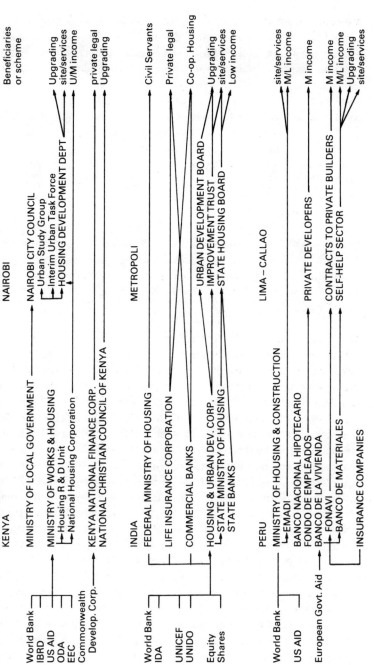

the regional development banks, the various dependencies of the United Nations, aid agencies of individual countries, such as USAID and Britain's Commonwealth Development Organisation and international charities. India's largest metropoli have also raised capital through issuing equity shares.The most important executive rung corresponds to central government ministries and dependencies who contribute funds from the national budgets. In Kenya and India additional funds may be allocated by city or state authorities but decisions are completely centralised in Peru.

The various authorities appear to identify with different sectors of the housing market. Central governments have concentrated in the past on completed dwellings which have been occupied by civil servants and other white collar middle income groups. State and city authorities have provided more basic housing for the 'deserving poor' such as the industrial workers schemes in Indian cities; they are also more likely to provide infrastructure and upgrade unauthorised districts. Projects targeted at the 'desperately poor' have been promoted by external funding channelled through national housing authorities.

The relationship between these institutions is not as clear cut as the figure would imply. While true for around 1980, many national authorities change their form frequently. Owing to this and the fact that two or three institutions, each with several executive departments, operate in each city, overlaps and omissions between jurisdictions are common. In Kenya, the National Housing Corporation (NHC) acts independently of the city Council's Housing Development Department (HDD) which it funds in part. They represent the state sector in Nairobi, while a separate national agency, the Kenya National Finance Corporation (KNFC) funds the private legal sector. Charities contribute to the unauthorised sector. The structure is dominated in India by the national Housing and Urban Development Corporation (HUDCO) which is funded by all sources, whether external, national, private or public. Again it participates through its own dependencies as well as by financing state ministries and their respective institutions. Despite government centralisation, Lima possesses the most segmented structure. Here EMADI, the national real estate administration, oversees the state's stock and organises sites, with or without services. The state also stimulates the private construction industry and participates in the market indirectly by earmarked taxes, which fund mortgages and supply credit for building materials.

The number of units generated by these institutions have been nowhere near sufficient. In 1975/7, the state sector in Nairobi provided about 1600 new units while private contractors built around 500 legal homes. Over the last decade their combined efforts never exceeded 3000 units a year, which is less than a third of that required (Hardoy and Satterthwaite 1981). In Delhi one new plot was provided for every 21 needed between 1961 and 1975. The ratio of those made available by Delhi's Development Corporation and those required in 1977/8 was still 1:16 (Sousson 1982). The Peruvian government provided about 28500 houses, flats, core houses, serviced and unserviced lots in the decade 1968/79, which satisfied less than 8 per cent of the deficit in 1980 (Sánchez and Calderón 1980). Whatever the state strategy, direct participation in the market (Nairobi) or structural reforms of land holding (Delhi) or finance (Lima), the shortages have increased. Most measures have benefited relatively prosperous income groups while the poorest quintiles have even been squeezed out of upgrading projects (Linn 1983). In all three cities the major discrepancies, which have arisen between the goals and the outcomes of housing policies, have been blamed on the misguided perceptions of their authorities and personal political and economic ambitions.

Nairobi's administrators inherited a deplorable situation arising from the discrimination practised during the colonial era. During the decade preceding independence, officials recognised that African housing was a means of encouraging political stability and economic efficiency in cities. This change in policy was expressed in the allocation of state land, not only to employers so that they could house workers but to individuals, who, with the aid of loans for building materials, could build permanent dwellings over time (Stren 1970). The measure was too little too late. The proposals were dismissed as humiliating on independence, for they were perceived as allocating Africans to poor if not slum dwellings, while Europeans and Asians continued to enjoy much better conditions. Although the NHC was created in 1967 on the recommendation of a UN technical mission, it devised tenant purchase schemes for heavily subsidised high quality dwellings. Squatter settlements multiplied to the east of the city centre and beyond the old city boundaries while units were built which were beyond their residents' means (Figure 5.2). Councillors feared that lower standards would lead to slums and were inexperienced in both

Figure 5.2

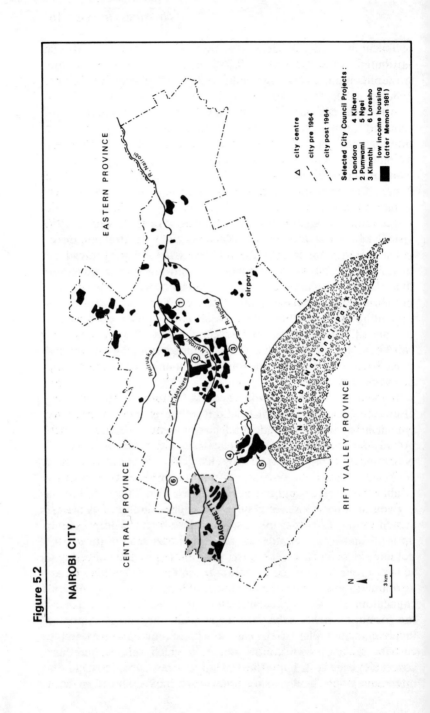

NAIROBI CITY

technical and financial fields. However, their actions can also be attributed to the fact that championing the poor or their housing was unlikely to further their political careers (Temple and Temple 1980).

Although the NHC's policy has focused on the poor subsequently, this is hard to detect in their estates. Of six projects offering units in 1977, Dandora, Pumwami and Kimathi were estimated as being within reach of 80, 50 and 40 per cent of Nairobi's households. As barely 20 per cent could afford to live in Kibera and Ngei and Loresho, whose plots averaged 700 and 2500 square metres respectively, they were clearly catering for a very select group (Chana 1984). The Kenyan standards Bureau still visualised 'minimum housing' to consist of two rooms with individual inside water connections and toilets, although landlords of unauthorised housing were renting single rooms not much more than three metres square, with iron roofs and mud and wattle or prefabricated wood-panel walls. Although 70 per cent of Kenya's cement had to be imported, the council was loath to authorise the use of landcrete blocks, as recommended by the University of Nairobi's Housing Research and Development Unit. It still indulged in eradication programmes which only exacerbated the problems of the poor. A study of Kariobangi, a council re-settlement site south of Dandora for those forcibly ejected from elsewhere, revealed the implications of chronic insecurity. The haphazard layout and high density of minimum shelters, which nobody dared to improve, heightened the risks of fire and cholera. Nevertheless the settlement represented an investment of around K£70000, a sizeable sum for a poor city to destroy wilfully (Kabagambe and Moughton 1983).

Even legal developments suffer from the rigidity of outdated standards. The World Bank sponsored Dandora project was held up for 18 months because the council's public health officers did not like the fact that individual sanitary blocks were arranged in a square so that four shared two common walls. The resultant delays attributable to 'misunderstandings between local political councillors and senior technical officers of the HDD . . . due to the former's lack of appreciation of what a large scale project involving innovative and demonstrative components involved', cost the scheme an additional K£1.38 million which was not recoverable from the beneficiaries (Chana 1984). Such conflicts often have obvert political overtones which expose the authorities to accusations of self-interest. For example, it was impossible for the city council to control unauthorised housing in Dagoretti before the mid-1970s, as it was the seat of a senior minister of the national government. Local Kikuyu landlords could exploit their initial advantages of being outside the previous city boundary with impunity long after it had been extended (Memon 1982). Another, perhaps more typical case, is unauthorised Kibera. This settlement had been favoured by the colonial regime as its original Nubian population could be trusted during the Mau Mau emergency. The Kikuyu penetrated the settlement since independence and after 1974, local adminstrators have had effective control over what is built or demolished informally. The result has been the emergence of large scale absentee landlordism which operates through the protection of political patrons. Readjustments in the clientage system take place when individuals move around the administrative hierarchy.

Most residents of Nairobi's unauthorised housing are tenants; the business is lucrative for the initial investment can be recouped within a year or 18 months and one can even use bank loans to build up rental enterprises. However, unlike Latin America, where profits may be gained by individuals risking eviction while establishing their home base, here landlords reap their profits because they are in a position to exploit links with the local administration (Amis 1984). A genuine policy to cater for low income groups would obviously curtail these lucrative opportunies.

The colonial legacy is also indelible in Delhi where separate authorities still represent the old city, and the bureaucratic and military zones. The city received contingents of displaced populations on partition but growth rates have been massive in absolute rather than relative terms. Delhi benefits from the multiplier effects of being the seat of the federal government and so of highly paid officials and foreign representatives. But awareness of this special role has also resulted in the adoption of planning policy of questionable utility.

In 1955 the Delhi Development Authority (DDA) was established and with the aid of foreign consultants produced the Delhi Master Plan in three years. Its cornerstones were to curtial expansion and to control land use so that development would conform to the physical structure envisioned for 1981. Following British practice of the period, migrants were to be diverted to eight

Figure 5.3

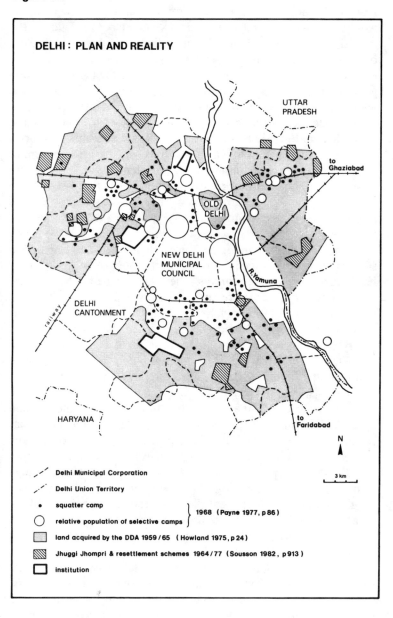

DELHI : PLAN AND REALITY

UTTAR PRADESH

to Ghaziabad

OLD DELHI

NEW DELHI MUNICIPAL COUNCIL

R. Yamuna

DELHI CANTONMENT

railway

HARYANA

to Faridabad

N

3 km

- - / Delhi Municipal Corporation

- . / Delhi Union Territory

• squatter camp

○ relative population of selective camps } 1968 (Payne 1977, p 86)

land acquired by the DDA 1959/65 (Howland 1975, p 24)

Jhuggi Jhompri & resettlement schemes 1964/77 (Sousson 1982, p 913)

institution

new ring towns situated outside the Union Territory; no more large-scale industry was to be permitted inside where land use would be specified and further development constrained by the imposition of a green belt. The operational mechanism was land ownership; state control over land was to ensure rational use, ensure access by all social groups and prevent the price escalation generated by free market forces. Between 1959 and 1965 the whole territory included within the 1981 urbanisable limit had either been expropriated or served notice to that effect (Figure 5.3) (Howland 1975). This involved 242.8 square kilometres, or 55 per cent of the total area, which was to be released in the form of integrated schemes composed of residential lots, their infrastructure and allowance for communal structure. Given the shortage of funds, the provision of more expensive houses and larger lots would generate capital to subsidise those destined for the poor.

None of these strategies succeeded. Delhi's population surpasses all the projections made while most of the ring towns have failed to reach their targets. The DDA seemed to be unaware that migration patterns are shaped by kinship networks through which members find their niche in the city. Their survival depends on casual employment and services rather than large-scale industry. Moreover individual initiatives suffered a set-back through the DDA's massive relocation programme of 1975–7 when approximately a million people were forcibly relocated at the city's periphery, sometimes even outside the Union Territory. Despite this action some 500 unauthorised colonies still remained in and around Delhi in 1979 (Sousson 1982). Moreover, the DDA has released land so slowly that developers have leapfrogged the frozen zone, while its distribution can hardly be considered impartial. By 1975, 69 per cent of the land had been allocated to high income groups representing 3 per cent of the populative. The poor, estimated at 76 per cent, had only received 6 per cent of the area (Howland 1975). Both the high cost and the method of allocation, involving a lottery system operating city-wide, deters applications from the latter.

Delhi's morphology and administrative mechanisms would seem the epitomy of bad planning. Land monopoly has converted the DDA into the largest speculator operating in the city, as its sluggish allocatory procedures have resulted in peripheral sprawl and ribbon development along all roads beyond its jurisdiction.

The cost of transport and servicing these is far greater than if more compact development had occurred within the Union Territory but it is the adjoining states of Haryana and Uttar Pradesh which face the consequences. Cross subsidies, which were the justification for adjudicating land to the rich, have not materialised either in the form of cheap housing or plots. The DDA is regarded by the bulk of the city's population as a punitive organisation whose actions are to be resisted or, preferably, ignored altogether (Sousson ibid.).

State intervention in the housing market has always been insignificant in Lima. Traditionally the capital was perceived as the preserve of bureaucratic, professional and commercial elites capable of housing themselves. When migrants arrived *en masse* to partake of its advantages, the traditional supply mechanisms were inappropriate. Entrepreneurs responded in the 1920s by constructing rooms around a lot supplied with communal sanitary facilities. The authorities rejected this solution and so encouraged concealment: landlords no longer provided any sanitation, as the rooms were not 'residential'. An urban planning authority was created in 1946 when small-scale squatting had already taken place north of the Rimac and on rocky outcrops. By the time a master plan appeared in 1965, mass invasions had been taking place on inland desert land for decades. Governments varied in their response but all attempted to raise political capital prior to elections with promises of 'solutions', 'improvements', and services. Under DL 13517 in 1961, the legal position was established: existing *barriadas* (shanty towns) were to be improved, provided they were on suitable sites which did not 'impede the city's expansion' or on land whose 'potential value did not justify its use for modest homes' (Lowder 1973). Thus squatters were cleared from valuable private land but generally tolerated on worthless sandy wastes (Figure 5.4).

A revolutionary military regime governed Peru from 1968 to 1979; it strived to transform both the structure of its society and its economy. Its principal goals were to assert national control over key sectors of the economy, previously owned by multinationals or by members of the indigenous oligarchy, address social inequalities and generate political support for its actions. Translated into housing terms, this involved nationalising industries producing building materials such as cement, stimulating the construction industry through financial measures and co-opting the

Figure 5.4

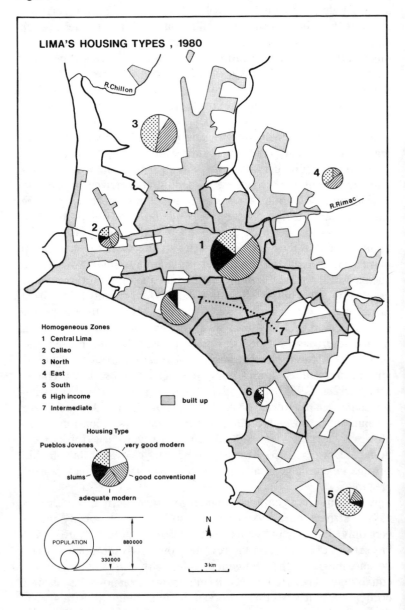

poor through granting *barriadas* legal status under the more dignified designation of *pueblos jóvenes* (young towns). Funds were channelled into the housing sector by two measures. First employees of 20 or more years standing were allowed to draw on their pension entitlement prior to retirement, provided that these monies were invested in housing. This enabled pension funds to build estates for the employees they guaranteed. In addition DL 22951 funded Fonavi from the proceeds of a 4 per cent payroll tax and a 3 per cent tax on firms benefiting from housing contracts. Fonavi builds houses destined for contributory workers. Cheap credit was also made available to self-help constructors.

These measures undoubtedly benefited the construction industry but the quality of the houses built ensured they reached only a few. Fully serviced middle-class estates proliferated on the good quality agricultural land situated between the established city and the far flung *pueblos jóvenes*, which had waited perhaps 20 years for their water supply. The doubts of the poor raised by these actions were confirmed by the interventions of Sinamos, the Military Government's agency designed to promote community development. A massive invasion took place in 1971 on the dry pampa south of Lima. The government adopted Villa El Salvador as a showcase, promising infrastructure, a transport service, an industrial estate and funds, all articulated by Sinamos. The settlers took it at its word but soon discovered that the regime was just as afraid of spontaneous initiatives as its predecessors. It refused to legalise their bank and used repressive tactics when the community rejected the leaders foisted upon it (Skinner in Ward 1982). Sinamos became totally discredited and was disbanded in 1978. However, as migration continued, the authorities were forced to designate two *bolsones* or areas where squatting is permitted.

Lima's experience over the period provides many morals for the promoters of self-help schemes. First such neighbourhoods were only tolerated on unaccessible wastelands while middle-class developments utilised more suitable intervening land subsequently. Not only did the poor subsidise the costs of infrastructure provision but the city bears the additional costs of servicing dormitories located over 30 kilometres from the major foci of employment. Secondly, while settlements developed when the economy was expanding, they could not maintain this during downturns when their structural weaknesses became apparent. Self-help infrastructure has proved to be short-lived in some circumstances; partly constructed and unmaintained buildings deteriorated rapidly and the older settlements have become grossly overcrowded. Understandably the second generation resists going through the whole process again in an unserviced *bolsón* 30 kilometres away. Thirdly, self-help has political attributes which make legislation a two-edged sword. The emphasis on neighbourhood development served to link their omissions with their inhabitants rather than to systematic shortcomings of the state. Their inequality was institutionalised for responsibility for services was devolved to the municipalities when they were revived in 1979 and their budgets were based on the revenue generated by property taxes and service charges. This mechanism ensures that poor unserviced neighbourhoods are likely to remain so. It is consistent with the post military (1982) regime's actions to strengthen capitalist structures in Lima's housing market. ENACE, the state property development agency which replaced EMADI, observes the private enterprise law, as does SENAPA, the new national agency responsible for the provision of water, electricity and sewers. Although ENACE-contracted housing developments and site-and-service programmes absorbed 80 per cent of state housing funds during 1981–3, these favoured only just over a quarter of the beneficiaries. However, it is doubtful whether that term is appropriate: although credit from the International Development Bank, the German and Japanese Governments underwrote SENAPA's activities, no element of subsidy was passed on to the consumers, who not only paid the installation costs but were also charged interest rates which were always greater, at times double, those exacted from industrialists. Self-help appears to have been rejected as a means for providing housing; only 3.5 per cent of lot holders in Lima have been able to use the Materials Bank, while FONAVI, to which the regularly employed are forced to contribute, has only benefited those who can afford modern housing (Arnillas 1985).

Conclusions

City housing markets mirror structures in society in which the weakest members occupy the least favourable niches. Market forces are reinforced by legislation and planning instruments. The status quo is disturbed when the disadvantaged population can no longer be considered a minority and when it attains sufficient education to articulate its demands, or when the costs of repressing it become too great. Most TWC authorities appreciate that they never will be able to supply Western-type houses *en masse* and that they cannot afford to destroy resources, whatever form they take. They are not yet convinced by the arguments that individual initiatives should be maximised by the adoption of more appropriate criteria for legal housing. Much research has illustrated the outcome of unsuitable policies. Less attention has been devoted to how administrative machinery can be improved and workable policies devised that gain societies' support without discriminating against a large proportion of their members.

6 SUPPLYING HOUSEHOLD NEEDS

City population growth exerts great pressure on the systems supplying them with consumer goods and services, which with the exception of socialist governments, have been provided predominantly by private enterprise. States have often intervened in response to political pressure to curb speculation during a period of shortages and hardship. However, such action is usually short term and aimed at controlling private entrepreneurs, not to supplant them. Government outlets may also be found distributing goods like grain or sugar but these operations are often an extension of state participation in production, processing or importing, rather than the outcome of a specific policy designed to supply city populations. Public intervention more commonly takes the form of price controls, the fixing of profit margins, the management of public markets and the imposition of standards. Thus in TWCs the quantity, quality and location of the goods on offer reflect very precisely their populations' effective demand.

Rapidly expanding populations not only force supply systems to expand their scale of operations but also frequently cause their reorganisation. There have been few city administrations or indigenous enterprises able to tap sufficient capital to stretch their operations to cater for much of the increased demand for goods and services. Under these conditions, the spontaneous appearance of scores of petty entrepreneurs is an effective and cheap response to a very real distributive problem. It is not worthwhile making technological innovations when *per capita* purchase power is very low and labour remains both plentiful and cheap. Moreover, the wants of the very small wealthy clientele may be satisfied through the import of luxuries, the employment of a large retinue of household servants and membership of exclusive institutions. The very skewed income profiles common in TWCs are reflected in their demand structures. Only when the expansion of the administrative, commercial and productive sectors generate a comparatively wealthy (in national terms), entirely urbanised 'middle class' of larger dimensions is effective demand created for a more sophisticated range of locally produced goods and a wider range of public services.

The analysis of the provision of goods and services is approached here from several angles. First the analysis of allocations made in household budgets is used to define the nature of demand in cities. Then the organisation of the distributive systems that attempt to satisfy those markets are examined. These in turn have given rise to particular spatial arrangements of outlets, whose form and configuration reflect the particular systems in which they are embedded. The data required for the first two approaches are neither easily obtained nor easily interpreted in the cross-national context for far deeper reasons than the mere logistical one of access to the relevant publications or the paucity of case studies.

Allocations made in household budgets are influenced not only by prices and income levels. They reflect a wide range of circumstances peculiar to a particular city in a specific country. These may include price controls which make certain goods artificially cheap; the characteristics of the housing market which are crucial in determining the cost of that element; the different transport needs which are imposed by the morphology of each city. Lifestyle, diet and clothing reflect climate, as well as culture. In addition, the ideal economic criteria for assessing the structure and efficiency of distributive systems are just not available. Admittedly, enterprises the world over are reluctant to discuss details of their investments, turnover and profits. Secretiveness is enhanced when entrepreneurial skills are still at the level of individual instinct and are considered to involve a large element of luck. Many reports reveal that the majority of petty traders and artisans are barely literate, keep no books and have little more than a hazy idea of business parameters; often their remuneration is the balance between the proceeds of the day and what is required to be able to operate on the following one. Only registered outlets operating in fixed premises, which represent a relatively small minority of entrepreneurs, are likely to keep records and even theirs may be rather rudimentary. Owing to the lack of comprehensive directories and the difficulty in assessing economic criteria, studies tend to be based on the number of outlets and on features readily ascertainable by field observation. This accounts for the emphasis in much of the literature on the outward form and distribution of retail outlets, rather than on the economic structures in which they operate.

The Structure of Demand

Man's most basic needs are food and drink. Although the population of any large city will not all be consuming exactly the same diet, studies invariably show that purchases in this sphere experience the lowest income elasticity, averaging around .6, which make it a most useful city-level yardstick for cross-national comparisons. Food and drink account for between a third and just over a half of household expenditure at city-level in the Third World (Table 6.1). As a rule the residents of capital cities allocate significantly less of their income to this sector than those of smaller cities and substantially less than is the case of the rural zones of their respective countries. The highest figure in the table for a Latin American capital city (46.6 per cent for Bogotá) is still lower than the lowest reported for a secondary city (51.7 per cent for Medellín). Comparable data for African cities all lie towards the upper end of the range, as do the statistics for Chinese cities, Kuala Lumpur, Manila, Chandigarh, Bangla Deshi cities and Colombo.

Worldwide expenditure on food and drink declines inversely with the increase in income. In most of the cities cited, the range is between about a third for the richest quartile to over 60 per cent for the poorest. Although wealthier citizens enjoy expensive meat, more fresh fruit and vegetables, imported goods and alcoholic beverages, their purchases still absorb less of their income than do the staple grains, roots and cheapest sources of protein of the poorer households' resources.

Income is the principal factor influencing allocations in household budgets. The household head's education, occupation, age and household size have seldom proved statistically significant once the effect of income has been taken into account. Undoubtedly substitutes made in some categories of expenditure conceal the influence of these variables. For instance, a child might be sent to an expensive private school or to a much cheaper state one; he/she might not attend at all either due to the lack of funds or owing to a shortage of school places. Likewise a sick man might resort to cheap herbal remedies because of his faith in their efficacy, or, to avoid the long queues involved in attendance at a public dispensary and the expense of the prescribed remedies. In all sectors of expenditure, real choice is the prerogative of the comparatively wealthy; income restraints determine the form and level of participation in urban markets for the majority.

Table 6.1: Breakdown of Household Expenditures

CITY	Date of Data	Food & Drink	Housing	Clothing	Health & Education	Transport	Other	Source
AFRICA:								
Accra	1977	53.9	16.0	13.7	7.5	6.7	1.7	Central Bureau Stats. 1982
Malawi	1968/9	41.8	17.0	15.9	3.0	5.5	.9	Humphrey & Oxley 1976
Nairobi	1968	45.1	23.1	10.0	2.9	6.5	11.1	Massell & Heyer 1969
Tunis	1970/1	51.0	18.0	12.0	6.2	4.6	2.0	INS 1972
Morocco (8 cities)	1970/1	44.7	22.6	9.3	5.8		17.6	INS 1973
ASIA:								
Bangladesh (30 cities)	1973/4	67.9	19.2	5.6	–	–	7.3	Islam 1982
Colombo (poorest 60%)	1973	59–66	9.3–12.4	7.3–8.1	4.4–8.7	.7–7.0	9.2–16.3	Municipal Welfare Report 1974
Malaysia (peninsula)	1973	38.28	–	–	–	–	–	Lam 1982
Manila	1975	49.4	–	–	–	–	–	Nat. Census Stat. Office 1975
Singapore	1977/8	31–55	–	–	–	–	–	Cheng 1982
LATIN AMERICA:								
Bogotá	1968/9	46.6	30.8	7.3	6.8	2.9	5.6	Musgrove 1978
Caracas	1968/9	35.5	33.3	6.3	6.4	6.8	11.7	"
Lima	1968/9	43.3	29.5	7.8	4.8	4.9	10.2	"
Porto Alegre	1974	40.4	29.4	6.3	6.0	4.7	13.2	Pereira et al. 1979
Rio de Janeiro	1974	41.9	29.4	4.7	6.6	5.5	11.9	"
Quito	1968/9	45.6	31.5	10.2	2.9	.3	9.5	Musgrove 1978
Santiago	1968/9	40.8	33.1	11.6	3.7	3.7	7.1	"

Purchasing power is the key to the structure of TWC markets. The large proportions of income spent on essentials are reflected in the importance of those sectors. However, the use of broad categories conceals real differences in the quality of goods and services consumed by income groups, which are only revealed by intra-city breakdown of the statistics. Then it becomes clear that the markets for food and beverages, non-durable goods and in Latin American cities, public transport, are mass markets dominated by the poorer, majority population, while elites monopolise the markets for modern durable goods. Of course the nature of these reflects national levels of development and wealth, as well as its distribution. The epitomy of a durable good in Latin American cities is the car. In 1969, the richest 5 per cent of the households accounted for 71 per cent of the expenditure on motor vehicles in Quito, but only 20 and 15 per cent respectively in Lima and Caracas, which also had much higher average household incomes. The range for households possessing domestic electrical equipment spanned a 25 to 40 per cent (Musgrove 1978). Meanwhile in China, a survey of 6500 families in 34 major cities revealed that 50 per cent of households owned a bicycle, a sewing machine and a watch, but domestic electrical equipment, other than a fan in southern cities, is virtually unheard of. Only 12 per cent of households possess a television (*China Newsletter*, No. 34, 1981).

The analyses of African cities present the evidence in different forms but come to the same general conclusions. Income elasticities for basic foods in Nairobi were very low, ranging from .285 to .599, but jumped to over 1.111 for all other sectors, even though this study was based on a middle income sample. In the poorer Malawi context, below average elasticities were reported for staple foodstuffs and clothing, while above average ones were attached to the more expensive range of foodstuffs, as well as to all durable goods and services. The holders of high status managerial occupations in Moroccan cities spent only 30 per cent of their income on food compared to the 41 and 50 per cent reported by office workers and sales personnel.

The data reported are far from complete and reflect conditions at a single point in time, mostly over a decade ago. It is difficult to assess their relevance now, although many are still being used by governments in contemporary market studies. This suggests that they assume that the rate of population growth, in association with the state of the economy, has precluded much increase in real purchasing power. Moreover change in consumption patterns over time is difficult to interpret, as it may reflect shifts in the relative costs of particular goods or services as well as differences in real wealth.

While the proportion of income spent on essentials declines with increasing income, one cannot assume that a decrease in expenditure in that sector indicates an increase in wealth. In the case of Abidjan, for example (Table 6.2), allocations ranged from 35 to 65 per cent in 1952, depending on the occupational rank of the household head; the corresponding figures for 1972 were 45 and 35 per cent. The key to this paradox lies in the speculative nature of the city's housing market during the intervening decade. The price of staple foodstuffs remained relatively stable while the cost of accommodation soared, such that the poorest families had to set aside a very high proportion of their income for shelter. The residents of neighbouring Accra on the other hand paid 2 per cent more for their sustenance in 1977 than they did in 1962. The cost of housing was not implicated here, allocations having remained comparatively low at 16 per cent. However, the Ghanaian economy has lurched from one crisis to another since the early 1960s giving rise to much political instability, associated disorganisation of production and mistrust in commerce. Ghana lost its eminent role as an exporter of prime cocoa and recent visitors to Accra describe scenes of hunger and great hardship resulting from the shortage of foodstuffs. Despite the substitution of cheaper foods, the residents have had to set aside more resources for its acquisition. Chile went through a similar period after the fall of the Allende regime and the imposition of one with diametrically opposed policies. Currently Peru is another example; high food prices in Lima reflect the real shortages of an economy overburdened with interest payments struggling after a major period of restructuring.

The changes reported for Tunis and Moroccan cities come nearer to the pattern expected after a gradual improvement in standards of living over a decade. The Moroccan figures are the more useful indicators, as they represent consumption in eight cities rather than the unique circumstances of one. There expenditure on food dropped 15 percentage points, housing, clothing, health and education, and transport all accounted for between one to three more, while the 8 per cent increase in the

Table 6.2: Household Budget Allocations in Abidjan, Ivory Coast

Group:	1952 expenditure (%)			1972 expenditure (%)		
	food & drink	housing/ durables	other	food & drink	housing/ durables	other
civil servants	35	30	35	45	45	10
employees	50	30	20	35	46	19
workers	60	25	31	25	55	20
casual workers	61	31	8	30	60	10

Source: Diambra-Hauhouot, A. (1972), p. 87.

'other' category acts as a sign of the broadening out of the market for durable goods. It would be interesting to have more recent data, for the price of food increased during the 1970s more than all the other sectors that make up the cost of living index, reaching 287 in March 1982, (1972/3 = 100), as opposed to a total index of 262.

All major TWCs have experienced the presence of foreign economic, if not political, elites whose tastes and lifestyles have differed greatly from those of the host population. Frequently their behaviour has been adopted by nationals aspiring to similar status, thus perpetuating these consumption patterns after the departure of expatriates, or even creating a larger demand for them. To this clientele, Western tastes are associated with modernisation and increasing development; they are favoured by those in salaried employment, whose lifestyles and education enable them to appreciate both their convenience value and greater quality. The goods in question are branded or labelled, factory made and sold by standard weights or sizes at recognised prices.

The trend can also be detected in the food sector. The common traditional eating pattern throughout the Third World consists of two meals a day. The main meal is usually prepared by boiling and is a porridge or stew, the principal ingredient being either a grain or tuber. This bland base is rendered more palatable by the addition of spicy sauces, which may contain green vegetables, beans or some type of animal protein, as well as condiments. Frequently an unleavened bread or pancake and beer, all made from the same staple, or a herbal tea, accompany the meal. The leftovers are eaten with a broth or small portion of vegetables or fruit for the second meal. The preparation of such meals based on fresh ingredients involves daily purchases and is time-consuming, regardless of the numbers to be fed. Despite the marginal productivity of many urban occupations, they nevertheless often involve long hours away from the home. This in itself encourages the purchase or preparation of snacks that can be eaten standing up or in the street and served from a piece of paper or leaf, rather than dishes requiring bowls and spoons. Bottled soft drinks are also easier to dispense than prepared infusions.

The next stage concerns foods prepared in the home. Those with greater purchasing power appreciate the storability, ease of preparation and versatility of processed foods, such as Western-style bread, noodle-type products and tinned sources of protein. However, many of these foods were or still are either imported, or as in the case of flour-based products, have a high imported content. This makes them particularly susceptible to price increases in inflationary conditions. These may not be passed on to the consumer immediately, for state policies promoting industry often subsidise their imported inputs. Such action often results in a far greater rate of subsidy to those with more income, as they consume a larger amount of these foods. This situation arose in Peru in the mid-1970s when the Military Government subsidised rice, wheat flour and cooking oil imports, as well as gasolene. The metropolis and especially its high income stratum benefited to an extent totally disproportionate to their population. Similarly bread production in Dar es Salaam accounts for much of Tanzania's sizeable imports of wheat, and Bangladesh's urban population consumes a disproportionate share of imported grain and cooking oil.

The clothing and footwear sectors have also undergone changes more profound than those dictated by mere fashion, as readymade clothing made to standard sizes and patterns gradually replace the purchase of cloth and the services of tailor and seamstress, while factory-made shoes gain favour over the products of the artisan cobbler. Furnishings of a Western type are adopted and domestic gadgets displace servant labour in the more developed cities. All these changes in the nature of demand recoil on the structure of supply systems, for the enterprises catering to traditional tastes are rarely able to serve these newer and expanding markets.

Supply Outlets

Given the nature of demand in TWC, it is not surprising that the most common retail outlet reported is that purveying foodstuffs, even when analyses are based solely on business conducted from fixed premises. These do not incorporate the vast numbers of market vendors and street hawkers, the majority of whom also trade in edibles. The hallmark of Third World food supply and distribution systems is their complexity which defies simplistic categorisation. They are made up of enterprises of very different size which conduct their affairs according to different codes, often exhibiting traits peculiar to a specific milieu.

The range in scale of retail outlets is very wide, stretching from the mobile hawker of a single basket of wares to the large supermarket in a modern shopping complex. Generally the smaller the city and the poorer the population, the more traditional the eating habits are likely to be and consequently, the greater the proportion of units retailing fresh foodstuffs. The storage potential determines the type of outlet in which an item is likely to be sold. Leafy vegetables and soft fruit spoil rapidly in high temperatures and must be dispatched quickly if they are to retain their value. Their handling charges and the risk involved pushes up their retail price, so making them an upmarket good sold at locations likely to attract the appropriate clientele. The fact that tubers and grains are much easier to transport and store renders them saleable by a much wider range of outlets.

The TWC consumer's major source of fresh food is the market-place, consisting of stalls both within a building or buildings and those without, as well as a large number of mobile vendors trading in the adjoining streets. Generally fees are charged according to whether the stall is provided or self-built, its permanence, dimensions and location; there is rough grouping according to type of wares on offer. Stall owners are independent entrepreneurs, each of whom acquires their own supplies and disposes of them as best they can. Rarely do they employ other than family assistants and most stalls are run by one person. Selling strategies reflect the standards current in the broader economy of the city: goods may be sold ungraded and by the pile or basket in the cities of the poorest countries or in the poorer districts of better-off ones. Such behaviour has been observed widely in all three continents. However, the common practices in well-established markets in larger or more developed cities include grading, sale by weight and for displayed prices, rather than being derived through bargaining. Competition between stall holders hinges on trade being attracted by the quality and variety of goods on offer, rather than being the outcome of the skill of haggling with customers, as in the former case.

Markets account for the largest single volume of trade in TWCs and cater to the widest range of income groups. Their service is extended by various forms of mobile trader. Some of these require a capital outlay at least as great as that of a stall and a market licence: these are the owners of tricycles or carts who ply fixed routes in the moderately well-off residential districts distant from the markets. They usually specialise in fresh vegetables, fruit, eggs or even fish and need to consider quality, given their clientele. A far more numerous group of mobile vendors, including modest hawkers equipped only with a basket or box, provide the same service in the poorer peripheral zones, only their stock consists of a small range of less perishable staples. Both of these types of vendor may vary their routes on a regular pattern or, adopting a form common in rural areas, become part of a periodic urban market cycle, which are common in Latin American cities, or of the night markets reported in South East Asia. Finally any sites that attract crowds, such as bus stations, factory gates or stadia, quickly acquire a complement of stalls and mobile traders offering refreshments of all kinds.

As cities expand rapidly in a territorial sense, transport difficulties curtail accessibility to markets and offset the higher prices fixed outlets are forced to charge to cover their greater overheads. In poorer districts 'corner shops' may be no more than shacks constructed of recycled materials and offer only the narrowest selection of durable staples, basic household goods and those goods which are delivered by the distributor, such as bottled soft drinks. Although these may have a recognised price, other practices of the outlet, such as the long hours they are open, the sale of minute quantities (one egg or a single cigarette) and the extension of credit to regular customers, are more like the market-place than the supermarket. In middle income districts, they offer the wider range of the small grocer but rarely any fresh food other than eggs; in Latin America many were also small bakeries, although this function is declining in major cities as factory production becomes more prominent. The well stocked grocer-delicatessen serves the elite and tends to be located in a central location or a purpose-built complex provided with ample parking space.

Most capital cities of any size, and others including a sizeable expatriate population, had acquired their first supermarket by the 1960s. Initially these outlets catered for the more pecunious element in the population and sold imported and processed goods, rather than fresh foodstuffs of local origin. Their prices excluded the average householder; even their staples were sold in too large a unit for those living on minuscule incomes generated on a daily basis and with little means of keeping food in the home. Since then local supplies have been incorporated and refrigerated equipment installed. Overheads have tended to decline with administrative experience and turnover increase with the fading of the elite image of this type of shop. By the 1980s supermarkets cater for a much wider range of income groups and earn their profits from greater sales at lower unit prices. Frequently they are established in poorer neighbourhoods before a traditional market.

In summary, retail units in TWCs are very numerous and very small. The population:trader ratio is far lower than that of developed settings, as demonstrated by the statistics reported for the Philippines (Table 6.3). Average threshold populations at comparable dates for grocery shops in Great Britain and the United States were 354 and 916 respectively (Dannhaeuser 1977).

Table 6.3: Population per Fixed Retail Outlet

	Fresh Food	Groceries	All Outlets
Philippines	167	187	145
Manila	118	194	76
Dagupan	81	91	47[a]

Note: a. Includes mobile vendors.
Source: Dannhaeuser, N. (1977).

Such low ratios reflect a purchasing pattern of frequent transactions at the micro scale consistent with the poverty of the majority of the population. In these circumstances the profits of large-scale enterprises stem from their high prices, for their turnover would have to be enormous before economies of scale would permit them to compete with the hawker on the pavement. The gradual evolution of systems in which profits are derived from volume of sales rather than prices is commonly regarded as a sign of increasing development, such as has been observed in major Latin American and Turkish cities.

It is common for the distinctions between types of retail outlets to be attributed to the ethnic group or nationality of the proprietor. In relatively new countries, this is a reflection of colonial organisation whereby indigenous institutions coexisted with those established for the expatriate population. The managers of the latter were either 'lesser rank' colonists, such as the box and trade *wallahs* in India's cities, or a third group, generally Middle Eastern in origin, introduced to act as a buffer between native and administrator. The Chinese assumed this role in South East Asia and are also represented on the western seaboard of Latin America, where they were introduced as indentured coolies to replace the slaves liberated in the nineteenth century. More recent influxes of refugees to that continent have also tended to be associated with trade and include those of Central European extraction, Catalans and Jews.

In the colonial situation, such groups served a separate market and operated under different conditions. Expatriate enterprises tended to be offshoots of import/export firms and served the elite; nowadays they compete with the multinationals. They still concentrate on higher order durable goods, such as vehicles and domestic equipment, or on luxury goods; Western commercial practices are observed. It may take some time before local suppliers can compete even for lower order goods, however, in Abidjan for example, the poorer population preferred to buy stylish second-hand imported clothing rather than misshapen and badly sewn local goods (Diambra-Hauhouot 1972). Buffer groups tended to serve an intermediate clientele of indigenous civil servants and the regularly employed, who aspired to better quality goods than those of the market-place but who could not afford the prices of the boutiques of the rich. Today they tend to run medium-scale grocery businesses, specialist outlets for the cheaper durable goods and services involving technology, such as garages, modern laundries and dry cleaners. Business practices are far more sophisticated than those of the market-place but are less likely to involve advertising and sales campaigns, such as maintained by the principal stores or branded goods, such as Coca Cola or Ford.

The Chinese stand out in this group owing to the segregation imposed upon this people by virtually every colonial power and which they now seem to prefer. Their enterprises cluster in Chinatowns, distinguished by *shophouses* in which several small enterprises share the open ground floor and adjoining pavement, while less accessible space is either allocated to professional services, storage or the accommodation of the traders' families. Chinese retailers are generally supplied only by Chinese wholesalers, in fact the latter tend to dominate the trade in the principal cities of the Philippines, Malaysia and Indonesia. The Chinatowns also have distinctive features reflecting their own specific needs, such as the high incidence of photographers peculiar to cultures worshipping ancestors (Jackson 1975).

Indigenous traders are over-represented in small-scale enterprise. For some observers, this dominance of small outlets is tangible evidence of how institutional mechanisms generate distinctive modes of production (Santos 1976). Many entrepreneurs could never meet the terms demanded by institutional creditors and have to manage on next to no capital; their goods are provided by a distributor or wholesaler and only paid for once they have been sold. Another common feature is for successful entrepreneurs to create additional outlets under the management of a trusted partner, rather than expand the existing business. Small-scale trade is highly competitive which ensures profit margins are low; a trader's hard won earnings can easily be eroded by misfortune, such as illness or theft. The acceptance of credit requiring interest payments and collateral is seen by many as an unjustifiable risk for the family's resources. Diversification on the other hand makes maximum use of labour, expands the service suited to the majority of the population and does not require the reorganisation of established practices. Nor should the gulf between traditional and modern business operations be ignored, as was discovered during the pioneering stages of chain stores and supermarkets. Stocking was relatively simple when most lines were imported but the task of maintaining a steady supply of local produce of the desired quality was so difficult that many enterprises found it easier to invest in backward linkages — market gardens, trucking enterprises and coldstores — than to attempt to organise dependable supplies from scores of independent small-scale producers.

While seeming chaotic from a Western point of view, indigenous trading is far from unstructured. The most successful small-scale traders are those occupying market stalls and there are always more aspirants than vacancies for these. When they occur, existing stallholders invariably select the successor, generally a relative of one of them and present the municipal authority with an installed candidate. Frequently stallholders form associations to lobby and intercede with the municipality, as well as to adjudicate between members and enforce market rules. Some of these can be very elaborate, the leaders of each market within the city forming a hierarchy culminating in a supreme authority, such as exists in Lagos. Another common feature of such entrepreneurs in African cities is their membership of some form of rotating savings association, whereby members pay a regular sum to an organiser who then dispenses the whole to each member in turn, claiming a share as payment for his or her labour. Members always risk the fact the organiser may abscond, despite the efforts to evaluate trustworthiness before joining. However, professional organisers of larger scale donations keep books, often bank the proceeds and are paid through the use of the sum in the interim period as capital for another enterprise or with the interest the sum generates over the cycle.

The existence of minority groups in certain forms of retailing should not obscure the fact that 'indigenous' traders in many TWCs are far from homogeneous ethnically. Indeed one could argue that the disparity between foreigners and nationals stems from scale of operation induced by distinction in purchasing power, while differences between nationals operating at the same scale are genuinely ethnic in origin. Most countries have certain cities, regions or peoples who are recognised as being particularly successful in trade: Antioquia in Colombia, Otavalo in Ecuador and Juliaca in Peru all have this reputation, while it is the Hausa in Nigeria, the Dioula of the Ivory Coast and the Ga in Ghana that are noted; in India the traditional trader casts, the Vaishya, still dominate the activity; among the Chinese, the same specialisms are associated with identical subgroups in totally unconnected cities.

Distinctions in trading characteristics between national groups may reflect cultural norms, affinities between members of the same group, or the relative position of a group in a city's social and economic hierarchy. In the first case, certain crops or goods may be considered as having male or female associations and are marketed by the appropriate sex. Market trading itself may have connotations with sex: women predominate among the Ga, which would never be acceptable to the Muslim Hausa. Further specialisation between groups often arises as a side-effect of inter-regional trade and reflects the linkages that occur between members of extended families or tribal groups active at different stages in the marketing chain. For some groups there is a significant overlap between their entrepreneurial role and a wide range of personal relationships, which contribute directly or indirectly to their business success. Such relationships include sources of credit, supplies, concessions and clientele and in turn, the trader may be expected to offer various degrees of credit and cheaper prices or make certain contributions. All these transactions reinforce the trust and co-operation required for a successful enterprise and are most likely to be found between kin and associates bound by the same religion and origin, as portrayed in Figure 6.1 for the traders of Kano. However, all resident ethnic groups tend to be represented among the market traders as this is the starting point for most traders. Dominance at this level may reflect the inability to compete for more profitable occupations, as is usually the case with women.

Trading systems

The organisation and scale of operations at each link involved in the transfer of foodstuffs from producer to ultimate customer reflect national and regional structure of land tenure, storage and the means of transport, credit and market information. The volume of produce and the extent of the supply area also condition the number and types of linkages. Every system generates its own particular set of constraints and mechanisms which further its reproduction; any change within them has repercussions on other parts of the system. Third World commercial systems are distinguished by inequality in the bargaining position of the actors involved; trade frequently takes place in a monopolistic or oligopolistic arena, between agents supported by commercial institutions and with better access to information on the state of the market and producers deprived of those assets and with no alternative destination for their produce.

A common outcome of the expanding scale of demand accruing from city growth is the absorption of more entrepreneurs at all levels of transaction, giving rise to more complex systems. Governments and better-off consumers often suspect that these are inefficient, that needless duplication of services and

Figure 6.1

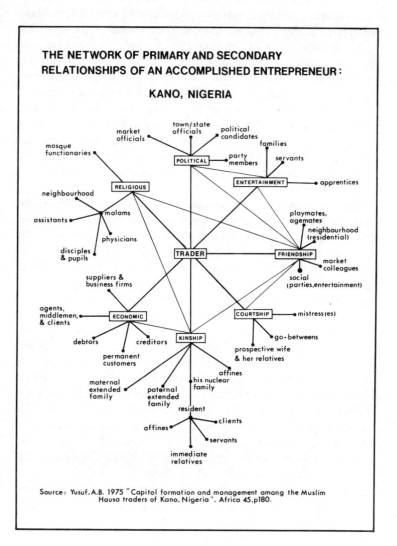

THE NETWORK OF PRIMARY AND SECONDARY
RELATIONSHIPS OF AN ACCOMPLISHED ENTREPRENEUR :

KANO, NIGERIA

Source: Yusuf, A.B. 1975 "Capital formation and management among the Muslim
Hausa traders of Kano, Nigeria", Africa 45, p180.

excessively long chains of intermediaries merely push up retail prices to no advantage of the consumer or producer. Municipal standardisation of units of trade, enforcement of quality controls and above all, the introduction of market services, have tended to rationalise structures in large cities, although evidence suggests that these processes can occur spontaneously in response to market pressure. More active forms of state intervention have often been less successful. The literature is liberally sprinkled with accounts of short-lived enterprises, conceived in haste and with inadequate understanding of the market mechanisms they are to replace, by administrators more accustomed to drawing up plans than to implementing them. Others may succeed for a time only to fall victim to political interference or changes in government policy.

State participation may occur at any point of the supply-distribution chain. In Jamaica, the AMC operated as a purchasing agency which streamlined the handling of produce between the farm gate and Kingston's wholesale market. Meanwhile in Turkey the state encouraged efficiency through competing with private outlets on equal terms. Most Latin American countries have separate agencies charged with stimulating the production of basic foods through a system of guaranteed prices and with selling it to the public; Ecuador operates rice and wheat programmes via ENAC while EMPROVIT distributes basic foods via its chain in the cities. Goods in state outlets are cheaper than elsewhere but not necessarily of equal quality. Governments have also used their chains to subsidise foods sold to vulnerable groups; however, schemes dependent on subsidies have tended to be the most prone to accusation of corruption and to suppression on changes in economic conditions.

An example of a composite, multiple-objective scheme illustrates the pit-falls. India's *Fair Price Shops* represent the desire to improve the efficiency of distribution networks via competition, while stabilising prices and supplying poorer citizens with necessities. The first aims are carried out by the Food Corporation of India, which procured up to 10 per cent of the domestic production of foodgrains from regulated markets throughout the country. These act as a buffer to even out the price distortions caused by highly localised zones of supply (Punjab and Haryana states) and demand (the lower Ganges valley). These grains, along with such items as cooking oil, salt and sugar, are rationed through the Fair

Price Shop network to those registered. Although a national scheme, the prices in the shops do fluctuate according to the region's income levels, needs and market conditions; on average they are about 30 per cent lower than those of alternative sources. Unfortunately, as in many state systems, 'the distribution is biased against the poor and its welfare content is eroded by irregularities and mulfunctions' (Ahmad and Singh 1982). The needy were less likely to have registered owing to ignorance and red tape surrounding the procedure and they were often sold surplus or substandard stock. In Delhi it transpired that the ratio of population per shop was much higher in poorer districts, which in itself rendered their service less adequate and harder to manage. Small-scale surveys indicated that the services deteriorated with distance from the apex of the national administrative hierarchy, so that service to the poor in smaller cities was likely to be far worse.

Such criticisms reflect the greater scrutiny to which any state enterprise is subjected. One could question whether it is realistic to expect an enterprise to satisfy both economic and welfare criteria, particularly in a country as vast and complex as India. Nevertheless, the formation of such large-scale agencies reflects a common tendency to intervene in markets and to attempt to remodel systems along Western lines, rather than to consider how local systems could be improved.

The simplest commercial system is that of the producer who sells direct to the customer. This was feasible in the very small capitals of newly independent inland countries, such as Mali, Upper Volta, Niger and Malawi, or in smaller settlements generally, but major cities cannot be provisioned by this method. The scale of demand calls for the surplus from a far wider area, particularly where there are marked seasonal regimes. Production and trade then become separate activities for all but a few large commercial enterprises. Multitudes of very small-scale producers may give rise to several echelons of intermediaries before economic loads are assembled for long distance transport, particularly where specialisation occurs. On arrival in the city, produce may be directed to entrepreneurs based in a wholesale market, channelled through a state agency, handled by the same intermediaries, or by a mixture of all three. Retailers purchase from all these sources, but those operating on a very small scale often acquire their stock from public markets. Bulk consumers, such as institutions and restaurants, may deal directly with wholesalers or shop in the market alongside everyone else. The provisioning system of any particular city exhibits unique characteristics as well as some of the general features described. The processes giving rise to them are best described in specific contexts.

Let us start with Suhum, Ghana (Schwimmer 1979). Being a relatively small settlement, one would expect a correspondingly simple commercial system. For green vegetables, the principal marketed good, this is so: 20 per cent is sold direct to the consumer by the producer. Half is handled by only one trader and only 30 per cent passes through a wholesaler. The distinctive element of this system is ethnic specialisation. The Ga and the Adaybe cultivate vegetables and so are their dominant traders, while the Akam and Guan handle cocoa and staples. Yams, however, are a valuable staple grown in the drier distant north; the commercial chain for them is much longer and more centralised. Producers sell to specialised assemblers who consign them by the lorry-load to the exclusive Yuhum Yam Sellers Association, whose members control the wholesale market. They in turn sell half directly to the consumer and channel the rest via retailers. A cross-section of ethnic groups take part in this trade, participation of each being reinforced by the vertical trading relationships that make up the chain. The third major element of local diet, fish, is handled by the Ga exclusively. Traditionally coastal assemblers established younger relatives in Suhum to organise local distribution. However, the construction of the new port town of Tema changed this pattern, for Tema Corporation built a cold store and refrigeration plant for the fish market. Seventy per cent of Suhum's fish now comes from Tema wholesalers who supply local wholesalers. These key entrepreneurs of the Ga Association sell over half themselves and pass the rest to specialised retailers, most of whom are second generation Ga. Coastal assemblers account for only a fifth of the supplies and very little comes direct from fishermen. Thus even in this relatively simple case, commercial systems differ according to foodstuff, its prominence in local diet and the location and identity of its producers.

Let us now turn to the other extreme, a strictly organised commercial system, such as found in socialist states, in this case China. Municipal Revolutionary Committees of large Chinese cities have six major organisations overseeing production, three of which are concerned with raw foodstuffs. The Second Commercial Bureau deals with vegetables, meat and poultry, sugar, salt and wine and non-staple foods. The Supply and Marketing Co-operative is particularly concerned with inter-regional trade in local specialisms, such as fruit, while the Grain Bureau also handles beans and the highly nutritious bean curd. Vegetable production is prominent in this structure because consumption has never been rationed, unlike grain, cooking oil or meat. Municipal boundaries have been drawn so as to include adjoining rural areas and thus maximise the degree of city self-sufficiency, particularly in vegetables. This policy reduces the problems of inadequate means of storage and transport of a perishable commodity, while expediting the cultivator's access to a major source of fertiliser, the night-soil generated in the cities. The intensity of cultivation declines inversely with distance; while the inner zones have extensive areas under continuous vegetable production with the aid of fertiliser, water control and the use of glass and plastic sheeting, outer zones are more likely to be dedicated to grain, orchards and industrial crops. Communes undertake to sow a stipulated acreage of a specific crop and to deliver a given quantity by a certain date to one of the Municipal Vegetable Company's linking stations. The latter offers a price between a pre-established floor and ceiling. The company is responsible both for co-ordinating production to maintain a steady supply and for weighing, grading and transporting the crop to the lead market; the latter performs both a supervisory and a wholesale role. It distributes supplies to smaller markets and neighbourhood outlets, implements the set prices and keeps the accounts for the retail side of the trade (Skinner 1978). In such a system change is likely to reflect state policy, such as to hold prices of necessities in cities stable while gradually altering the terms in trade in favour of the producer, so as to equalise living standards and discourage migration. However, systems do not always function as smoothly as they ought, even in China, as is implicit in the more flexible arrangements which production teams, even households in some instances, are now being allowed to make directly with linking stations or particular markets, or even to sell direct to the consumer.

The supply and distribution systems of the majority of major cities lie somewhere between these extremes of simplicity and structured hierarchies. Three cities of approximately the same size (population around 600 000) at the time reported, illustrate this range in Figure 6.2. The connecting lines in these indicate linkages without any connotation of strength, for even in-depth studies find

Figure 6.2

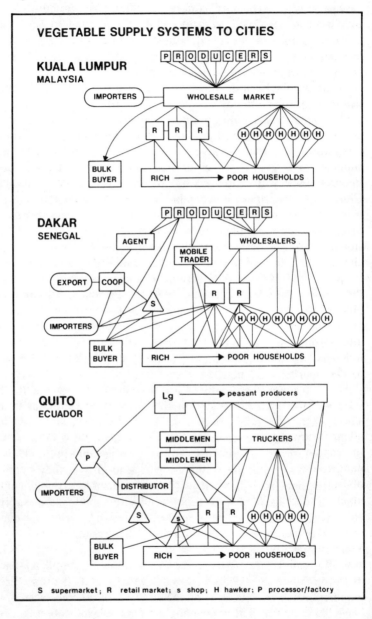

S supermarket; R retail market; s shop; H hawker; P processor/factory

it next to impossible to measure actual flows of goods or cash. The case of vegetables is traced again in view of their prominence in diet and market-place trade.

Paradoxically, Kuala Lumpur's system is made up of aspects associated with both simple and highly rationalised structures (Jackson 1975). On the one hand extra-market outlets do not compete in the sale of fresh vegetables, not even for exotics destined for the elite market. On the other hand, a small group of traders operate a wholesale market which handles virtually all produce, regardless of origin. Supplies come from three sources: temperate vegetables, especially Chinese and English varieties of cabbage, are grown in the Cameron Highlands some 220 kilometres away; seasonal deficits are made up by imports from China, Taiwan and Indonesia. Green legumes and herbs come principally from the more accessible lowland of Selangor. Chinese market gardeners in both peninsular areas dispatch regular con-signments by specialised truckers direct to the wholesaler; these charge a 5 to 10 per cent commission on the retail price and also frequently provide credit in cash and kind. The wholesalers supply three major and eleven minor markets, as well as a few bulk buyers and a multitude of mobile vendors; the larger markets also perform a minor wholesale function for these traders. Everybody attends the markets, but only the poorer, less demanding house-holds are likely to purchase the lower quality ware of street hawkers.

The contrasts within Dakar's systems result from different standards being applied in the various segments (Arnaud 1972). This is quite common in cities subjected to colonial administrations involving a large expatriate population. Dakar was the capital of French West Africa before it became that of inde-pendent Senegal. French influence is evident from the vegetables of European origin in the local diet, the practice of importing luxury foods and the presence of supermarkets which cater to the elite. On the other hand the commercial system handling local produce was primitive in the extreme in the early 1970s. Vegetables were sold by the sack or basket rather than by weight and no effort was made to grade them. There was no wholesale market; traders performing this function established themselves on any convenient waste land and producers brought their wares to them. A minority of mobile traders assembled loads at village level. For the most part this trading system was exploitative of everyone but the *bana-bana* who performed the wholesaling function. Producers had to absorb the cost of transporting their bundles of highly perishable commodities in total ignorance of the state of supply in the market. Not being satisfied with the ample opportunities for price-rigging that such conditions gave them, the *bana-bana* rarely paid producers for more than part of their load, claiming that sales were poor. Promises to cancel the remainder a day or two later, provided additional supplies were brought, could not be resisted by those unable to remove or store their goods. This meant that producers were in fact subsidising the costs of wholesaling and retailing. Wholesalers also gave retailers credit over several days, covering the cost with elevated prices; they in turn had to deal with the same trader so as to receive more supplies and to return the sacks and baskets. It is not surprising that large-scale producers able to attain the quality demanded preferred contracts for regular consignments to supermarkets or institutions; they received less than the retail price but more than from the *bana-bana*. Above all, the purchaser provided transport and paid for the transaction on collection.

The origins of such an inefficient system are difficult to pin down. Small-scale production could be very well organised and achieve high quality, as the regular exports of green beans to France by Synjamar, the syndicate of market gardeners, proved. However, efforts to achieve scale economies and streamline operations of the local market failed. Unicoop became notorious for gluts and scarcities and the inexperienced handling of imported potatoes, while the state enterprise (La Sodania) collapsed with sizeable debts. Instead of displacing the intermediaries, producers used both entities to offload poor quality goods unacceptable to them. Moreover *bana-bana* domination is unlikely to be broken by a central wholesale market, while its proposed location at the periphery of Dakar would increase the transport problems faced by the majority of retailers.

The complexity of Quito's supply system reflects the city's transformation during the 1970s and a corresponding reorganisation in production and distribution networks. Ecuador was atypical for a small country in that until recently the capital was overshadowed in the commercial and industrial sphere by Guayaquil, the port which articulated the tropical primary export economy. However, the oil from the eastern *selvas* fuelled the state administration as well as the *sierra* (highland) economy. Quito expanded rapidly and became a rival focus for *serrano* migrants. The increased purchasing power and scale of market demand speeded up the implementation of agrarian reform measures, which resulted in the creation of specialised commercial-scale units alongside peasant holdings using labour intensive methods. Thus some production networks were rationalised, as the larger suppliers dealt directly with processors, wholesalers and bulk buyers, rather than the numerous layers of specialised intermediaries. The latter included truckers who brought up rice, plantains, avocados and fruit from the coastal lowlands or the eastern *selvas* to the major markets; central place based wholesalers of the coast or *sierra* who consigned local produce to Quito-based wholesalers or sold it to independent truckers, and also mobile Quito-based wholesalers who would visit surrounding districts at regular intervals.

Meanwhile the distributive network was becoming more fragmented in response to increasing income differentials and areal sprawl of the city. Quito has about two dozen municipal markets of which half a dozen dominate the wholesale trade (Cazamour d'Artois and Moya 1984). Markets sell a wide range of goods but a few specialise in durables rather than in perishables. The smallest are exlusively retail and have a periodic cycle of peak activity. The municipality inspects and controls its markets, endeavouring to improve sanitary conditions and to prevent overspill into undesignated areas, especially by unlicensed itinerant hawkers, whose forestalling tactics obstruct the traffic in adjoining streets. However, the dirt, confusion and crowded atmosphere of the markets attracts those who prize low prices above their personal comfort and who are prepared to journey to the central and southern districts of this very elongated city. Middle and upper income groups clustered in the northern sector tend to patronise supermarkets where goods are preselected, washed and packaged and self-service is the norm. They are often part of a larger complex, the most up-market of these are situated in the midst of a huge parking lot and would not look out of place in any American city. Apart from a large supermarket and chain store, some two dozen specialised outlets provide for all recurrent domestic needs. Besides the shops, there are cleaning and personal services, high order services, such as banks, post office and payment offices for domestic water and electricity bills; one can relax afterwards over coffee and pastries or a coke and chicken-and-chips at McDonald's. Apart from these major outlets, small shops are common in residential neighbourhoods and offer a small range of the less perishable vegetables and fruit as well as groceries and household goods. Mobile hawkers are most common near workplaces and transport depots; they visit poorer outlying districts but are less evident in upper-class ones.

The trading systems described so far are for fair-sized cities in poorer countries and are correspondingly less developed than those of far larger and more cosmopolitan metropolises. Supermarkets, for instance, were introduced in Latin America in the 1950s, and by the 1970s chains with over a hundred branches apiece existed in São Paulo, Buenos Aires and Mexico City. Major department stores have long operated payment by instalment schemes and provided back-up services for durables; local and international credit cards were widely used in the 1970s. The numerous branches of banks and mutual savings societies are testimony to the much higher income levels than current elsewhere. Poorer households patronised department stores particularly for durables, indicating that these outlets were utilising a profit strategy based on high turnover rather than high prices; richer groups continued to patronise specialised outlets. Television has long been a medium of mass advertising, particularly for branded goods and chain stores.

Another trading system common in most TWCs is that in which the organisation is undertaken by the distributor, who either appoints managers to their own outlets or invites locals to apply for concessions. The obvious example of this is that of gasolene, for in most countries the source of supply is either a multinational, its local subsidiary or a state company which has taken over their network. Chainstores, whether supermarkets, or retailing clothing, domestic goods or fast food are often run on the concession principle.

Wherever very low incomes predominate, the metropolitan cities have an unassailable market advantage which is reflected in the concentration there of manufacturers of domestic consumer goods. Specialised goods, particularly those produced under licence and requiring strict quality control, such as pharmaceuticals and toiletries, are supplied to the whole nation from there and their populations absorb much of the modern kitchen equipment, china, furniture and stationery. As elsewhere, the producers' salesmen tour the retail outlets of chains and independents and compete with alternative suppliers. The quality and choice of clothing, shoes, household textiles and other fittings is also far greater in the metropolises and they are often available at lower prices, given the proximity to the producers and the scale of production. These sectors display a greater range in type of producer and outlet, as cheaper substitutes are provided by craftsmen. However, even goods made from recycled materials benefit from the more plentiful supplies of oil cans and drums, packing cases, rubber tyres and bottles available there. Such goods are often retailed in the street by the craftsman and at the site of production.

Spatial Patterns

The location of goods and service outlets reflect the historical morphology of any city, as they arise in response to need. Population density and purchasing power are independent variables which determine the quantity and quality of goods and services that can be absorbed at any location. Obviously the significance of the transport factor is related to the scale and morphology of the city, but in a TWC it is heightened by the inadequate service of most public systems and by the lack of provision for private vehicles in older and in predominantly pedestrian designed cities. Also land values and rates seldom relate directly to land uses in cities of indigenous origin in Africa and Asia.

Many studies in those continents are convinced that central business districts (hereafter CBD) do not exist in their cities. Given the lack of, or irrelevance of data for the usual economic criteria used to define CBDs (land values, rents or rates), analyses have depended on the observable features of the outlets. Usually a heterogeneous collection of enterprises are encountered, operating from an assortment of buildings of varied age and state of repair and offering different types of good and service by different means. The identity of the population determines the existence and rank order of a particular type in adjacent districts. Other elements may appear in response to external needs, such as those of tourists or pilgrims. Capital cities always acquire a certain range of high order services attached to their rank and to cater for administrative and diplomatic personnel. In very small capitals the clientele for these may be so limited that the result is 'the unadapted White city — an agglomeration of Blacks created by and for the Whites, a centre never integrating with its city' as in the case of Niamey, Niger (Laval 1981).

The simplest analytical technique to analyse CBD functions is the location coefficient, which requires only the numbers of each type of outlet. Even this measure may not identify a distinctive hierarchical order of types of outlets. When applied to the *sūq* of Omdurman, the most traditional of the three cities which make up Greater Khartoum, the types of outlet which achieved indices of over ten included a mixture of traditional trades, tourism and modern commerce, being, in descending order, middlemen and commission agents, wood and ivory carvers, silversmiths, tourist shops, hide buyers, tobacco sales, harness shops and banks. The most ubiquitous functions, such as food outlets, laundries, bakeries and millers, carpenters, wood and charcoal sales and bars also achieved their greatest concentration in the *sūq* (Kuhn 1971). Even in contexts which developed under considerable external influence, such as Oran in Algeria, the centre can best be defined by 'the intensity of land use rather than the standard indicators of high order functions . . . [being composed of] . . . a motley of low grade bars and shops . . . juxtaposed with high order professional, personal and administrative function, all over layered by residential land use in the upper storeys even at the heart of the city' (Thompson 1982).

External influence is responsible for much of this hetereogeneity. Small cities which did not attract a large alien element were able to adapt to changing systems, accumulating additional outlets. This was particularly prominent in those Indian cities where the significance of river transport was eroded and then replaced by the railway. The eventual result was often a linear commercial structure with outlets stretched out between the termini of the different forms of transport. The former commercial centres of Dacca and Patna were adjacent to the wharfs and wholesaling is still concentrated there. A separate node arose alongside other colonial institutions and the intervening axis became filled in as demand rose. Type of outlet is related to location on this continuum. At the long established end in Dacca, the narrowness and circuity of the alleyways ensured pedestrian dominance and traditional forms of trade were maintained, while at the other, wide streets and pavements are associated with such Western features as vehicle access, window displays and high rise blocks offering office space for banks and import/export agents (Majid 1970). In Patna wholesaling activities, food and general stores are prominent in the first; automobile showrooms and specialised high order goods (electrical, radio and hi-fi, leisure, watches) at the other end, while the intervening shops concentrate on cloth and general household needs (Dayal and Thakur 1976).

The principal disadvantage of the CBD concept for TWC contexts is the assumption that spatial accessibility mirrors a unidimensional hierarchical structure of commerce and does not admit intervening variables, such as an extremely asymmetrical income distribution and ethnic segregation. This is evident from the way accessibility is usually defined in terms of cost or convenience as if they were constant for the total population. The colonial heritage of most sizeable cities of Africa and Asia consists of an indigenous market, *sūq* or bazaar, located apart from the *new town* and its administrative functions and attendant shops. Indeed colonial administrators often placed the native bazaars out of bounds for their nationals. The 'buffer' commercial groups' enterprises performed that function literally, being physically located between the designated ethnic zones. Such segregation terminated with colonialism but its legacy consists of patterns in which income distinctions have replaced ethnic ones. Additional outlets in these areas obviously reflect the purchasing power and shopping patterns of the clientele they hope to serve.

The relative importance of market and other outlets reflects the ratio between poorer and comparatively richer populations. Additional facilities arise from individual initiative and appear where opportunities are perceived. As much city growth can be attributed to the influx of relatively poor migrants and their descendants, it is the market retailing system which comes under pressure first and which also absorbs more traders. Initially this expansion may just overflow into adjacent streets, but this process is limited. Original market-places were centrally located; much expansion leads to conflict with neighbours and traffic obstruction. Furthermore there is a limit to the area that can be served by a central point, especially to a predominantly pedestrian clientele. Consequently new traders seek a focal point elsewhere and over time a hierarchy of markets may emerge to reflect the manner in which, in West Africa at least, the '*per capita* income surface declines from the centre of the city to the rural fringe' (Sada 1978). The original market usually remains dominant, as the largest in terms of the number of traders, items for sale and population served, being the kingpin of the wholesaling system. Markets appear to repel one another, as new ones may relocate several times before establishing a satisfactory catchment area. In Monrovia, Liberia, the boundaries tended to fall at 20 minutes' walking distance (Handwerker 1979). When incomes rise, other forms of outlet can begin to compete, appearing first at focal points and later in residential areas.

Many West African cities, however, included a larger indigenous element during colonial days than was common elsewhere and the restricted sites of the coastal capitals dictated the direction of future development. *Villes neuves*, new towns and especially constructed garden suburbs were much more prominent features of North and East African cities and in cities of the Indian subcontinent. Here state administrative offices tended to be located apart from those of private commerce, giving rise to CBDs composed of specialised zones. Town planning regulations inherited from colonial ordinances often still forbid the establishment of service and retail outlets in the exclusive residential districts. However, the assumption that residents would shop at distant centralised points, made when servants were plentiful, upper-class women idle and the whole city very much smaller, are not necessarily true today. Elites undoubtedly have refrigerators and cars, but not the middle rank civil servants; even if they did have a car, it is unlikely it would be available to the wife during the day. As a result new outlets may appear, surreptitiously in disused garages in the case of Dakar's SICAP estates; new clusters of facilities at focal points on the periphery of such areas include both modern and market features. At other sectors of the periphery, where expansion is in the form of shanty towns, the new facilities operate from stalls, counters at windows or the front rooms of homes and in the open air.

As cities grow, new institutions added after independence or those requiring much space, such as a university, are established away from the centre in less congested districts where traffic is lighter. Conditions in the indigenous nuclei often deteriorate under the pressure of overcrowding and lack of physical repair; redevelopment there and in central districts generally tends to squeeze out small-scale entrepreneurs from profitable locations, for administrators favour uses which can contribute more to city revenues, while the poorer clientele may also be under pressure to relocate nearer the periphery. Eventually economic and amenity considerations in combination with the transport problems lead to the transfer of the wholesale market to a peripheral location accessible to national routes. This move tends to accentuate the disparities in resources between traders, placing those without vehicles at a great disadvantage. If the area is designated as ex-clusively industrial or commercial, it also curtails the opportunities for casual work which supported a sizeable population at the old site.

When location patterns are examined at city level, the analysis has usually been based on the number of outlets and functions in each cluster; any effort to weight these, so as to take into account scale or quality, has had to be on subjective criteria for the specific case. Even so, a number of interesting features are revealed by these exercises. In Nairobi, a city distinguished by strict ethnic residential segregation in its colonial phase, the number of functions showed little relationship to the number of outlets or the population served by each complex (Kimani 1979). The author argued that the variation in scale of operation accounted for this, as a specialised quality grocer could perform the service of a great many *home shops* in poorer areas. Further analysis of catchment areas revealed that shopping clusters in African (poor) areas de-pended on a dense local population, while those in the old Asian or European zones had much larger catchments of sparser populations with a much higher income. A factor analysis of functions also indicated segmented characteristics, reflecting the proportion of different socio-economic groups in the population (Tiwari 1979). The first and last factors selected modern pro-fessions (legal, medical and financial) and low order trades (butchers, grocers, wholesalers, bar owners and clothing retailers) respectively. Intermediate groupings seemed to reflect an under-lying dimension of technology and education, in which the order of selection indicated the frequency of demand of those skills. The third factor picked out plumbers, furnishers, decorators and tyre retreaders; the fourth was associated with metal workers, mechanical engineers, car showrooms and stationers, while the fifth included opticians, estate agents, auctioneers, travel and safari agents, architects and educational suppliers.

A more conventional analysis based on Davies' location coefficient yielded functional indices ranging from 397.6 to 7.5 for the 41 commercial clusters in Benin, Nigeria (Onokerhoraye

1977e). The natural breaks in the continuity of the indices served to devise the five levels of the hierarchy. At the apex stood a core incorporating the principal commercial streets and the principal market on which they abutted. The zone served the daily needs of the rich, as indicated by the slightly higher prices for perishables than quoted in other markets, but the special needs of the whole population, for durables in the market area were cheaper than elsewhere. The main sources of food were found in the subsidiary markets which distinguished the second and one of the third order centres. The third and fourth levels offered smaller specialist outlets for durables and mini-supermarkets under Nigerian management. The lowest level only provided a limited range of provisions, immediate needs and personal services from *home shops*, stalls and temporary structures.

Latin American cities do not exhibit the features just described, as their populations enjoy a higher average standard of living than is common elsewhere. Some developed mass transit systems in the early part of the century and all expanded in response to economic forces unfettered by colonial powers. There has been no counterpart for centuries of the ethnic segregation imposed in certain African and Indian cities; with few exceptions, differences between 'natives' and more recent arrivals reflect the disparity in opportunity between city and elsewhere rather than substantial differences in identity. Consequently, large Latin American cities have much more in common with Western ones and similar CBD structures can be identified. However, these may have become split as the congestion in the original core makes that area less attractive to modern functions and residents alike. Most building materials were relatively short-lived, particularly *adobe*, and require constant maintenance. Some cores became symbols of historical roles centred on immobile institutions, such as the cathedral, president's palace and town hall; they have become the focus of tourist curiosity, but the narrow streets, absence of parking space and pollution caused by the slow-moving traffic, have long encouraged both state and private offices and commercial enterprises to move elsewhere. The former tend to choose locations on major boulevards, while the latter often have either shifted to or become the focal points of upper-class residential districts. For example, Bogotá's *Multicentro* was originally conceived as a 'city within a city'; it is situated in the most exclusive residential area. Quito's Av. Amazonas, crowned by the ten-

storey-plus Hilton Hotel and American Bank in a street of exclusive shops and offices still containing a few two-storey family
houses converted to other uses, is in Mariscal Sucre, a middle-class
district well to the north of the original centre and away from
working-class zones. Lima now has two subsidiary CBD's; one was
originally conceived by a major department store and has since
acquired a great complement of specialised outlets, chain stores,
professional functions and commercial offices, while the other is a
very much up-graded shopping and banking centre of the upper
class district of Miraflores.

In all these examples, the original initiative was taken by private
enterprise and grew spontaneously, rather than at the instigation
of a planning authority. At a smaller scale, this has been the
hallmark of the location of most commercial clusters; it is
especially evident in new middle-class housing districts in which
developers start by building a shopping complex near a major
access route, so as to encourage custom for the subsequent residential development. Neighbourhood markets with their
associated tradesmen, workshops and artisans still exist, but the
wholesale markets have long since been moved to what was then
the periphery; by the 1980s most of these are again embedded in
the urban fabric and sprawl over adjoining areas. On the whole the
contrast between market and fixed outlet is decreasing as supermarket chains are competitive in price and often reach estates
before markets are established, given the transport problems
created in cities now spreading over several hundred square
kilometres. Mobile hawkers also compete with markets.

Far Eastern cities present yet another commercial pattern, for
few other peoples seem capable of living at the densities which the
Chinese tolerate. Western style CBD functions can be distinguished in the redeveloped areas of Hong Kong, Singapore and
Tapei, but commercial districts take different forms and coagulate
into clusters with similar uses. *Shophouse* cores have been
identified in Kowloon and Taichung just outside Hong Kong's
CBD. This location has been attributed to the tradition of combining business and residential premises, while the cellular
structure would appear more related to business practices than to
criteria concerning access by clientele (Leeming 1978). New government estates outside the established areas are more likely to
contain commercial nuclei which are access oriented, given the
selection of their residents on homogeneous economic criteria.

Conclusions

The structure of retailing mirrors income distribution within TWCs. Effective demand is highly skewed, giving rise to a small but high income market and a mass one with very low individual purchasing power. These may be supplied efficiently by specialist shops, much of whose stock is imported and by public markets, hawkers and neighbourhood outlets selling essentials respectively. These sectors are not watertight: wealthy families do buy market produce, although a servant probably performs their transactions and the poor do purchase factory-made and processed goods, particularly standardised items produced in bulk, such as school uniforms, cooking oil and matches. This overlap is also evident in the organisation of distribution, as hawkers may be financed by wholesalers or manufacturers to sell factory produce in the streets. Changes in commercial structures are induced both by increases in population and in income which can occur independently. The penetration of capitalist systems is very uneven, being spearheaded by imports, the production of standard consumer durables and processed foods and bottled drinks. Local foods may continue to be produced and sold by traditional systems long after other sectors have been restructured; this will always be the case when sizeable proportions of TWC populations remain very poor and hawking represents an interim occupation for many new entrants to the labour market.

Government intervention in the distribution of goods reflects the authority concerned. Municipalities are concerned with health measures and maintain order, while central authorities instigate economic and welfare measures. All municipalities employ inspectors to ensure that food is offered for sale in a state fit for consumption. Their main targets are those sold or prepared in the street, for even if the ingredients and products are satisfactory, the hygiene of the vendors and their utensils must be suspect when hands, plates and spoons are washed in a public fountain or a bucket of much-used water. Municipalities also control where outlets are sited. Most have relocated abattoirs and wholesale markets at the periphery, where they are accessible to producers and do not interfere with other activities. Periodic campaigns to 'eradicate' hawkers from central districts are also common but usually a tacit code of behaviour evolves and is observed: tourist wares may be offered in prominent places, snacks and sweet stalls are permissible outside sports venues, work sites and places of entertainment but fruit vendors and games of chance tricksters must operate in the back alleys. Authorities also attempt to discipline parking in commercial centres.

The economic measures wielded by central government have much wider significance. The principal weapon has been price control, exerted either to control speculation or to cheapen particular goods. The latter include concealed subsidies attached to the imported materials of processing industries and those applied to basic necessities. A number of governments have experimented with offering bonds or rations to the especially needy but these have rarely succeeded in reaching their intended population; government participation in distribution has had a poor record generally. The failure in marketing has been attributed to their inability to appreciate the roles played by the various members of TWC supply systems.

7 MODELS OF THIRD WORLD CITIES

TWCs have been structured by processes which differ in nature or scale and strength to those active in Western cities. A great deal of attention has been paid to the impact of specific factors, such as migration or the role of the state; if these differ significantly in TWCs their interaction should give rise to cities structured by fundamentally different forces. The search for a general model to explain the internal mechanisms of a TWC is a long-term quest for synthesis and is not easy, even at the level of an individual city. The validity of cross-national comparisons when social and economic variables are involved is debatable and most attempts at modelling have focused on a single concept which can be defined precisely. A wide range of approaches have yielded a very considerable number of models of TWCs which can be divided into two main schools: the descriptive and the dynamic (Table 7.1).

The descriptive school consists of deductive models based on a single city at a specific time. They depict land uses, population and social groups within a city and compare their distributions. Some examine a morphological aspect which is then related to the characteristics of the inhabitants of the areas of interest while ecological models reverse the process. Morphological and density models are examples of the first case, for they concentrate on land use and population density classifications and their distribution patterns; the occupants of each type of area are examined only to shed light on these. On the other hand ecological models are based directly on small areas' population characteristics. These data are manipulated statistically so as to isolate their common elements; the spatial patterns of scores for these are related to city morphology at a later stage.

The members of the dynamic school focus on the processes which explain the allocation of social groups to specific types of locations within the expanding city; the dependent variable is the land and its use. They imply that a site's use and type of occupant is determined by the identity of the decision-makers in a particular setting. These range from the omnipotent authority, such as a colonial power or in South Africa, to those desperate to find a niche in the cities, such as recent immigrants. They also differ in power, for most TWC municipalities are supported by the legal framework but lack economic resources, while entrepreneurs and elites are rich in resources but need the co-operation of the state to safeguard their investments.

It would be wrong to deduce from the order in Table 7.1 that there has been a progressive evolution in model design from the descriptive to the dynamic. Descriptive models are still being devised, while some of the dynamic ones have been in existence for 20 years. Neither is there necessarily an association between type and explanatory power. It is true that many descriptive models have often contributed more to our understanding of TWCs though their authors' realisation that 'non-Western' social and economic structures are responsible for patterns which do not parallel those of North American cities, than from the subtlety of their concepts. The focus on decision-makers in the models of the dynamic school emphasises the workings of the various subsystems that make up a given society, rather than these being offered as an excuse for the poor fit of a model. Their concentration on human behaviour in a relatively narrow sphere of action is attractive for cities of varied size. Geography and culture may be compared usefully and it often provides insights into the causes of change over time.

Morphological Models

Such models have been constructed for cities of all the major regions of the Third World. Their common elements include a central concentration of commerce and retailing outlets and a series of residential districts differentiated by their degree of attachment to that core and their residents' use of space to display status. The models indicate that indigenous elites, being closely associated with the activity of the core, tend to remain there when means of transport are rare, slow or expensive and when public utilities are provided at a far slower rate than the city's population is incorporating new territory. Members of the educated and professional classes are more aware of the vectors of disease and choose to display their status in more Western terms, that is, space. Their knowledge and lifestyle encourages them to shun the traditional centre but the spatial concentration of utilities there

Table 7.1: Models of Third World Cities

A

DESCRIPTIVE MODELS OF TWC STRUCTURE

Focus	Data	Methods	Examples
PHYSICAL MORPHOLOGY	Town plans; land uses; architectural types	Observation; classification; delimitation of zones; historical dating	African city; *bazaar* city; Islamic city; SE Asian city; Yoruba city; Latin American city
DENSITY GRADIENTS	Census tracts: Gross population densities; relative location; average land values; amenities	Correlation; linear regression; tests for negative exponential curve; analysis of residuals	Accra, Lagos, Jos, Nairobi; Tapei, 12 S Korean cities, Poona, Varanasi, Madras, Bombay; Bogotá, Cali, Lima, Quito, Santiago, Piracicaba
SOCIAL ECOLOGY	Social and economic indices by census tract, or survey data for cluster samples	Segregation indices; principal components analysis; spatial patterns of factor loadings	Cairo, Alexandria, Algiers, Rabat-Sale; Accra, Benin, Douala; Bombay, Calcutta, Madras, Poona; Rio de Janeiro, Santiago, La Paz, San Juan, Ponce

B

DYNAMIC, PROCESS-ORIENTED MODELS OF TWCS

Focus	Data	Methods	Examples
USER INITIATIVES	User identities, wealth, power and methods	Sample surveys; property registers; descriptive statistics	Accra, Kumasi, Lagos, Lusaka; New Delhi, Karachi, Manila, Kuala Lumpur; Lima, Mexico City, Monterrey, La Paz, Caracas, Rio de Janeiro
ENTREPRENEURIAL INITIATIVES	Adverts, sales, property and land registrations, bank loans, mortgages	Analysis of transactions by organisations	Douala, Lagos, Abidjan; New Delhi, Bangkok; Buenos Aires, São Paulo, Lima, Quito, Mexico City
STATE INITIATIVES	Identity of decision makers; context pressures and policies; identity of implementors	Participant observation, sample surveys, attitude surveys	Dakar, Lagos; New Delhi, Bangkok, Metro Manila; Mexico City, Bogotá, Valencia, Lima, Santiago, São Paulo
	Impact of legislation on location; lifestyle and occupations of specific groups, often racially defined	Observation before and after implementation	Colonial cites; Durban, Pretoria, Salisbury, Natal

discourages its abandonment altogether. They tend to dominate adjacent neighbourhoods while the poor, especially if recently arrived or of a low status ethnic group, cannot gain admittance to the established city and so must share the unserviced periphery with large scale or objectionable land uses, such as airports, military installations, large industrial processes and the city's rubbish dump.

The actual forms generated by these principles vary with the scale of each city, its level of economic development and whether its society is structured on ethnic or class lines. The three examples pictured in Figure 7.1 are all drawn on the classical isotopic plan. However, the United Nations' 'African' city model would seem only applicable to the West African cities with populations of around 100 000. It appears in a volume discussing Africa south of the Sahara, which eliminates cities of Arab origin (described in Figure 2.1, p. 30); moreover the presence of an indigenous core excludes cities which had expatriate origins, while the absence of a port rules out capital cities of the littoral. What one is left with is the West African urban heartland. The model organises different ethnic groups into a single dimension through the medium of density; a ring of low density government uses and associated housing districts of the colonial regime, sandwiched between the original pre-colonial city and that of past independence developments, is still evident. The emphasis on residential districts also suggests that productive activities only take place in the core or the periphery, which is highly unlikely to be the case — a centre small enough to supply its residents entirely from the outlets in the core would be unlikely to attract large-scale industry to its periphery — or merit the title of city today.

Although its Latin American counterpart was based on far larger and more Westernised cities, it displays some of the same attributes (Griffin and Ford 1982). Once again the classification of the residential areas appears to imply a scale ranging from dense to sparse. The central zone is 'maturity', with the full range of utilities and so it remains desirable to middle-class residents. Adjoining areas are gradually consolidating and improving as services diffuse from the core. Once again new arrivals are forced to the periphery, where they squat on wasteland, or share zones of 'disamenity' with industrial and uncongenial uses, or suffer from their repellent characteristics. The major difference between this and the African model is the role of the elite, a car-borne,

Figure 7.1

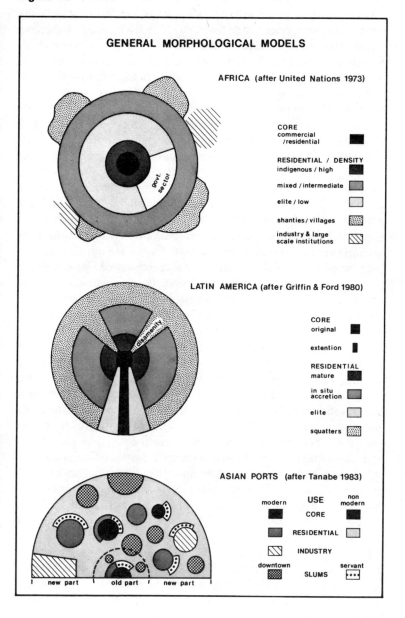

educated and highly Westernised one in this case. This class constitutes a market for exclusive goods which encourages the development of a spatially distinctive district to cater for its needs; the model represents this as a spine off the original central business district. Members of the elite associated with it cluster in a sector which cuts across the more slowly evolving outward diffusing patterns of the rest of the city. This model is applicable only at an extremely general level. It is doubtful whether its base, Tijuana, a city on Mexico's border with the United States and Bogotá, a large inland capital, could be considered as 'typical'. Most Latin American capitals have populations of many millions; their roles as the reception point of Western innovations and of the largest streams of migrants and as the central decision-making authority of their respective nations make a gradual and even outward diffusion of public utilities highly unlikely, even when the elite are catered for by a separate sector. Neither does the model seem tailor-made for intermediate-sized cities which are seldom the recipients of large volumes of squatting migrants at their periphery. This model appears to be over-influenced by the outward appearance of the cities' physical fabric. Other observers have put much more weight on fluidity of spatial movements in response to migration, industrialisation and individual social and economic mobility (Bähr and Mertins 1981).

The size of Asian port cities renders some type of multiple nuclei model essential but the bipolar classification adopted is revealing, as it represents the perception of their local authorities. Whereas the previous models had taken pains to avoid dividing areas according to a culturally loaded 'modern-traditional' or 'Western-indigenous' dimension, this is what the officials have focused on. However, it is not the labels that are important to them but the underlying economic structures that characterise each land use. 'Non-modern' industry is not represented because it is intermingled with 'non-modern' residential zones and the core; 'slums' originated both in association with specific modern uses and as the consequence of villages being engulfed by the expanding city. This model would appear to be based on the 'formal-informal' division of production, although those terms never appear in the text. It conveys an impression of the heterogeneity and complexity of contemporary millionaire cities and, unfortunately; of their authorities' bewilderment rather than their awareness of the need to adopt a flexible approach to city management.

Morphological models have also been devised for specific cities (see Figure 7.2); their designers have been influenced by the Chicago School's theories and their contribution to rings and sectors. Yadav scrutinised the social, economic and physical characteristics of Delhi's *localities* (neighbourhoods) in search of similar patterns. His task was rendered more difficult by the lack of data for the area under jurisdiction of the municipal committee and the *cantonment*. His statistically tested solution introduces a new explanation for a system of rings. Once beyond the historical core classified as a 'pedestrian zone', it would appear to be the attitude of the state which influences the type of neighbourhood, through the degree of security granted to their residents. Thus the inner circle was 'regularised' *post facto*, a process which is diffusing outwards to a zone of 'primarily planned developments', while beyond this neither legal nor planned 'sporadic' development continues. There are obvious similarities here with Griffin and Ford's ideas only they would seem more valid in a city where land banking is the cornerstone of municipal policy, rather than in Latin America's context of free market forces.

McGee's early model of South East Asian cities pays much more attention to the identity of the various groups involved in structuring the city. For him the classification of the commercial core as modern or not was immaterial: what was significant was whether its entrepreneurs were Chinese, Indian or Western. Sectors were more likely to represent these in such socially segmented cities. Residential types were classified by morphological criteria: although the Western housing introduced by the colonial authorities could be found flanking and extending the government sector, the space demands of such neighbourhoods had forced more recent developments out to the periphery, where they competed with disadvantaged groups unable to acquire more convenient sites. However, here intensive agriculture only admitted discontinuous development; large scale industrial uses had to locate still further away. This model uses Hoytian sectors to cater for ethnic variables, while rings represent a density function which allocates uncompetitive land uses or users of land to the periphery.

The rapid expansion of TWCs frequently leapfrogs certain sites (for example, marshlands) while engulfing long established rural communities further away which maintain their original character and function. In Jakarta spontaneously evolving and traditional villages, known as *kampungs*, occur throughout the city and con-

Figure 7.2

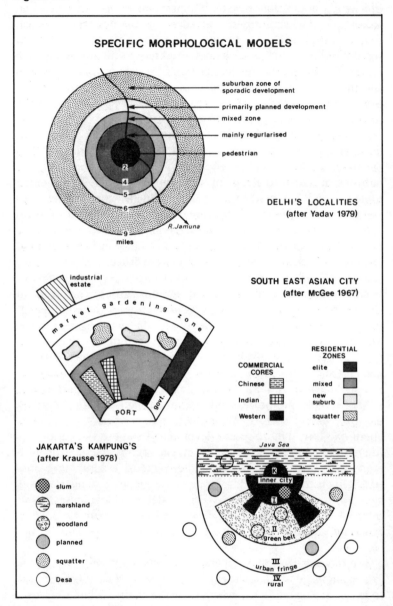

SPECIFIC MORPHOLOGICAL MODELS

suburban zone of
sporadic development

primarily planned development

mixed zone

mainly regurlarised

pedestrian

2
4
5
6
9
miles

R.Jamuna

DELHI'S LOCALITIES
(after Yadav 1979)

industrial
estate

market gardening zone

PORT

govt.

SOUTH EAST ASIAN CITY
(after McGee 1967)

COMMERCIAL
CORES

Chinese

Indian

Western

RESIDENTIAL
ZONES

elite

mixed

new
suburb

squatter

JAKARTA'S KAMPUNG'S
(after Krausse 1978)

slum

marshland

woodland

planned

squatter

Desa

Java Sea

K
inner city

I

II
green belt

III
urban fringe

IV
rural

trast sharply with the rest of its physical fabric. It is tempting to denote them as shanty towns but this would be inappropriate: *kampung* improvement is a key element of Indonesian urban policy and many are legal entities whose residents have every right to remain there. Krausse's model was designed to counter the tendency to evaluate *kampungs* merely by their physical characteristics by drawing attention to their diverse origins, roles and inhabitants. Both the traditional business core, the *kota*, and the newer extension to the south contain high density *kampungs* on restricted sites whose residents are dependent on the activities of those districts for their livelihood. They are distinct from the long standing woodland communities studding the surrounding green belt, which are smaller, less densely populated and contain a more varied range of occupations. The urban fringe contains both planned, legal *kampungs* designed for those displaced by redevelopment elsewhere and genuine squatter settlements, particularly in the undrained marshlands. The city extended its boundaries in 1975 to encompass a swath of rural land served by long standing villages called *desa*.

Sound descriptive models are based on carefully recorded observations throughout the city in question, but some would appear to be based on more impressionistic evidence. All concentrate on physical forms (the pattern of the street grid, the location, architectural style and function of buildings and their ethnic associations) in delimiting zones. Often these are classified in terms of the historical development of the city and the explanation of their contemporary roles is made through comparisons with Western models and the author's intuitive knowledge as to how circumstances differ locally. They serve to draw attention to very obvious features of the inherited fabric at specific points in time but explanations as to who occupies, where and why, lie beyond their scope.

Density Gradients

The attractions of a model, which transforms a characteristic of city form into a simple and easily comparable statistic, are obvious. Density gradients link the theory about how a city's population resolves the conflicting costs of space and transport to the urban forms which result from the transformation of their solutions into space. They are relatively easy to calculate, being based on the gross population density of census tracts and the straight line distances which separate them from a pre-established central point. The simplest equation takes the negative exponential form. Gradients have been calculated at various periods in time for American, British, West European, Japanese, Australian and New Zealand cities. These indicate that lower gradients evolve over time, as income increases, transport develops and the total population of the area expands. Higher income allows increased expenditure in housing, addition to transport networks allows greater distances to be inhabited and larger urban territories encourage the growth of subsidiary service centres, which relax the need to travel to the centre. It appears that under free market conditions the tendency to equilibrium would cause the exponential pattern to reappear, albeit at a less steep gradient, after such changes.

Similar calculations have been made for TWCs of various sizes. The equations for single dates confirm that the gradients observed for smaller cities are indeed the steepest while studies conducted in the same city, for example, Bombay (1881–1961), Seoul (1965–73) and Bogotá (1964–78), all display steadily decreasing gradients between consecutive periods. A few, such as those for Greater Poona (1881–1961) do not. The pool of studies is small, so overall conclusions must be tentative. However, TWCs differ in their rates of expansion, their patterns of income distribution and the structure of their housing markets; they have developed in response to exogenous forces more often than endogenous ones. Why should they display any similarity in patterns and trends in density with Western cities of comparable size, even at this very general level? This is the question which has motivated many studies.

Although cities have been grouped into size categories in Table 7.2, there are still many other dimensions which reduce the validity of comparison. The original model makes assumptions about the role of scale which may be invalidated by the TWCs' different levels of economic development and its impact on their populations' levels of consumption. Systematic variations attributable to scale may be assessed more realistically by comparing cities with a common history, such as those of a single country. Brush's thorough study of 24 Indian cities, chosen to represent the full range in size and function, came to the conclusion that a regular continuum of decreasing gradients related to population did not exist. His graphs revealed four different types, each of which corresponded to particular evolutionary patterns. Poona and Varanasi dated from the pre-colonial period and had retained, or intensified, residence in their cores; Bombay, Calcutta and Madras, being colonial foundations with Western-style CBDs handling their commercial activities, had much lower central residential densities. Hyderabad's two cores represented its indigenous and colonial roles; this was reflected in a subsidiary peak density denoting the second focal point. Meanwhile a few more recently founded industrial centres had been planned around their industrial works instead of a business core. Consequently Jamshedpur had a very low gradient compared to other settlements of its dimensions.

Brush attributed the differences observed to the history of the city in question but as this is unique, it is the identity of the actual factors involved which interest us here. In India the state constrained the free market assumptions postulated by the model through the allocation of land to specific uses or users. This was common in most colonial regimes, but the demarcation of local goverment jurisdictions and the implementation of planning or housing policy can have similar effects. Thus the gradients for Indian cities were influenced by the presence and location of former *civil lines* and *cantonments* whose use of space contrasted greatly with that of the indigenous population. Similar patterns may be observed in African cities: the gradient for the eastern sector of Accra is much flatter than those to the west or the north due to the presence of the Government Reservation Area. The gradient in Lagos actually increases with distance owing to the fact the city was grossly underbounded until recently. The enforcement of stringent municipal by-laws on construction standards within the city encouraged settlement at its periphery where these were ignored; despite subsequent encapsulation in the metropolitan zone, the old boundary stands out as a divide between different standards and densities of housing. The same occurred in Kampala.

An underlying and reinforcing factor of state action is segregation. Despite contemporary rhetoric, state actions have seldom had the same impact on all groups in the past. The classic case of this is Nairobi, whose overall gradient conceals the dramatic contrasts evident between sectors associated with the

Table 7.2: Population Density Gradients[a]

	100 000–500 000	500 000–1 million	1 million–3 million	Over 3 million
AFRICA				
Accra	0.65 (N) 0.40 (W) 0.36 (E)			
Nairobi	0.60 (range 1.31 to + 0.32)			
Lagos			(positive equation)	
ASIA				
Gaya	0.862	Bangalore 0.528	Hyderabad 0.348	Bombay 0.102
Hubli	1.384	Grt. Poona 1.072	Madras 0.235	
Jamshedpur	0.232		Busan 0.11	Seoul 0.19
Suwon	1.031		Daegu 0.67	
LATIN AMERICA				
		Kingston 0.327	Belo Horizonte 0.27	Buenos Aires 0.121
		Cali 0.21	Recife 0.190	Rio de Janeiro 0.07
		Monterrey 0.19	Bogotá 0.12	São Paulo 0.115
			Cali (1978) 0.27	Bogotá (1978) 0.11
			Guadalajara 0.41	Mexico City 0.173

Population at Time of Study

Note: a. All gradients take the negative exponential form unless indicated to the contrary.

Sources: Accra: Bobo 1977; Nairobi: Kimani 1972, Tiwari 1972; Lagos: Okpala 1978; Indian cities: Brush 1968; South Korean cities: Mills and Song 1979, Mills and Tan 1980; Kingston: Newling 1966; Latin American cities in 1970: Ingram and Carroll 1981; Cali and Bogotá in 1978: Gregory and Ingram 1982.

European, Asian and African residents. As late as 1969, the earlier colonial segregation policies are revealed by their respective density gradients. That for the European population was flattest while the Asian was steepest; but the gradient for the narrow wedge of territory into which discrimination forced the majority African population actually increased with distance. Undoubtedly, if gradients were constructed for contemporary South African cities, the same phenomenon would appear. However, although legal measures produce the clearest patterns, similar local effects can arise from ethnic or religious associations; density decay patterns in Nairobi were also associated with communities whose focal points were the mosque, Sikh puja or Catholic church, respectively. In West African cities, intergroup rivalry or even hostility can constrain an individual's choice of location quite independently of income and as effectively as a legal measure.

It is difficult to disaggregate the effect of the factors described above from the more narrowly conceived economic ones envisaged by the model, especially when the latter have seldom been isolated or tested in Western contexts. Its theoretical base assumes that free market forces will distribute people according to their ability to choose a desired amount of space at particular locations (distance from the centre). The lack of any other qualitative variables suggests that urban infrastructure can be assumed to be ubiquitous, or at least residence in specific areas does not deny one access to it wherever it is located. But basic urban utilities, services, even made-up roads and personal security, are certainly not evenly distributed throughout the built-up area of TWCs. Densities cannot be taken as indicators of welfare levels, nor indeed of the growth rates experienced by the cities. The model requires modification to take these circumstances into account but the inclusion of transport, as suggested in Western contexts, would seem inadequate. It is not the cost of overcoming distance to a resource that is in question so much as its very existence. Utilities in Latin American cities of the mid-1960s, for example, were still concentrated in the centre, while the middle classes of even the capital cities seldom owned cars. Consequently this social group lived centrally and at the highest densities in Santiago, Lima, Bogotá and Quito (Amato 1970). The rich had already left for the spacious periphery while the poor resided at intermediate densities and distances. Public transport and car ownership was even less developed in the small (population of 150 000) but rapidly growing city of Piracicaba in São Paulo's hinterland in the late 1970s. Here holders of high incomes were still concentrated in the city centre at the highest densities and car ownership made no significant impact on the gradients (Dawsey 1979). The same could be said of Jos, a slightly smaller city in Nigeria, where the rich made the shortest journeys to work (Ayeni 1976).

Economic elites of course can choose where to live and pay for the additional cost of providing service connections to greenfield sites. This was brought out in the Accra study which incorporated variables representing transport costs, rent and a full range of utilities (running water, electricity supply, waste disposal services, private toilets and baths) in the density equation. The availability of electricity was the only one to exhibit a positive correlation with housing density; only the possession of a bath, rent and transport costs were statistically significant. This analysis concluded that while living at the periphery of Accra may be more spacious, it is also far more costly, which reflects the quality of the dwellings as much as their location (Bobo 1977).

The distance factor is a difficult one to translate into monetary terms or to evaluate. The model assumes the expansion of transport networks will lead to lower densities. Suburbanisation did occur in the presence of mass transit systems in Buenos Aires, Rio de Janeiro, São Paulo, although metros in Caracas, Santiago and Mexico City were built subsequently. However fares for these are usually a flat rate regardless of the distance travelled. Furthermore while cars may be convenient in the suburbs, their utility is sharply reduced when employment remains concentrated in historic centres with narrow streets within which parking space is minimal. In these circumstances the decentralising tendencies of non-car owners are conditioned by the capacity of public transport rather than by its cost, while most car users are influenced by the location of employment and the physical structure of the city.

These conflicting tendencies may be avoided by substituting land values for transport costs in the equation. These reflect the relative merits of location in a much wider sense than sheer distance to a hypothetical centre. Unfortunately land value data are hard to collect and to assess; most studies have been based on a small sample of properties in a few census tracts. Nevertheless these have revealed interesting aspects about the expansion of cities. The largest number of studies is for Latin America where levels of development might lead one to expect closer parallels to

Western patterns. The land value gradients reported are similar but generally flatter; over time they get flatter still. However, the usual explanations for such flattening, decentralisation and urbanisation, need verifying. These cities' spatial expansion reflects their increase in absolute population, rather than their existing population's acquisition of a higher income which is translated into a greater consumption of space. Amato translated both density and land value data for four Latin American cities into quotients representing the case for six socio-economic classes (Table 7.3). The exercise revealed that land values generally declined with distance from the centre and they fell far more sharply in sectors occupied by lower income class groups. He concluded that on the whole richer people occupied more expensive land relative to that of other groups at comparable distances from the centre and that they also occupied it at much lower comparable densities (Amato 1970).

Table 7.3: Density and Land Value Quotients for Social Classes

	Lima		Bogotá		Santiago		Quito	
Social Class	Density	Land Value	Density	Land Value	Density	Land Value	Density	Land Value
1 high	381	147	375	133	363	68	164	50
2	1 048	131	710	151	211	45	224	30
3	1 020	84	738	99	613	6	238	19
4	1 056	95	824	71	–	–	332	9
5	1 533	89	874	60	838	5	220	8
6 low	1 137	53	890	56	–	–	350	10

Source: Amato, P. W. (1970), pp. 453–4.

When Mohan and Villamizar studied land values 15 years later, they also found that denser populations were associated with lower valued land at the same relative location in Bogotá and Cali. Examination of the city-wide pattern revealed that a land market was working such that values were increasing at a more rapid rate in the outer rings than in the centre. Although there was a considerable difference in absolute price, a catch-up mechanism was at work. This became evident when sectors occupied by different social classes were examined. They concluded that 'while the rich substitute for land with capital, the poor substitute for land by crowding' (Mohan and Villamizar 1982). The rich can choose to build vertically in more central locations or to buy a car to reach more distant ones, but the competition for land everywhere in the city causes the poor to pack in more people.

The steeper gradient of land values in smaller cities, the decreasing slope over time and the more rapid increase in values at the periphery have also been observed for the South Korean cities of Seoul, Busan, Daegu and Suwon. Gregory and Ingram concluded that the rate of increase in land values is related neither to the size of the city nor its rate of population increase. The explanation is the market forces which determine the rate of return on urbanising peripheral land *vis à vis* alternative investments. Elsewhere land value gradients have revealed the impact of some of the constraints on those forces. The graph of land values and rents against distance from the centre are incomprehensible in Lagos unless one appreciates that the centrally located and high quality housing is very highly subsidised by the government; the figures for this stock bear no comparison to those of the open market (Sada 1972). Similarly Nairobi's land value gradients portray significant differences in slope when disaggregated by sector. The consistent pattern of residuals generated by the gradient model led Kimani to 'wonder whether or not a deliberate attempt had been made to under- or overvalue certain properties on a racial basis'. Even after inserting population density in the equation, the remaining sectoral patterns of residuals 'reinforced the idea that racial segregation had had a powerful influence on land evaluation' (Kimani 1972).

In this discussion, a model based on the rational economic logic appropriate to an egalitarian context subject to free market forces required the addition of political and social variables to explain its limitations. We now turn to a set of models which confronts the social organisation of TWCs directly.

Ecological Models

Social area analysis, a procedure based on the Chicago School's research and refined by Shevsky and his Californian associates in the mid-1950s, has been applied to a number of TWCs. The underlying theory assumes that the spatial patterning of social groups in a city can be explained by a few underlying independent constructs. These 'components' or 'factors' are derived from social and economic indices representing a large number of small areas within a city, usually census tracts, by either principal components or factor analysis. The factors commonly identified in North

American cities have been named as socio-economic status, lifestyle or familism and demography; they represent the economic basis of the household, its behaviour according to its size and stage in the lifecycle and whether it has migrated or belongs to a distinctive ethnic group. The structure of society is revealed through the interactions of these factors, while the social morphology of the city can be ascertained from maps based on each area's score on a particular factor. These analyses permit intra- and inter-city comparisons unimpeded by the distraction of their unique physical features.

The statistical manipulations required by these techniques are problematical in TWCs. The primary source of data is the census but these are held infrequently and their results are usually published only at aggregate level after some delay. The techniques are also affected by the scale at which the studies are conducted and the number of units on which they are based. TWCs are rarely divided into appropriately sized census tracts and boundaries are amended long after they have been overrun at the periphery. The choice of scale is usually between districts, which are few and provide too crude a lattice, or an unwieldly number of sub-districts. Some researchers solve this problem by grouping the latter into 'homogeneous zones' or by sampling but these operations may also introduce errors. Tests have revealed that analyses based on 500 or 600 data units contribute little more than what can be ascertained from about 100, which is considered an acceptable number for the techniques.

Table 7.4 lists the factors isolated and the proportion of the common variance attributed to them in analysis of a sample of TWCs selected to represent both size groups and geographical zones. Despite their date of publication, most are based on censuses for 1960 or 1970 owing to the data problems mentioned previously. The factors listed in the table illustrate the differences between TWCs and North American cities and between the TWCs of different continents. The factors common in North American cities do not appear clearly: 'status' may be associated with lifestyle, ethnicity or migration; it may be achieved or traditional. The demographic factor may be represented by male concentration or dominance, by a stage in the lifecycle, migrants or an ethnic group. Traits associated with the lifestyle factor are subsumed in the forementioned. While every city regardless of size generated a factor representing some facet of migration or

Table 7.4: Factors and Their Variance Identified in TWCs

	100 000–500 000 people	%	500 000–1 million people	%	over 1 million people	%
A **F**	BENIN 1975 1 Economic status 2 Household size 3 Urhobo 4 Other ethnic groups (Onokerhoraye 1977a)	 38 15 13 10	RABAT 1971 1 Status/Ethnicity 2 Housing Quality 3 Male dominance (Abu-Lughod 1980)	 50 17 12	CAIRO 1960 1 Status/lifestyle 2 Male dominance 3 Social disorganisation (Abu-Lughod 1969)	 52 10 9
R **I** **C** **A**	DOUALA 1964 1 Migrant status 2 Lifestyle/urban villages 3 Traditional/modern 4 Migration/social rank 5 Newcomers (Clignet and Jordan 1971)	 30 25 17 15 13			ALGIERS 1966 1 Occupation/lifestyle 2 Dependants 3 Migration (Eichler 1977)	 39 23 10
A **S**	ALLAHABAD 1961 1 Traditional status 2 Achieved status (Singh 1975)	 31 23	LUCKNOW 1961 1 Achieved status 2 Traditional status 3 Male concentration (Singh 1975)	 20 19 13	CALCUTTA 1961 1 Achieved status 2 Male concentration 3 Traditional status (Singh 1975)	 20 16 16
I **A**	JAMSHEDPUR 1961 1 Achieved status 2 Traditional status 3 Male concentration (Singh 1975)	 22 15 14			TAPEI 1976 1 Occupational status 2 Farmers migrants 3 Family status (Hsu and Pannell 1982)	 27 15 11

		%
PONCE, P.R.	**1970**	%
1	Socio-econ. status	a
2	Housing quality	a
3	Born elsewhere	a
4	Women's status	a
(Loar 1980)		

LA PAZ	**1976**	%
1	Status/life cycle	38
2	Population structure	28
3		
4	Occupations	12
(Thomas and Wittick 1981)		

RIO DE JANEIRO	**1960**	%
1	Status/life cycle	40
2	Migration	27
3	Life cycle	23
4	Possessions	11
(Morris and Pyle 1971)		

SAN JUAN, P.R.	**1970**	%
1	Socio-econ. status	a
2	Housing quality	a
3	Born elsewhere	a
4	Women's status	a
(Loar 1980)		

SANTIAGO DE CHILE	**1970**	%
1	Socio-econ. status	45
2	Familism	36
(Bähr and Riesco 1981)		

L
A
T
I
N

A
M
E
R
I
C
A

Note: a factors listed accounted for 'at least 5% of the variance'.

ethnicity, the latter was most prominent in Africa. Society in Asian cities seemed to be split between family-inherited and occupationally-based status systems, while economic status and lifecycle variables' are closely intertwined in Latin American cities.

The variables highly correlated with status in the United States are occupation, education and income. Association between these can only arise when TWCs require and reward certain skills. When many of these studies were conducted, the proportion of non-manual jobs was very low and restricted educational opportunities ensured that most expertise was acquired on the job and over time. In Latin America, for example, this is evident from the factor loadings for La Paz, where higher educational levels were associated with office employment, while paradoxically lower ones were attached both to areas of unskilled and of professional classes. In Santiago, where education had been more widely available for a much larger period, its loadings echoed that of other desirable amenities, such as running water and consumer goods in the home. Outside Latin America, ethnic and cultural factors cloud such relationships, for state education may be perceived as Westernisation or at least as a challenge to traditional values. Jews and Christians, who do not share this view, often score highly on this factor in Indian and African contexts compared to Muslims and indigenous elites. However, esteem reflects the code of the ethnic group in question and Jews and Christians, despite education and wealth, rarely figure highly in city-wide society. This situation arises with parallel status systems: in Douala the second factor contrasted those displaying Western class-based criteria with those of the traditional female Ga elites, while the fourth distinguished between the dynamic merchant Pahouins from Yaoundé, the principal commercial city of the Cameroons, and the less active residents. This sort of dualism is complicated by the institution of caste in India but as this is not recorded in the census, its role can only be assessed indirectly.

A factor as ambiguous as this would seem unlikely to yield clear-cut spatial patterns in TWCs. Multiple value systems, such as portrayed by achieved versus traditional status in Indian cities, generate separate focal points, while juxtaposition in space may reflect broader language or source regions in common. It might also indicate a need to separate antagonists, for local groups in Douala maintained a greater degree of segregation between them-selves than with foreigners, or long distance migrants. Unless a city's neighbourhoods are differentiated by housing or their access to desirable utilities, there is no reason why they should be structured by other than traditional kinship conventions and associations with the land. Only where housing is transformed into a marketable commodity can the economic element become instrumental in allocating households in space and even then income may not be correlated highly with either education or social esteem.

The lifestyle factor in the United States associates small households with educational attainment and high rates of employment; this is rarely observed in TWCs. Sometimes the presence of joint and multiple generational families has been the cause; in others, greater wealth has allowed nuclear families to include domestics in. their households. In either case, the household is large and contains a mix of age and skill groups. But population structures have been distorted far more by migration. Mass migration, particularly if it takes the form of transient residents of one sex, such as in Muslim societies, cannot but generate incomplete communities with distinctive lifestyles. This accounts for the 'male dominance' observed right across North Africa, from Rabat to Alexandria and Cairo, and the 'male concentration' in North Indian cities. The population dynamics of different ethnic groups' migration to West African cities often results in lifestyle being inextricable from migration and ethnicity. The 'bourgeois', Westernised migrants with their smaller families are distinguishable from those following more traditional patterns; they in turn are divided between those who migrate as a family, leave their family behind or dispatch their children to be reared in a rural environment. Further, migrants to TWCs can rarely be considered as part of a single phenomenon. Migrants' behaviour and aspirations are very diverse; a capital city attracts a great many comparatively well educated applicants seeking university admittance, posts in the national bureaucracy or commerce. Such candidates are unlikely to have much in common with those driven to migrate by a drought or flood, even if they do stem from the same region. These differences often contribute to such factors as 'infertility', 'newcomers', 'family size' or simply 'population structure'; they may also be named after the ethnic group concerned.

Quite a few studies isolated a factor strongly linked to the physical fabric of the cities. This factor associates different construction methods with specific neighbourhoods and their residents: the *medinas* in Arab cities still contrast with the *villes neuves* of colonial days. Accra's 'density gradient' factor contrasts the makeshift conditions at the periphery with the established city, while the 'urban villages' stand out from the more recent developments which now engulf them. An analysis of Benin's house types yielded a building materials component which accounted for 66 per cent of the variance. Spontaneous developments are most likely to display such contrasts, which is why the analysts of Rio de Janeiro decided to examine its widely scattered *favelas* separately. Surprisingly their removal did little to clarify the factors, while no factor directly linked to employment emerged within the *favelas*. These were structured purely in terms of their residents' period of migration, life-cycle stage, family size and residual combinations of these characteristics (Morris and Pyle 1969).

Comparisons of social area analyses emphasise the discrepancies which occur between individual cases but this is partly a product of the choice of variables. The Latin American examples tended to include variables representing urban amenities and material possessions as surrogates for income; these correlated highly with occupation and may explain the importance of the socio-economic status factor there. Undoubtedly income, especially if assured and regular and community affiliation, as expressed via ethnicity, religion and migration history, are the main factors underlying TWCs' structure. These are associated with a settlement's functions but not necessarily with its size. However, it is difficult to acquire data to test these hypotheses. The technique has highlighted the conflicting structures prevalent within many TWCs, as well as indicating some superficial similarities between them. Nevertheless, it is still a descriptive device which has rarely been applied to a city for more than one point in time. As such it cannot reveal much about the processes by which individuals are allocated to specific spaces. These require a dynamic portrayal of the sorting mechanisms.

Users' Initiatives

All major TWCs have been stimulated by migration and have experienced rapid expansion of their built-up areas. Two dynamic models concentrate on the identity of the users who have occupied new land and how they urbanised it over time. A great deal of research has catalogued the forms this demand has assumed when such development is undertaken by the poor. J. F. C. Turner translated his observations of the evolution of Lima's *barriadas* into a model; this combined the personal attributes of the user and his changing circumstances with length of residence in the city, with the satisfaction of his housing needs. However, it is not just the poor who have taken the initiative in adding areas to the city. A. S. Morris attributed this role to the rich in the case of Caracas, while the role of the traditional chiefs cannot be ignored in many West African cities.

Turner's model is a most sophisticated contribution to this sphere in that it allows for both the continued expansion of the city and the changing personal circumstances of those that contribute to its growth. It depicts the characteristics of each at three stages in time and traces their logical evolution (Turner 1967, 1968). At the initial stage, when a city's growth rate is comparable to that of the nation's natural increase, he assumes that the additional population can be accommodated through densification, the in-filling of the existing built-up area and only minor accretion at the periphery. These possibilities are exhausted when growth rates surpass 5 per cent per annum. During this transitional stage, some filtering takes place in the housing market, as the members of the elite abandon the core but the majority of the growth at the periphery stems from migrants wishing to consolidate their position in the city.

Here the model incorporates a number of assumptions about the selectivity of the migration process and links them to the formation of shanty towns (see Figure 7.3). Migrants are indifferent to housing quality on arrival, being young, male, single and at a disadvantage in the labour market; their prime consideration is to gain access to sources of casual unskilled employment, such as that provided by a city's wholesale market or provincial bus termini. As these occur in the centre of small cities, nearby slum property or temporary housing on waste lots is acceptable. However, while these living conditions may be appropriate for such 'bridge-headers', they are not for the upwardly mobile 'consolidators' who have secured a stable job and acquired family responsibilities. For them security is the dominant concern, for a fragile economic base can be easily undermined by an inopportune illness or an unfortunate theft. Regular outgoings on rent represent a threat at this stage, while the cheapest housing in slum property provides unacceptable conditions in which to rear children. Now the most attractive proposition is one in which no regular outgoings are demanded and the individual is free to consolidate his housing base as and when the means materialise. Such accommodation is achievable in shanty towns at the city's periphery.

A further stage of the model allows for both the varied fortunes of these spontaneously generated neighbourhoods and their significance for new arrivals to the city. The first shanty towns were small in scale and clandestine; they occupied worthless land and were under constant threat of removal. The continued demand for land and the survival and growth of shanty towns accustomed the authorities to their presence. Further invasions were conducted on a massive scale and resulted in better layouts, more generous plots and more suitable sites. These are easier to develop while some of the earlier ones either never evolve beyond the temporary shack stage or take far longer to do so. Although residents at the periphery cannot make use of the facilities in the established city, self-help and support from charitable institutions eventually cause the authorities to relent and provide utilities; private enterprises and state services are acquired gradually and turn the fledgling dormitories into more rounded communities. Fresh migrants need no longer undergo an urban 'apprenticeship' in the core; their forerunners, willing to provide shelter and advice on job opportunities, are established at the periphery. Furthermore job decentralisation makes the former locations less attractive. Finally the bestowal of land titles provides the official seal of approval on the new neighbourhoods. From then on moves are associated with the perceived character of the neighbourhood by 'status seekers'.

The attraction of this model lies in its ability to integrate various mechanisms governing change. However, it has been criticised for presenting rather too rosy a picture of neighbourhood development. Constraints rather than choice guide most actions of the poor and what was achievable in the Lima of the 1960s, at the height of an import-substitution boom, was not a decade or two later during economic stagnation and recession. The sheer competition for employment, the growing demand for educational qualifications and the decreasing availability of land for new invasions means that the migrant arriving in the 1980s faces a far tougher task than his predecessors in acquiring either a job or a home in Lima (Dietz 1982). These sorts of changes cannot be

Figure 7.3

CONSTRUCTS OF J.F.C. TURNER'S MODEL

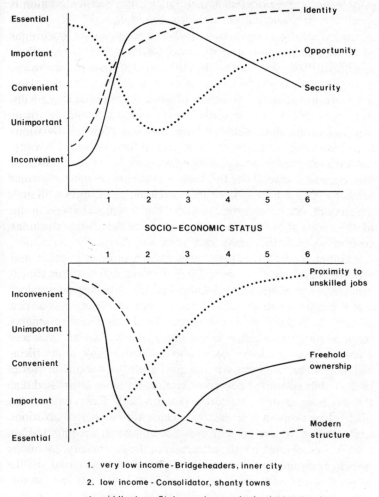

1. very low income - Bridgeheaders, inner city
2. low income - Consolidator, shanty towns
4. middle class - Status seeker, serviced neighbourhoods
6. upper income - Elite, exclusive neighbourhoods

subsumed by the rate of population growth, which fuels the processes described by the model.

Other criticisms are directed at the model's assumptions.
Nobody doubts the role of migration in stimulating city growth,

but the links between migrants and shanty town evolution have proved less direct in Latin American cities. Many studies have demonstrated that the migrant presence in them reflects their proportion in the city's population. Migrants are over-represented in specific settlements, but this does not constitute a reliable norm on which to base a general model. Furthermore the model implies that individuals and neighbourhoods consolidate in tandem. Evidence for specific cities throws doubt on this; the very stresses implicated in this type of urban development cause the withdrawal of some households, the incorporation by others of a floating population of renters to help finance it and, once the hazards of eviction and the inconvenience of the lack of utilities have been overcome, the arrival of more pecunious buyers on the doorsteps of the pioneers. The temptation to sell out for a 'large' sum, at least far larger than they have ever possessed, is tempting for those who have been living at survival levels for years. Furthermore the increasing attractiveness of such neighbourhoods renders their untitled residents more exposed to the machinations of the unprincipled property dealers, while the actual costs of 'regularisation' may force some to sell out.

Another sphere of criticism concerns the processes operating in the established city. Can one really assume that removal from the city centre is a sign of upward social mobility? The circumstances suggest that it might well result either from ejection or the inability to gain admittance to this desirable location. The concentration of utilities, services and white-collar employment in the centre makes it attractive to the middle classes, who are both unable to afford the high costs of private transport and unwilling to face the inadequacies of the public systems. They were certainly far more centralised than the very poor, as discussed earlier (Amato 1970). Rent controls have made older properties artificially cheap on a number of occasions, while vertical redevelopment provides up-market accommodation; both processes reinforce the attraction of the central city. Moreover housing is becoming scarcer there as CBD activities expand and the increase in car ownership is reflected in wider streets and parking lots. Little cheap housing is to be had there and congestion is likely to force out the foci of unskilled employment before those of the white-collar workers. It is not really surprising that the renters of Mexico City's central 'slum' property had higher household incomes than the owners resident in the peripheral *colonias proletarias* (Conway and Brown 1980).

The value of a model is greatly enhanced if it is generally

applicable. There are four prior conditions to be met before Turner's can be relevant. The first pair concerns state permissiveness and the availability of land; these determine whether shanty towns can be established and at what scale. The second refers to the volume and characteristics of the migrants who generate the demand for housing and how the city's housing market reacts to this pressure.

Shanty towns can only exist with the tacit condonation of the state. After all, squatting on land without the prior permission of its owner, or building houses where master plans dictate otherwise, constitutes an illegal act which insecure governments are more likely to interpret as a direct challenge to their authority, rather than as a result of a people desperate for somewhere to live. One can find accounts from just about every corner of the Third World which describe how military bulldozers have razed 'shanty towns' to the ground at some time, while more active repression has included dumping truck-loads of their residents a great distance away in open country. Such actions often decrease when politicians are seeking electoral support and when the scale of the phenomenon makes it puerile. Small, scattered shanty towns are more likely to be cleared repeatedly than where the same number of people are sheltered in a few, very large zones. Over time experience guides potential squatters away from unacceptable sites, such as those that offend the state's sensibilities or cause negative overspill effects on adjoining private property. Cities such as Lima, Dakar and Karachi, which have desert wasteland in the vicinity, are more likely to acquire such settlements than those whose periphery can only be occupied at the expense of intensive market gardening, or with difficulty, owing to the nature of the terrain. Seasonally-flooded land is involved in coastal Jakarta and along the ravines traversing Kuala Lumpur, while construction on stilts is necessary over the tidal swamps of Guayaquil, Recife and Manila. Steep slopes and exposed bedrock are facts of life to countless shanty towns the world over. Any potential for evolution and improvement cannot but be retarded by the characteristics of such sites, especially in cities subjected to uncertain and contradictory policies.

A high proportion of migrants to Latin American cities become permanent residents; they have every incentive to build up a secure base for their families' futures. This is not necessarily the case elsewhere. The average age on marriage is generally lower in

Muslim, Hindu and many African societies. Migrants from the former are more likely to be males who have left their wives and young children in rural villages which are perceived as safer, more peaceful and where it is cheaper for them to live. In many parts of Africa, a sojourn in the city is considered as an essential 'rite de passage' for every young man, apart from an economic necessity. In the former case, ties with the home village need constant maintenance via remittances, visits and local investments. In the latter, a large proportion of the migrant stream is temporary. Such migrants do not generate a demand for family accommodation, nor do they possess a long-term perspective. Shanty towns would appear ill-suited to their needs. In East and West Africa they seek cheap rental accommodation provided by congenial ethnic residents (Kliest and Scheffer 1981). Dormitory accommodation provided by caste groups has served the same purpose in large North Indian cities (Berry and Rees 1969). These patterns of migration were reported frequently in the 1960s and early 1970s; they probably change as many participants appreciate the degree of commitment required if an economic niche is to be obtained in the city. However, the formation of Latin American style shanty towns would seem unlikely, given the different structure of the family. A house in many West African contexts is not perceived just as a shelter for one's wife and children, but as the potential base for a new lineage in the city and the prestige associated with that position. Aspiring migrants need to acquire a large building both as a speculative business — tenants help to pay the rent — and as a means of exerting authority over the group. This is harder to do and involves more than overcoming market forces. The effective gatekeepers to the land are the traditional chief and the prior residents with whom the applicant must ingratiate himself. It does not require a mere commercial transaction, as would be the case in an established Latin American shanty town (Peil 1976). New development at the periphery in Lagos houses both natives and migrants and reflects both the decay of the core and the northwards shift of industry towards the new state capital of Ikeya (Afolayan 1982). In neither case does the settlement perform the roles associated with shanty towns.

As we observed in Chapter 5, unauthorised housing is ubiquitous and takes a great many forms in TWCs. Its appearance is undoubtedly linked to migration and it is a mechanism by which fortunate individuals can consolidate their position in the city.

Turner's model portrays the ideal case, which is clouded by the complexities of reality. In many cities constraints imposed by the state and site availability have prevented self-help development from attaining a basic standard. The model has had a powerful influence on the policy of international consultants and aid donors; the Turner pattern of evolution may become more possible as more states espouse site-and-service schemes in response, provided land is available.

Meanwhile Morris states the case for the expansion of the city being directed by the choices of the rich (Morris 1978). The elite after all are the group with the means to satisfy their whims and they are in contact with foreigners and so most likely to be influenced by their tastes in housing. The old built-up cores of Latin American cities became congested before technology permitted renovations on the vertical scale, but imported cars enabled their owners to escape and yet retain access to their offices and the city's services. European and American culture in the 1920s equated status with the dimensions of the landscaped surroundings of large houses. This called for space, but the choice of area was constrained by what was available at the time. Thus the Caracas elite, flush with the profits of the coffee boom, left the city for the comparatively distant estate of Los Chorros which was put on the market at the time. Status-conscious development, however, exhausts space quickly; subsequent aspirants to this lifestyle were forced to replicate it wherever owners of rural estates were willing to sell. Individual suburbs expanded according to how fashionable they were perceived at the time; this depended either on the identity of their pioneers or on the nature of the surrounding land uses: large parks and high status institutions, such as the university complex, constituted an attractive force, unlike the jails and cemeteries. Subsequently, when the vast investments required to connect such areas to the city's water mains and sewers had been made, it was possible for less wealthy individuals to diffuse outwards and fill in the intervening spaces in a more modest style. By the mid-1970s the valley floor was fully occupied and the elite were on the move again, this time to the hilly, fresher environment of its southern regions, where difficult topography demanded a high rate of initial investment and so guaranteed the exclusivity of the development.

The rich may constitute a minute proportion of most TWCs populations but they consume land and utilities at a greater rate.

The point Morris makes is that their influence on which areas of the periphery are serviced and urbanised is paramount, for the social overhead capital invested in them directs future development long after the original inhabitants have left. The poor can do no more than make use of the sites rejected by all other groups. The model thus provides a healthy reminder of the economic underpinning of TWC evolution, for the elites' skeletal development can serve a far greater population when filtering and densification takes place. A review of the historical development of La Paz would seem to confirm this progression (Lindert and Verkoren 1983). Even in Lima the rich developed a whole series of exclusive neighbourhoods, ranging from coastal Miraflores and Barranco in the 1920s to hilly Monterrico in the late 1970s. This pattern is fostered by contexts in which income distribution is highly skewed and land markets are unfettered by effective planning controls. The stimulus for diffusion stems from the increased demand of the middle classes for modern housing. It is unlikely to arise where these groups remain very small, or impecunious, or where ethnic affiliations condition locational opportunities. Moreover the diffusion of the middle classes can no longer be considered as a spontaneous response to vacated elite suburbs; some of that elite, in their entrepreneurial roles, are actively directing this demand to estates planned with government directives and support. This type of development will be examined next.

Entrepreneurial Initiatives

Profits motivate all entrepreneurs taking initiatives in urban development; they may be made in a variety of ways. One mechanism commonly responsible for the suburban forms of many Western cities was transport. The constructor of a tramline or railway generated both income and future clientele by selling off the land alongside. The low income and technological levels of TWCs made this type of development comparatively rare; most entrepreneurial initiatives have concerned land development and the promotion of housing schemes directly.

An exception is the case of Buenos Aires which was studied by Sargent. Mode of transport underpins his 'dynamic model of urban morphology', although he starts by identifying the sets of variables associated with three interacting 'forces' — the spatial, occupational and temporal (Sargent 1972). The last named represents variables which stimulate change, such as population growth, technological innovations, the state of financial markets and the perceptions of both speculators and buyers of land. These broad conditions have a varied impact on socio-economic and ethnic groups, as they are filtered via income, cost differentials, the location of employment and their perception of the environment. Their reactions are translated into space via the introduction of transport networks, the patterns of land ownership and land speculation, development schemes and the presence of government controls and services. Land occupation patterns are the result of a three phase nested structure: the settlement 'sphere' is a direct product of the 'speculative realm' which arises in response to the transportation framework. Sargent based his model on land sales and the successive improvements made to the transport network centred on Buenos Aires. The nature of the transport determined the frequency and spacing of the stops and so the continuity, density and distance from the centre of settlement (Figure 7.4). Trams and trolley buses were associated with continuous development which trailed off rapidly with distance, while railroads supported clustered settlement around each station for greater distances. These patterns of settlement arose naturally from the pressure of rapid population increase where no planning controls fettered the free market forces acting on land at the city's periphery. Consequently the chain which translated the demand for land into settlement was comparatively short.

The preconditions of this pattern of settlement then were rapid population growth, economic expansion and suitable terrain; these stimulated a variety of speculative developments of which transport is just one example. In Buenos Aires it was particularly prominent because the city's rapid growth coincided with the introduction of the technology which fixed routes in space. The scale of the city then reinforced the need for mass transport and so subways and commuter trains remained important. Elsewhere the role of transport was less prominent. In Caracas, for instance, a train company developed the small suburb of El Paraíso, the first to break out of the confines of the colonial city. In Lima, too, tramlines stimulated growth around the villages of Barranco, Chorillos and Miraflores. But in both cases the real spurt of population increase occurred after the introduction of motor

Figure 7.4

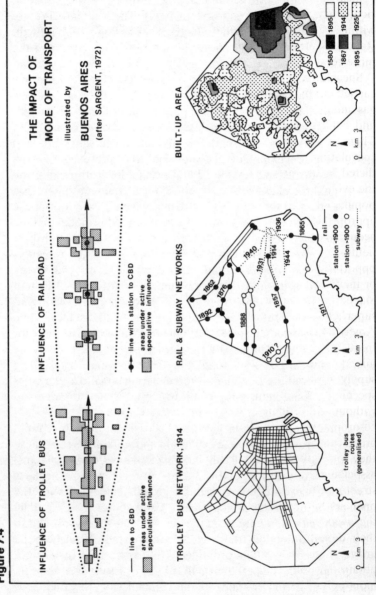

THE IMPACT OF
MODE OF TRANSPORT

illustrated by

BUENOS AIRES
(after SARGENT, 1972)

INFLUENCE OF TROLLEY BUS

— line to CBD

▨ areas under active
   speculative influence

TROLLEY BUS NETWORK, 1914

— trolley bus
   routes
   (generalised)

0 ——— 3
    km   N ▲

INFLUENCE OF RAILROAD

•—— line with station to CBD

▨ areas under active
   speculative influence

RAIL & SUBWAY NETWORKS

—— rail
● station <1900
○ station >1900
······ subway

1862 1876 1892 1888 1857 1911
1940 1931 1914 1944 1936 1865
1910 ?

0 ——— 3
    km   N ▲

BUILT-UP AREA

1580 1867 1895

1895 1914 1925

0 ——— 3
    km   N ▲

vehicles had provided a more flexible form of transport for the rich, while the poverty of the masses still restricted them to sites within walking distance of their employment. In these circumstances, Morris' emphasis on the actions of the elite would appear more relevant.

Speculative development in Latin America's cities was also carried out by the utility companies which provided water, sewers, gas and electricity. Impecunious municipalities granted franchises and concessions to private companies to install these services. Their actions were always motivated by profit and often by speculation. At first sight, their participation might seem as predicted by the 'private city' model developed from observations of the evolution of Philadelphia at a similar period. It depicted a city population engaged in the private search for wealth, as appropriate to a society motivated by individualism and acquisitiveness. The basis for such an urban system was competition; this mechanism provided both the economic opportunities for its citizens and the constraints on their arbitrary or inefficient behaviour. By this means private interests could be made to serve public welfare. This comparison is only relevant at a superficial level, for the economic and social structure of Latin American cities was different (Greenfield 1982). Utility companies frequently gained an exploitative image. Whatever the initial promises, every major city could cite examples of maladjustment of supply to need. Services were used to attract buyers to new speculative developments while densely populated districts went without; elsewhere there was duplication and lack of co-ordination, particularly of trolley-bus routes. The developers' greed caused a whole host of long-term problems for the cities, for they packed in as many lots with street frontages in their associated developments as possible. This gave rise to chaotic street plans, strangely shaped plots and little allowance for public open space or neighbourhood services such as schools. But it was the weak bargaining position of city authorities, attributable to their dependent financial context, that contributed more to the image than the companies' style of development. In order to obtain the utility, the concessionaires often had to be awarded a monopoly. Unfortunately contracts seldom established the responsibilities of the holder to extend the service to all parts of the city and its population. It was extremely difficult to do this later: most utility companies were foreign-owned and, like the national government, raised their capital on the stock markets of Western Europe or North America. The possible repercussions of a lack of confidence on the foreign exchange market, caused by a government imposing conditions on such companies, were so severe that few dared to intervene unless the deficiencies constituted a health or safety risk. São Paulo's municipality, for example, took over the water and sewer company, while gas supplies and the transport and electricity company remained in private hands.

Infrastructure influenced the spatial pattern of a city's growth but was rarely the cause of it. São Paulo could not have supported such activities without the investments of the coffee barons, just as Lima owed its modernisation in the 1930s to the owners of cotton and sugar haciendas up and down the coast. The patterns described are peculiar to Latin America, because private enterprise was constrained in the colonial contexts elsewhere at these periods. When independent countries emerged after the Second World War — in Asia and Africa, technology and the form of foreign intervention had changed. Urban utilities may still be designed and installed by foreign companies via contracts with the state, but generally a parastatal company takes over their administration on completion and the development is planned.

Contemporary entrepreneurial action is more evident within the restricted field of housing where two systems may be discerned. Here the framework is that of finance, not transport. The financial systems determine the scale of demand by defining eligibility to housing: mortgage criteria enable the middle classes to claim modern, mass-produced units, while the certified poor are assigned to low income or site-and-service schemes. The former is the preserve of local entrepreneurs: in Latin America legislation passed in the 1960s and 1970s served to channel private and institutional domestic savings into the housing sector. However, the planned low income arena has been occupied by international finance and charitable funds. The speculative realm defines both the nature of the product and its location in space. Private developments reflect market conditions directly, while state intervention usually filters those affecting the sponsored sector. The contemporary settlement sphere is far more constrained: legal development involves planning permits and agreements with utility companies; accessible land of suitable dimensions is far scarcer and subject to intensive competition. Both systems are fuelled by massive backlogs in demand.

The complex mechanisms involved in providing mass housing in either of these spheres are the focus of the 'managerialism' approach to urban analysis. Urban development is the tangible result of transactions between multiple agencies, each operating under financial, legal and temporal constraints. The identity of each enterprise grants it particular advantages unassociated with the skills required to construct houses. Entrepreneurs operating in the middle-class market in Latin American cities, for instance, need both personal and professional links with landowners, government agencies, financiers and local society. As the greatest profits stem from the top end of a restricted market, the goal is to devise an elite-modelled product cheaply and to promote it to an aspiring status-conscious group. Only those well placed to respond to the social values of that group are likely to succeed, given the highly speculative nature of the market, particularly at times of economic recession and high inflation. Such developments are often sold as a way of life rather than as mere housing. On the other hand international agencies dominate the second arena; here economic criteria play a greater role in the formulation of the project, while political considerations determine whether it is acceptable. The proposed development must satisfy city authorities and local society, rather than the potential users. The agency may be the initiator of the negotiations, rather than a suppliant, but nevertheless it is more constrained in its actions through the need to work with the plethora of often uncoordinated and jealous public authorities, each more concerned about their roles in the political system than with the implementation of a particular project. This type of development is common on a small scale throughout the Third World (Payne 1984).

The managerial approach focuses on the identity of those active in urban development and the factors which stimulate or constrain their operations. It is primarily system-oriented and emphasises economic criteria. Studies reflect on the spatial repercussions of their mechanisms, but the approach is aspatial; analyses establish the factors operating in a particular development's context, but rarely are these woven into a city-wide model of urban structure. Those that attempt this have tended to focus on the intervention of the state as a representative of private interests, rather than in its own name.

State Initiatives

There are two principal schools of thought concerning the state's role in city spatial organisation: the Marxist, which stresses repressive instruments wielded to further dominant socio-economic class interests and the structuralist, which tempers such tendencies in view of the large numbers of the dominated. Marxism and the French school of urban sociology have inspired both approaches, especially the writings of Manuel Castells.

The Marxist model conceives a repressive state whose instruments eject the poor from desirable locations, deny them access to resources and force them to the unserviced periphery or unsavoury sites of the cities. This is the politicised counterpart of the 'private city' model, where the state is pictured as colluding with dominant interests so as to further the profits of property capital. Its instruments underpin various dimensions of city organisation. The legal code and municipal by-laws establish the rights of private property, define acceptable forms and the uses to which it can be put according to location. Planning is the medium which arranges the city to suit particular 'interests'. The nature and pattern of public investment is a means of benefiting groups in a position to gain overspill values through ownership of adjoining property. The state also employs repression directly to protect private property, to hinder if not hound the less well endowed and to silence opposition.

The repressive tactics are felt mostly by the weaker groups and increasing class segregation results in the spatial plane of the city. The inner city provides a major scenario for such action: the poor are systematically weeded out of sites with lucrative development potential by planning mechanisms which both define and condemn substandard property or objectionable land uses. State investments in water mains, roads and services enhance the land values of private proprietors at the expense of taxpayers not so favoured. At the periphery the poor's hard earned services often render them more vulnerable to 'gentrification' owing to the increased burden imposed via the state's taxation of property and lumpy charges for regularisation. Thus the structures of production (land and housing) and financial markets (credit) effectively prevent the poor from participating in formal property production systems, while informal ones are constrained whenever they seem likely to provide a viable alternative.

Such arguments have arisen from analyses of protests stemming from urban renewal schemes and shanty town formation — both conflict scenarios. Every large TWC can provide examples in which small-scale entrepreneurs, tenants and squatters have been evicted at some time, but it requires a conceptual leap to sustain that such action is part of a deliberate and systematic policy to suppress the poor. In Manila, for example, evictions are the consistent actions of a highly repressive state but other income groups suffer in different ways. Moreover, the impact of economic policies varies with the scale at which it is examined; hardship caused to a minority is not necessarily an indicator of a consistent policy of class domination. For example, politically — and economically — weak groups, such as tenants, smallholders and petty entrepreneurs, rather than richer residents were dislodged by the siting of a route for a new link in São Paulo's metro system. Consequently the route cost the city less in compensation to property owners and a mass transit system patronised by many poor groups was improved at the expense of those displaced. It is even harder to associate either political or profit motives to a state which prevents squatting on a municipal rubbish tip or on an unstable river bank. Certainly national social and economic systems are responsible for the desperate poverty of their occupants and those within the city allocate them to such dangerous sites, but surely the charge is that the state has failed to provide better opportunities, rather than that of repression attached to their location.

Given the growth rates experienced by major TWCs, constant repression would seem a very expensive economic and political proposition. Large deprived populations with no hope of improving their conditions constitute an economic burden and a direct political threat which cannot be ignored. Moreover the sheer scale and complexity of the city hinders a concerted policy. The demands of low income groups take varied forms according to the context in which they arise. The state, in the view of the structuralists, attempts to diffuse potential conflict by remoulding these into acceptable forms which can be propagated by its policies. In order to achieve this, it mobilises its own resources and seeks to channel those of independent organisations. Only when these measures fail to quell discontent, will it threaten or suppress those demands it either cannot or chooses not to meet (Burgess 1981).

The mechanisms used to attach low income groups to the state's political machine are manipulative and filtered through a great many departments and quasi-autonomous agencies. Similar forms have been observed in many of Latin America's major cities. Patron-client relationships arise from the selective allocation of resources and permissiveness concerning squatting and illegal sub-divisions of land for low income groups. The provision of utilities, or intercession with those charged with such provision and the promise of regularisation of tenure are used to promote political support. The mechanism involves a reciprocal deal which requires skilful manipulation by both the community and the state's representatives. Paternalism reflects an asymmetrical power relationship in which the petitioners lose their separate identity. Their leaders are co-opted as cadres who are absorbed into the lowest rung of the politico-administrative ladder. Either way, individual neighbourhoods become associated with the sponsors who helped them to improve their material well-being and a potential class-based threat is transformed into a series of dependent areas, each of whom's particular circumstances can be blamed for any breakdown in public provision. In addition site-and-service schemes provide abundant scope for the creation of acquiescent political support. Patronage and favouritism often direct the selection of participants, while the threat of exclusion may always be wielded to quell discontent.

Given the limited resources in TWCs and the fact the state is the largest single source of urban investment, it would be a foolish government which did not use such mechanisms to foster a favourable political climate. The structuralist model is realistic in that it casts the state in the role of an arbiter who cannot afford to ignore the demand of any social class. Moreover, the state must balance private economic interests with the broader goals desirable at city-wide level. Consequently it is quite possible for it to supply utilities to some low income developments, to condone or to regularise others, while at the same time using force to clear a particular site. This approach would seem generally applicable: the processes observed in Mexico City, Valencia and Bogotá could be best accommodated by it (Gilbert and Ward 1985); the continued appearance of illegal colonies in Delhi has been attributed to 'political nepotism and municipal corruption' (Bose 1974); the state's allocative systems were so well understood in Nigeria that the federal government intervened (Onyekwere 1984). The disadvantaged, whether in class, caste or ethnic terms, always will end up concentrated in less favoured locations, unless a radical change in the ideology which structures society takes place. Even in communist China the inherited physical fabric limits the degree of equality in living conditions that can be attained.

An extreme type of repression is fuelled by the concept of racial superiority rather than by social or economic criteria. States developed discriminatory policies and maintained them by force at various times. In pre-colonial days their spatial impact was evident from the 'strangers' quarters' located outside a city's walls or within a particular ward, where the occupants could be watched. European colonial regimes made distinctions based on race and considered non-whites inferior. The spatial consequence was segregation, as illustrated by Dutt's descriptive model of the colonial city in South Asia. This bears a strong resemblance to Calcutta; the 'native' or 'Black town' is separated from the European and each generated its own business core and residential extensions (Dutt in Brunn and Williams 1983).

Some of the mechanisms used to assign populations to their designated areas within cities by colonial regimes were reviewed in Chapter 3. New sites allowed planners to express power and status relationships in city's morphology (see Figure 7.5). The distance between groups was used to symbolise their disparate status and where topography made this impractical, railways and non-residential land uses or areas inhabited by buffer groups could be used as physical barriers to enhance distinctions (Home 1983). When cities already possessed substantial indigenous populations, the desired pattern was achieved via a combination of legislation, coercion and investments in the urban environment. Even so, absolute segregation was probably never achieved and was certainly not maintained, given the relatively short period of colonial control and the rapid expansion of most cities after independence. Such spatial patterns can be surprisingly enduring, although the basis for distinction changes: in contemporary Rabat, for example, selective immigration has fossilised the contrasts between the various parts of the city centre by identifying each with an economic class (Findlay, Findlay and Paddison 1984).

In one case this has not been so. The dominant-dependent relationships established by colonialism elsewhere not only continued in South Africa but have been reinforced by the capitalist systems underpinning industrialisation. The roots of the

Figure 7.5

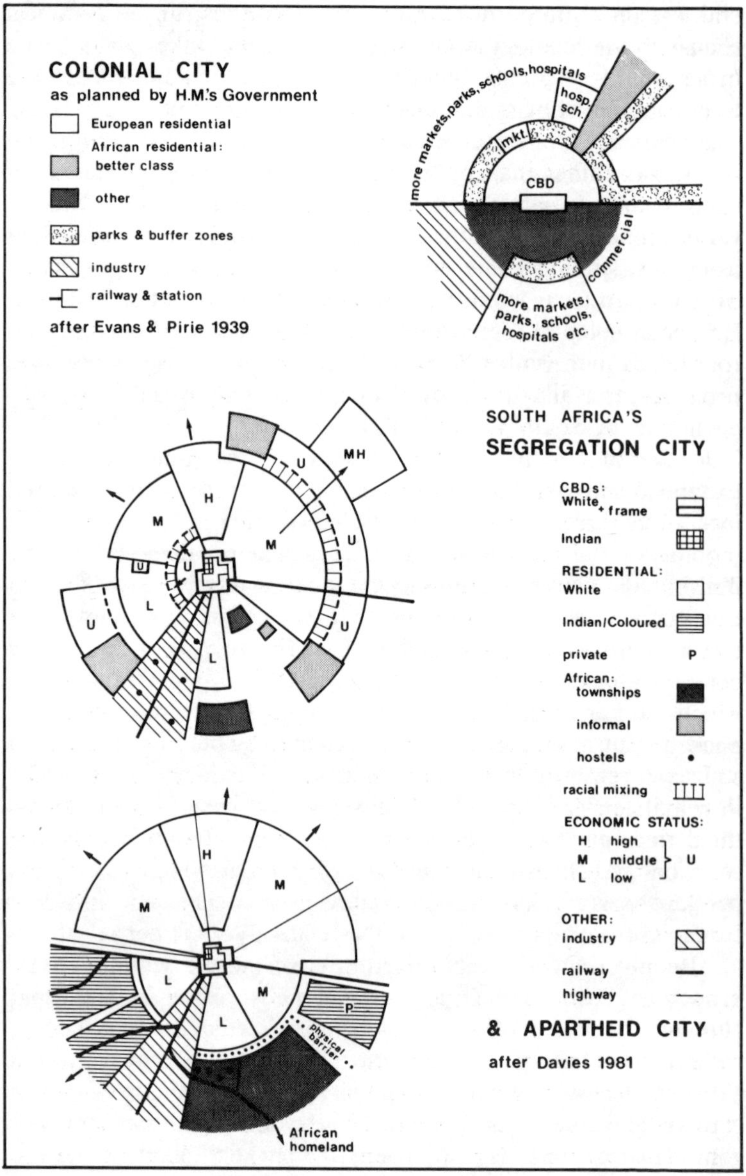

COLONIAL CITY
as planned by H.M.'s Government
European residential
African residential:
better class
other
parks & buffer zones
industry
railway & station
after Evans & Pirie 1939
more markets, parks, schools, hospitals
hosp. sch.
mkt.
CBD
commercial
more markets, parks, schools, hospitals etc.
SOUTH AFRICA'S
SEGREGATION CITY
CBDs:
White + frame
Indian
RESIDENTIAL:
White
Indian/Coloured
private P
African:
townships
informal
hostels
racial mixing
ECONOMIC STATUS:
H high
M middle
L low
U
OTHER:
industry
railway
highway
& APARTHEID CITY
after Davies 1981
physical barrier
African homeland

'segregated city' date back to measures adopted by individual states prior to the formation of the Union. These became progressively more repressive and seem to have been instigated by officials rather than the white population at large; indeed they had to be introduced by stealth as they ran contrary to British policy at the time. In Natal residential segregation was evident from the 1870s and led to the political exclusion and finally to the suppression of the commercial activities of Indians and Africans. Owing to the presence of a prosperous Indian community who were British subjects in Durban, the criteria for citizenship had to be changed to race and 'respectability' rather than property: British subjects could hardly be excluded by legislation designed for the 'native, coloured and uncivilised'. Here the action was prompted by jealousy over the Indian community's greater economic success (Swanson 1983).

As South African cities grew, the discriminating mechanisms enhanced economic distinctions between the races. Poor wages, lack of education, restricted job opportunities, constraints on mobility and family life and the lack of investment in public housing all contributed to the deplorable and depreciating conditions of African city lifestyles. Consequently they were prime targets for the spurious arguments concerning disease common in colonies elsewhere. The outcome was the 'segregation city' in which Africans not employed as domestic servants were either packed away in barrack compounds of their employers or forced to squat wherever possible. Low pay prevented them from competing in rental housing markets while legislation progressively denied them the right to own urban property. Other non-white groups were better off: at least they had their families intact, an independent source of income from trade and were not entirely barred from owning property.

Although all these mechanisms furthered segregation, sporadic growth over time had not fashioned homogeneous ethnic areas (Figure 7.5). As Davies has shown, the CBD had sectors controlled by the Indian or Chinese communities, as well as that of the Whites; there were areas of racial mixing responding to economic class criteria, as well as racial enclaves in otherwise homogeneous zones (Davies 1981). The sponsors of apartheid ideology rejected even this degree of spatial co-existence. The Group Areas Act of 1950 sought to clarify urban spatial arrangements such that the absolute minimum of contact occurred between racial groups.

Enclaves were not permitted; each group could only expand at the periphery of their respective sector and either man-made or physical barriers, such as buffer zones of sterile ground, were to separate peoples. Whenever possible transport routes were to avoid crossing other groups' sectors and grant direct access to employment. The workplace was the only context where racial mixing was permitted and even here ownership of enterprises was constrained on racial grounds. Davies and his colleagues have traced the impact of such laws on the structure of South African cities over 20 years. Populations were moved to achieve the desired patterns; most upheaval was born by non-whites and highly competitive Indian and Chinese traders lost business through their removal from the CBD. The Asian and Coloured populations have been allowed to acquire property within their restricted zones, but the locations of the disenfranchised and impoverished Africans symbolises their status in the eyes of the dominant society. Despite their greater numbers, they occupy comparatively little space, as they are allocated to high density mass public housing schemes or distant townships connected to the 'White city' by high speed commuter trains. Die-hard apartheid supporters would rather they were removed further still to distant 'homelands'.

Although the 'apartheid city' is undoubtedly the picture the Afrikaaner official would like to see, its achievement has not been smooth. Violent resistance has attended the displacement to the homelands, or to isolated townships such as Soweto, or to the destruction of squatter camps like Cross Roads. The model can only be implemented by constant repression on a scale few governments have cared to emulate. Although rustication has been used in China and various countries have striven to control city-ward migration, nowhere else have men been locked into a system of dependent labour relations which forces them to work in the city but never allows them to become part of it. Fortunately the mechanisms which have produced the spatial patterning of South African cities are unique.

Conclusions

Models serve to clarify thought and summarise findings; they reveal as much about the attitudes and analytical tools applied to TWCs as about reality. Frequently models and theory developed in Western contexts have been applied to a TWC to test whether similar patterns can be found. The value of these experiments lies in the explanations offered when they were absent. There are limits to intuition, however: morphological models identify different building forms but the history of these is of less interest than the identity of their present occupants and the roles that they play in contemporary society. Ecological models define and locate social groups within cities but again the explanation for these patterns lies elsewhere. The attraction of the dynamic types of models lies in their focus on a process — migration, land purchase, service provision, the impact of legislation. Social groups are defined and located through the analysis of a specific mechanism. The approaches can be repeated and tested in different cities and so contribute to a model of general application. Despite the criticism of Turner's model, for example, recent analyses of migration within West African cities (Afolayan 1982) suggests that the intra-city migration patterns are not that dissimilar to those observed within Latin America, although the housing forms involved correspond to those peculiar to local society. There are similarities in the observations in Latin American, African and Asian cities as to how authorities attempt to raise political capital from their dealings with low income groups. The state plays a prominent role in certain aspects of TWC morphology through the provision of utilities and major low-income housing schemes. At present increasing attention is being focused on the relationships between international funding agents and the state and their implication for the forms of development adopted within TWCs.

8 CONCLUSIONS

The framework guiding the analyses in this book stems from the premiss that TWCs are different from Western cities because of the position their countries occupy within the international economic system, as this conditions the manner in which their societies and their economies evolve. Well documented research has illustrated the implications of the uneven penetration of capitalist structures in TWCs by focusing on the modes of production within them and their respective labour-absorptive capacities. These studies have led to the rejection of dualist models in favour of schema depicting systematic polarisations; these illustrate how less favoured groups can survive and indeed be interdependent, as well as dependent, on capitalist production. The analysis in this book contributes to the parallel debate concerning modes of distribution. It has concentrated on how flows of resources are structured and consumed by different groups and how these patterns have changed over time. It is apparent that dualist models of consumption suffer from similar shortcomings to those of their productive counterparts for groups vary their 'choice' of market according to the goods or service in question. A more fundamental query arising from the analysis concerns whether other types of mechanisms are also responsible for structuring TWC societies.

Much controversy surrounds the nature of the structures and mechanisms associated with capitalism in Western cities. This arises from different theoretical approaches about how the economic and political elements of society interact. They have given rise to concepts that illustrate the role of the components which reinforce or regulate capitalist mechanisms. Their validity has been tested by examining the changes that take place in the built environment and the conflicts which arise between the various classes that produce and own it on the one hand and those that work and live in it on the other. An equally extensive debate concerns how political and economic interactions reflect and shape the structure of the state. Our interest in these is whether they can explain whether the subordinate position of the Third World within international capitalism causes systematic differences in the structure of consumption within their cities.

Let us examine some of the relevant concepts devised in the First World. Pahl, for example, has concentrated on the role of urban managers — conceived as individuals who control access to both private capital and resources, as well as those who implement the more diffuse goals of the state — by examining the impact of their respective *gate-keeping* practices. The former express their activity via discrimination and the red-lining of particular neighbourhoods, while the latter determine service provision levels and shape plans (Pahl 1975, 1979). Rex, on the other hand, distinguished between classes corresponding to roles in the productive process and those arising from position in the housing market, which reflect type of tenure, or personal attributes (age, race, family composition) which affect access to types of tenure (Rex and Moore 1967).

Discrimination also affects *housing classes* but these often cut across those devised utilising production criteria. Castells' concept of *collective consumption* subsumes both these areas of interest by emphasising the role of consumption as a means of reproducing the workforce and as one peculiarly urban, given the agglomeration tendencies inherent in capitalist productive systems. He explains the increasing interventions of the state in the provision of communal services and infrastructure, which contribute to both production and consumption, by the reluctance of individual firms to invest in support systems whose contribution to profits is indirect, difficult to assess and over the long term. He then argues that the continued privatisation of profits and socialisation of costs leads to the politicisation of consumption and the emergence of inter-class alliances to confront monopoly capitalism (Castells 1977). Harvey's conception of state intervention is as a mediator between different circuits of capitalism which arise from the overaccumulation within the primary industrial sector. Momentum is maintained, when profitable investment opportunities in industry are insufficient, by diverting excess capital into the secondary circuit which aids production indirectly (via fixed capital assets and physical infrastructure) and into a tertiary *consumption fund* composed of support for the former (research, scholarships) or reproduction of the labour force (social expenditures in housing, for example). He agrees that the long-term planning and commitment bound up in these activities discourages firms unless the state intervenes in the capital market and subsidises their investments by such devices as development grants, cheap loans and tax exemptions (Harvey 1973, 1979).

All these concepts attempt to provide a theoretical framework which is both verifiable and capable of explaining behaviour. They are concerned with access to resources and particularly the exchange processes which lead to their consumption, although it is recognised that these need not be different from those involved in production. The filters that regulate access to resources may be strictly economic, that is purchase power which is determined by an individual's participation in production, culturally determined, or politically defined, as when the state contributes to the welfare of those unable to work, or provides goods and services generally and to specific groups. Let us relate these to TWCs.

The dualistic or polarised approach to production within TWCs stems from the fact that large proportions of their populations work in labour-intensive rather than capital-intensive enterprises; these have no access to finance capital and rarely attain profits beyond those required to sustain a very low standard of living. Such entrepreneurs' consumption is constrained not only by their lack of purchasing power but also because their occupation does not generate a predictable income which confers trust in capitalist financial circles. Thus they are debarred from credit purchase systems, particularly those granting sufficient funds at reasonable terms to permit investment in capital equipment or in reproduction, as in the case of housing, education and health. This does not result in parallel economic systems, for those not employed in capitalist enterprises are nevertheless linked to them; they utilise their products in their manufactures, provide some minor service for them or recycle their residues. The position occupied by the Third World is responsible for this asymmetrical relationship. Labour-intensive enterprises combine resources differently and are generally much smaller. One would expect consumption patterns to reflect a similar polarisation.

Capitalism confronts very skewed income distributions within TWCs. There are very wide differentials between the highest and lowest deciles; income is concentrated in the top two or three deciles; the poorest groups barely attain subsistence and often supplement their earned income through subsistence strategies, such as by planting a fruit tree or keeping a few chickens, or through contributions from elsewhere, such as when migrants receive a sack of grain or potatoes from relatives. These traits do not affect the capitalist enterprises producing primary commodities, simple manufactures and assembled goods for export; indeed they benefit from cheap labour. However, they do constrain the domestic market for consumer goods to the extent that imported and artisanal products may be adequate to serve small city markets. This is the stage when dualism most applies, as the quality and type of goods reflect clearly their respective mode of production. Capitalist penetration requires encouragement from the state: import-substitution industries often remain dependent on imported machinery, parts and the subsidies granted by the state because the restricted market does not offer sufficient returns on further investment. Often the very poor depend on the 'excessive' consumption of the wealthy for survival, for they employ them as servants, hand out tips for trivial services such as shoe-shining, carrying market baskets, car-washing or minding and throw out goods which may be recycled via charitable or scavenging activities. Here, gross disparities in acquisitive power are reflected in the markets for different types of goods. State services are limited given their lack of fiscal resources and those that are provided are easily monopolised by the wealthier groups, who are also able to supplement them with private services. The polarisation of consumption would appear similar to that of production visualised by Santos.

The fortunes of export activities affect TWCs directly. The expansion of export sectors result in the absorption of more labour by commercial activities, by the processing and manufacture of exports, or by the bureaucracy, owing to the increased contributions to the state. Nearly all these activities are concentrated in cities and stimulate demand both for services and for goods. The rates of population increase of most TWCs do not mean that the numbers of the very poor are reduced but that the increase in the middle deciles' purchasing power now makes the capitalist production of certain consumer goods more profitable. Western lifestyles become more fashionable to the upper classes; they resist paying higher wages and observing the labour codes where domestics are concerned but are prepared to invest in consumer durables to replace them. This process is uneven, for export-led economies, unless based on a dominant supply of a key resource, are always vulnerable to world market price fluctuations and the policies of the dominant trading blocks. Moreover, the state in many Third World countries is increasingly becoming the majority shareholder of key sections of their economies, which would suggest that it is more likely to provide infrastructure in support of production rather than the reproduction of the labour force. This state of affairs still results in restricted markets for consumer durables, especially when a country only pos-esses a few cities; however, it may stimulate the market for a different form of consumption by the newly pecunious classes. The outcome visualised by Harvey, a boom in urban real estate designed for the middle classes, has been observed. Once again consumption assumes different forms according to the individual's degree of integration with capitalist production networks.

The polarisation of consumption would seem likely to endure for some time yet in TWCs, given the fact that the profitability of Western technology is determined to a great extent by scale economies. In countries with few cities and a small total population, the internal market cannot reach these unless improved communications and increased rural incomes allow industries to serve a national market. Unfortunately, restructuring of production in the countryside, the cause of migration to the cities, rarely seems to lead to increased standards of living for the majority. More densely populated countries possessing many cities have greater opportunity to develop products appropriate for their particular needs and of reaching the thresholds demanded by capitalist production processes. Even so, markets for manufactured goods expand comparatively slowly.

The dimensions of total consumption in TWCs are an indicator of income levels. However, cultural factors may influence both an individual's income through his participation in production and his type of consumption quite independently. In the first case religious or cultural taboos cause individuals to shun particular occupations regardless of their economic potential. This behaviour reserves opportunities for those not so constrained. Individuals may also prefer to employ kin, or those that share their religious or ethnic origins, regardless of their ability. Specialisation by ethnic group is often fuelled by migrants finding employment with their contacts. Similar patterns in consumption are also evident in heterogeneous societies whose constituent groups have different dietary preferences and lifestyles. Cultural allegiance may be expressed in the built environment through customs concerning property. When groups perceive land historically occupied by them as a communal possession of all members, segregation is highly likely. Moreover, although the guarantee of free access to such land undoubtedly reduces living costs within the city, its possession does not grant the benefits associated with landownership in capitalist societies. Its occupants are not free to sell it, nor to allow others to occupy property they have built without the prior consent of the larger group and its leaders. While these rights are increasingly being translated into monetary terms, the fact they exist at all means that such land and property cannot be considered as a commodity exchanged on an open market. A similar situation arises where Islamic laws are still observed and individuals may inherit an unalienable share of a property.

This dimension corresponds to an alternative non-capitalist structure of society which may take several forms. In the *ascriptive-hierarchical* ranking system, birth into a particular group determines an individual's occupation, lifestyle and consumption levels. Many pre-colonial societies were structured on these lines but the caste system in India developed the principle so that the rank of thousands of subgroups was translated into distinctive production and consumption patterns. It must have always been difficult to observe all the institutionalised traits outside the home, given the heterogeneity of population in large cities. Nevertheless the hierarchical organisation of society has endured. The colonial regime may have tried to improve the conditions of the *untouchables* but it also incorporated the traditional elites into its administration, while the members of low castes performed menial and demeaning tasks. This rough hierarchical order is still observable today in Indian cities, although there are cases in which caste rank does not reflect economic rank, such as when leather workers — a scorned group owing to their association with slaughtering — were able to dominate the modern shoe industry or when traditional metal working castes were employed in iron and steel plants. Official state policy is aimed at eroding caste distinctions, which is why caste status is not recorded by the census but the institution is still the dominant criterion in the selection of marriage partners and plays a significant role in occupational behaviour.

Corporate kinship societies are also structured by non-capitalist principles. Access to resources for both production and consumption is mediated by membership of a clan or at least a group with a common ethnic, linguistic, religious or territorial origin. A number of these groups may occur within a single city and their strength is in direct proportion to their size or their dominance of particular activities, rather than to their position on a single social prestige scale. They are common, for example, in West African cities, particularly where land is associated with them, in Malaysian cities where the Chinese, Indian and Malayan communities dominate different sectors of the economy and in those Central American cities where many members of migrant contingents only speak an indigenous language. Most states seem indifferent to such structures unless they have overt economic and political implications. The Malaysian government, for example, discriminates in favour of Malays in an effort to increase their participation in key sectors of the cities' administration and businesses.

State action within TWCs obviously supports production and finance capital. It does this through investments in physical infrastructure, subsidies for industrial production (such as cheap energy), legal provisions which establish the environment in which business is conducted and the physical planning of the cities. These measures reinforce the class consumption structures associated with capitalism in a number of ways. Firstly, planners have imposed the Western practice by which workplaces are separated from the home. Not only does this ensure future investments in roads and increase the costs of servicing outlying dormitories but such provision discriminates against those unable to afford private transport — unless the state is prepared to subsidise the developments by providing mass transport. Secondly, the availability of privately-consumed public services such as potable water, sewers and electricity often reflects not only the ability of potential customers to pay for the service but also their capacity to fund the installations. Large-scale industrialists may be wooed by the provision of fully serviced estates but private householders have to convince the agencies that it is worth their while to service them. Thirdly, state social support systems benefit those engaged in capitalist enterprises: social security systems apply only to those in regular registered employment, who, through this condition, are also eligible to apply for credit and mortgages from state banks. Fourthly the deficiencies in state provision of goods or services, such as primary education or public cleansing, reflects the state's inability to raise sufficient fiscal revenue from the productive process or from profits, whether reaped by individuals or companies.

Superficially state behaviour under conditions of peripheral capitalism would seem to reinforce Western patterns, only the impact of those actions accentuates economic class differentials to a greater extent, given the incomplete and uneven penetration of capitalist structures and the reduced wealth of the state, which prevents it from subsidising those marginalised by it. Non-capitalist structures assure some groups access to particular resources but it is difficult to evaluate how widespread or significant these are. Let us assess whether the evidence presented in previous chapters supports this interpretation of consumption structures.

Consumption in TWCs

Administrators are the state's representatives within cities. In Chapter 4 we examined the position of city administrators within the state hierarchy and the respective responsibilities to cities of the various tiers of government. As in cities the world over, municipal jurisdictions seldom coincided with the functional area of the city and local governments were often formed into larger authorities in order to co-ordinate services. These circumstances render effective administration particularly difficult when city populations are growing rapidly. Nevertheless administrators did not appear to fall into Pahl's two gatekeeping categories of designers of policies at national level and their local implementors. Local authorities appeared to have little power, not because the level of national development was reflected in small budgets generally but because central governments intervened directly in many functions of the city. Decisions to construct state housing, highways or water systems were frequently taken and implemented by national ministries in both small countries with only a few cities and in very large federal states, such as Brazil. Frequently this was attributed to the international financing of such projects, which required the intervention of central government as guarantor. This distinction is also associated with the role of planning, which is frequently the responsibility of national or regional authorities rather than those of cities. (This pattern is often repeated in the private sector, such as when banks assess the credit-worthiness of potential customers at state or national level, rather than in the context in which they reside.) Consequently local gatekeeping is restricted to resources whose characteristics must be assessed locally, such as property.

Both Castells and Harvey theorise about the amount of state revenue levied, from whom it is exacted and how it is spent within cities. Castells visualises an indirect reduction in the costs of production through the state's investments in infrastructure. Within many TWCs such investment is financed overseas, either through soft loans extended by development banks for the specific project, or through general loans by the World Bank to governments. The link to international capitalism is much more direct and bound up with national policies, rather than those explicitly attached to a city and the production within it. A similar point is relevant to Harvey's arguments that overaccumulation in the production circuit will cause the diversion of investment into others. The mere presence of multinational companies in TWCs already indicates their need to colonise new markets; their investment strategies are unlikely to be conditioned by the profits accumulated within a single city or country. In addition, opportunities exist to penetrate sectors of the economy presently in the hands of petty entrepreneurs. Local entrepreneurs would appear more likely to diversify their investments into other circuits, as their alternatives are more restricted and they are more likely to develop closer ties with the state, particularly at local level where they are useful in planning contexts.

The state adopts a more independent role when it attempts to pre-empt a portion of the profits arising from the urbanisation process. These consist of the enhanced values of land, which is one of the few profits that is universally recognised as belonging to the city, rather than to a higher tier of government. Local government also has greater say in how the public services for which it is responsible are allocated. The legacy of past investment automatically benefits those able to command favoured locations in a market economy but there is more scope for manoeuvre when services are extended. Both class and clan interests can exert powerful pressures on such decisions when their scarcity converts them into political rather than mere economic issues. Local governments have often used the offer of provision as a political tool to secure the votes of the deprived. This mechanism is only effective where the franchise does not exclude citizens on the grounds of illiteracy or migrant status.

In conclusion the state influences consumption in cities at numerous levels. Central government intercession with international agencies is responsible for the introduction of particular types of goods and services designed elsewhere; it itself often intervenes directly in the provision of others. These developments are usually imposed on the city from above and may cause many unforeseen repercussions. Local government's role in the city is constrained by the resources and authority vested in it by higher tiers. Frequently its scope for action is narrow and its impact on consumption is limited to the local policies attached to minor services.

The housing delivery systems depicted in Chapter 5 form a segmented market, for which Rex's concept of *housing classes* is appropriate as these cater for distinct clientele. The state housing market operates through a kind of ascription, as eligibility for housing usually rests on employment by the state, or support for the state, rather than on criteria relative to need or to the ability to pay realistic rents for it. On the other hand, the private legal sector caters for the economic classes considered reasonable credit-risks on capitalist criteria. Both ascriptive and economic class traits characterise the unauthorised sector, for while access to particular sites may depend on the identity of the individual, most residents are simply too poor to participate in the open market for housing. The combination of these housing classes within particular cities served to illustrate how they were reinforced both by the state and capitalist structures.

The state in most TWCs demonstrates the influence of external consumption levels through its maintenance of stringent building standards. These reflect in part its own self-image for it inherited stock from its colonial predecessors in many African and Asian countries. It is also expressed in their unwillingness to accept more realistic standards for site-and-service programmes. These projects, often funded by external sources, are a means of incorporating less pecunious classes in the market, as they extend small amounts of credit to enable them to pay for the land over time. However, this finance reflects Harvey's mechanism working at the international level, through the donations by wealthy nations to agencies who allocate it to peripheral nations and to peripheral groups within those nations.

There are also some cases where the state does contribute directly to private investments in housing. The Peruvian government has chosen to do this through fiscal measures: the proceeds of a payroll tax funds a housing bank and the state places contracts in the private sector for the construction of basic housing; a tax on the firms benefiting from this work supports the building materials bank. This intervention seems to benefit Lima disproportionately and is closely tied to the fortunes of the national economy. The type of housing produced is only within reach of relatively pecunious groups. A more indirect way of favouring these groups was observed in Delhi, where the state development authority's release of land reflected open market principles rather than those of need, which was one of the criteria used to justify its land banking activities.

The persistence of the unauthorised sector, despite state dis-approval, underlines the inability of legal market structures to cater for the mass consumption of housing. The scale of the sector in most large TWCs has forced authorities to develop a *modus vivendi* with their inhabitants. Not infrequently the price of regularisation and services has been the taxation of improvements to which the state did not contribute. The sector, despite the pejorative terms attached to it, is made up of a wide range of quasi-legal types of housing as well as squatters on vacant lots. It survives because it is profitable: traditional chiefs gain in stature through the allocation of land to migrants and landlords have found that high profits can be generated by comparatively little investment. It is the only way the poor can hope to gain a secure home. When they build or contract others to build new homes, they consume the materials and services of both capitalist and petty entrepreneurs. Their consumption of housing is spaced out over the long term for they endure extremely poor living condi-tions while gradually improving their homes; some of these never evolve beyond a very basic shelter.

In conclusion, TWC housing markets display substantial differences to their Western counterparts. State housing is usually allocated according to partisan rather than economic rationale. There is some evidence to support Castells' and Harvey's hypotheses about how the state supports the provision of private legal housing but this sector is exceedingly small in most TWCs. Traditional housing allocation procedures persist where indi-genous leaders control access to land. Western cities have no counterpart to the unauthorised housing class which absorbs the majority of poorer residents. The state's inability or unwillingness to assist its activities means that it is forced to regularise the *fait accompli*, rather than to guide its development. Its increasing acceptance of unauthorised housing solutions has been interpreted in Latin American cities as a desire to create political support and to dissipate latent class unrest through the creation of a petty bourgeoisie. Such actions would seem to benefit petty entrepreneurs elsewhere, as a much higher proportion of housing is rented.

The most widespread forms of consumption were discussed in Chapter 6: food, clothing and household goods are mostly produced and distributed by the private sector. The state participates indirectly when it subsidises production or provides grain storage facilities, or when it subsidises the consumption of needy groups. The latter measures are not widespread and seldom seem to achieve their objectives. The number, type and scale of retail outlets reflect the skewed income distribution within TWCs. The preponderance of units selling food, much of it in unprocessed form, is an expression of the minimal purchase power of the mass market. Indeed the logic of scale economies often bars the poor from shopping in capitalist outlets, for goods are sold in too large a unit for those with erratic daily earnings and no means of storing food hygienically. Paradoxically these housewives probably spend more for comparatively poorer quality goods, owing to their need to make frequent small purchases. A certain threshold standard of living must be attained before a household is able to benefit from Western distribution systems.

The comparison of the distribution networks of fresh vegetables in five cities served to illustrate the variety in structure between TWCs. In most cases tiers of petty capitalists made up the chain between producer and consumer, those for perishable goods being the shortest. The interactions within the chain in undeveloped markets reflected the asymmetrical power of the parties, such as when the *bana-bana* in Dakar delayed the payment of producers. Frequently, both producers and wholesalers had to rely on intermediaries for transport. The organisation of the chain often revealed ethnic and kinship ties between producers and distributors, as in Suhum, Kano and Kuala Lumpur. Modern capitalist structures could exist side by side with more traditional systems, as the desire of supermarket chains and food processors to control their supplies led to backward investments in production and transport.

Similar divisions are evident in other types of consumption. In the clothing market both the very rich and the very poor resort to made-to-measure tailors and seamstresses; however, the former utilise imported models and materials and offer their wares in tasteful boutiques. While the latter are more likely to be working from a market stall, at home or any convenient public place. Factory production, most commonly associated with standardised items like shirts and underwear, may be sold in permanent shops of varied status, as well as in market places and by hawkers. There is usually a choice between craft and factory-produced simple consumer goods too. Petty manufacturers convert recycled metal into stoves, sinks and paraffin lamps, the sorts of goods required by the majority of the population. Their factory-made equivalents are often only useful to those with homes equipped with electricity and running water. Even the production of major consumer durables such as vehicles may include craft substitutes, such as the upholstering of cars or the wooden bodies attached to flat-bed trucks to make buses. However such items, and consumer durables generally in the more wealthy cities, are the products of capitalist enterprises and their consumption is encouraged by the availability of the hire-purchase and credit systems offered by large-scale retailers and franchisers. These can make certain items, such as televisions, available to a very wide clientele.

Physical access to retail outlets is a major factor forming consumption patterns, particularly when these entail frequent purchases by clientele without access to transport. Daily needs are still supplied mostly by markets in smaller and less developed TWCs but these can only serve a limited radius. Hawkers without means of transport do not really extend this, indeed they mostly compete with the fixed outlets in the markets. This type of distributive system is threatened by the reallocation of markets to outlying locations and because the area of major TWCs cannot be served from a few fixed points. In more pecunious cities supermarkets may be established in new neighbourhoods before markets owing to their superior investment in transport and wholesale acquistion of stock. Small multi-produce shops soon appear in new neighbourhoods and are able to overcome transport problems because producers of processed and manufactured goods, bottled drinks, cooking oil and soap, for example, are prepared to deliver supplies and offer credit. If markets are the focus of mass consumption, the shopping centre is that of the monied classes. This is where international styles of consumption and methods of shopping are copied. Outlets devote space to displays, have regular promotion campaigns and end of season sales and utilise self-service.

To conclude, purchase power determines the frequency and unit of consumption, as well as the type. The skewedness of effective demand in TWCs is reflected in the ratio of outlets catering to basic needs to all others. The increased area of TWCs and the relocation of food wholesalers has often resulted in a restructuring of retailing in favour of the more capitalised entrepreneurs. The market for processed and manufactured goods is often extended through the willingness of the producer to deliver goods and supply credit to the retailer. Outlets of bulky and heavy luxury goods must also provide a delivery service for customers. State intervention is very slight and usually indirect, such as when it subsidises producers or curtails imports.

Polarised consumption patterns cannot but shape the spatial structure of the TWCs. The descriptive morphological models analysed in Chapter 7 revealed how districts with distinct layouts, building materials and architecture reflected their respective date of creation and their builders. Their arrangement was a product of the status of their occupiers and their functions but many cities outside Latin America bear the signs of dual status systems stemming from their indigenous and colonial roots. Today such dualism is more likely to correspond to polarised consumption patterns, as districts are identified with economic elites and un-authorised housing. However, while the former are an economic class, the residents of unauthorised housing span several. The magnitude of the housing deficit means that the regularly employed, even in low-paid white collar jobs, can be found in that housing class, as well as the itinerant labourer or hawker. The friction of distance and the polarisation in consumption of means of transport is reflected in the higher distance-decay functions of TWCs, particularly when employment opportunities have re-mained concentrated in central locations within smaller cities. When attention was turned to their social ecology, the factors isolated in many African and Asian cities revealed the co-existence of non-capitalist social structures based on ethnic groups and their characteristic family compositions and lifestyles. However, the difficulties of application of social area analysis and the latitudes that the method allows for the subjectivity of the interpreter must place doubt on its usefulness. This is illustrated by the fact that Berry and his associates and Singh based their analyses of Indian cities on the same census data but identified quite different sets of factors.

The dynamic set of models illustrate the mechanisms which underpin different aspects of consumption in cities. Turner and Morris focus on the roles of the homeless and of elites respectively in the creation of new housing districts. Sargent depicted the impact of the introduction of transport on the development of land. The speculative developments undertaken by utility companies, apparently with the connivance of a weak state have attracted such tags as *the private city* or even *the manipulated city*. These models illustrate most clearly the mechanisms of unfettered capitalism. The structuralist model of the cities focuses on the interplay between their economic and political dimensions. The framework allows for the superficial inconsistencies of the state when faced with similar circumstances. Unfortunately, much of the research in this sphere has concentrated on the impact of a single event or its implications for a single or very few areas, usually composed of unauthorised housing. There is an urgent need for more city-wide studies particularly of African and Asian cities. One consistent city-wide state policy that has achieved notoriety is that of *apartheid*. This institution solves the dilemma posed by city economies which depend on cheap, servient labour in a society which rejects the basic human rights of the majority of its subjects. Davies has spelt out the economic and spatial implications of pursuing this policy over time. Here a dualist model of consumption is entirely appropriate.

There are many instances in TWCs in which the state's influence on consumption patterns favours not just class interests but those of specific administrators or entrepreneurs. This informed use of power was evident in Nairobi when residents of a particular district under the 'protection' of a minister openly flouted the city's planning regulations. Another district developed under the patronage extended to certain entrepreneurs by officials. Certain *jhuggi jhompri* in Delhi seemed to live a charmed life considering the widespread implementation of clearance schemes until the identity of their champion was appreciated. The opposite circumstances are more common in most cities: police attention is drawn to specific settlements which just happen to house union leaders or be alongside an official's recently acquired land. There is an underlying strand here which suggests the existence of institutional practices which cannot be classified simply as corrupt or as reflecting class interests. Let us examine these further.

The salient features of these acts are as follows: they are not founded in law and so cannot have contractual obligations; they occur between individuals of different classes and groups; they are based on the principle of reciprocity between unequal partners, in which the promise of goods and services are exchanged for loyalty; they are voluntary and while specific relationships may terminate, the system as a whole is long enduring. The system concerns the use of patrons to mediate the access of a particular group or person to goods or services. They are commonly observed where the state is responsible for the provision of most communal services, such as roads, public lighting and security and in respect of privately-consumed public services, such as water, schools and medical facilities.

These relationships occur, according to Eisenstadt and Roniger, whenever the structure of society and the authority of the state are ambiguous (1980). We have noted that several status systems exist in many TWCs and these are not necessarily cohesive internally. City economic elites, for example, include industrial, commercial and land-owning groups as well as being members of the state with whom they may be linked or be against (Walton 1977). In many societies the boundaries of the kinship are unclear, as traditional patterns of bilateral or multilateral descent give rise to extended families, while the household unit is becoming restricted to the nuclear family. The state is also often fragmented into a host of vertical networks, each with a very narrow scope of action. Their interactions are surrounded by mistrust which gives rise to numerous controls and counterchecks. The impetus for this *transactional model of patronage* is the desire to exchange concrete services for social insurance, for protection against arbitrariness, exigencies and demands. The price of this security is the patron's control over the client's access to markets and public goods. It is most effective when a single market is involved, such as that of services provided by the public sector and when resources are segregated through the fragmentation of authorities responsible for them.

Patron-clientage flourishes when the state is insecure and has a very fragmented structure, especially in association with a society which lacks a clear stratified structure. The introduction of capitalist structures requires both the state and society to develop international links and results in increasing material differences in the standard of living enjoyed by those incorporated by them. The increased competition over consumption stimulated by these changes causes individuals and groups to seek means by which to assure their position in society. As a model, it would seem appropriate to cities such as Lahore (Qadeer 1983), Bombay (Michaelson 1979), Lagos (Barnes 1977), Ibadan (Aronson 1978) and Nairobi (Amis 1984) and probably in smaller, less developed Latin American cities. Although the practice has been described in particular contexts in many TWCs, there is insufficient evidence to claim that it is the dominant mechanism organising consumption.

In conclusion, this book has detected numerous ways in which consumption patterns within TWCs differ from those in capitalist societies and these cannot be attributed to lower purchase power alone. Large-scale capitalism, represented by international companies and institutions, has greater impact within TWCs but these are also structured by indigenous cultural principles. Consumption patterns reflect the contradictions between these influences; patron-client structures are one way in which they may be bridged by individuals.

GLOSSARY

adobe	sun-dried brick in Spanish-speaking countries
audiencia	regional Supreme Court in Spanish colonies
bana-bana	indigenous wholesaler in Senegal
barriada	low income, quasi-legal districts in Peruvian cities
basti	groups of unserviced rented huts erected for tenants in Karachi
bazaar	market in Asian cities
bustee	cluster of generally unserviced huts either rented by landlords or built with their permission by tenants in Calcutta
cabildo	town council in Spanish colonial cities
caliph	traditional supreme civil and religious ruler of Islamic regions
camara	town council in Portuguese colonial cities
cantonment	British military quarters attached to Indian cities
civil lines	area set aside for British colonial officials in India
colonias proletarias	low-income, quasi-legal housing districts in Mexican cities
cordon sanitaire	strip of vacant land between neighbourhoods to prevent spread of contagious disease in French colonial cities
donatarios	areas granted to nobles to administer in the name of the Portuguese crown in the sixteenth century
ejido	a plot of land held in usufruct for agricultural purposes in Mexico; land held in reserve in Spanish colonial towns
ejidatario	a holder of an *ejido*
encomendero	a holder of an *encomienda*
encomienda	a territory administered in the name of the Spanish crown
frei zone	German equivalent of *cordon sanitaire*

Government Reserve Area	district set aside for European residence and institutions in British colonial cities in Africa
haras	city quarters in *medinas*
harasa	equivalent of rates paid to support city watchmen in *medinas*
hikr	a property tax exacted on conquered cities by Islamic rulers
homelands	territories to which the South African government would like to consign all her black population
ḥubūs	land endowed according to Islamic law in North African cities
jaqir	revenue raised from particular tax area in Mogul Empire
jihad	proselytising raids in the name of Islam
jhuggi jhompri	cluster of generally unserviced huts either rented or built by squatters on waste land in Delhi
kampung	indigenous village embedded in Malaysian and Indonesian cities
kharaj	agricultural land tax calculated as a fraction of yields paid in Mogul India and some Arab empires
kotwal	equivalent of city manager in Mogul cities
lotissement	lot provided for the landless in French colonial cities
madrasah	Islamic religious school
Maghreb	Islamic area of influence in North Africa
mahajar	head of guild in Mogul India
medina	Islamic city
mercedes	land grants in early Spanish colonial period
mestizo	man of Spanish and American-Indian parentage
mohulla	ward in Indian and Pakistani cities derived from Arab *maḥallah*
mohulladar	community recognised head of a *mohulla*
muftī	Islamic magistrate
mugli	latrine connected to a pit capable of being emptied from outside the property in Indian cities
muḥtasib	inspector of morals and behaviour in the *sūqs* and other public places in Arab cities
mulk	private land and property in Arab cities

obraje	textile workshops in Spanish colonial cities
octroi	tax exacted on goods entering a city in Pakistan and Northern India
pedicab	bicycle-drawn cab which serves as a taxi in South East Asian cities
pol	indigenous sub-district in some Indian cities
pueblos jovenes	term introduced to upgrade image of legalised *barriadas* in Peruvian cities
qāḍī	Islamic judge; supervises pious foundations in cities
sanda	dry pit latrine in North Indian cities
selva	tropical forest, especially Amazonia
serrano	highlander in Latin America
sierra	mountainous regions in Spanish-speaking countries
shanty town	umbrella term for area of unserviced or inadequately serviced huts made of non- durable materials which lack legal recognition
sharī'ah	Islamic Law
shaykh	traditional headman of a guild or ward in a *medina*
shiqu	urban districts in Chinese cities composed of both inner and suburban sub-districts
shophouse	multistorey property subdivided between retailing, workshops and residential accommodation in Chinese cities
stool chief	paramount chief in West African cities
ṣūfī	Islamic mystic
sūq	traditional market-place in a *medina*
swish	tamped mud construction in African cities
tank	a pool, pond or reservoir in Indian and Pakistani cities
trishaw	tricycle cab in some South East Asian cities
ulamā	scholars versed in Islamic Law
vila	Portuguese town status
villa	Spanish town status
ville neuve	new town set aside for expatriates in French colonial cities
waqf	land endowed according to Islamic law in Middle Eastern cities
zamindar	large-scale landowner or rent franchiser in Mogul India

REFERENCES

Abiodun, J. (1976), 'Housing Problems in Nigerian Cities', *Town Planning Review*, 47, 338–47

Abu-Lughod, J. (1980), *Rabat: Urban Apartheid in Morocco*, Princeton, New Jersey: Princeton University Press

—— (1975), 'The Legitimacy of Comparisons in Comparative Urban Studies', *Urban Affairs Quarterly*, 11, 13–35

—— (1971), *Cairo: 1001 Years of the City Victorious*, Princeton, New Jersey: Princeton University Press

—— (1969), 'Testing the Theory of Social Area Analysis: the Ecology of Cairo', *American Sociological Review*, 34, 198–212

Aderibigbe, A. B. (1975), *Lagos: The Development of an African City*, Lagos: Longman Nigeria Ltd

Adrien-Rongier, M. F. (1981), 'Les kodro de Banqui: un espace urbain "oublié"', *Cahiers d'Études*, XXI (81–3), 93–110

Afolayan, A. A. (1982), 'Residential Mobility Within Metropolitan Lagos', *Geoforum*, 13, 315–25

Ahmad, A. and Singh, A. K. (1982), 'Public Food Distribution Systems in Indian Cities', *GeoJournal*, Supplementary Issue 4, pp. 27–47

Akpan, N. U. (1982), *Public Administration in Nigeria*, Lagos: Longman Nigeria Ltd

Alperovich, G. (1980), 'Determinants of Population Density Gradient in Tel Aviv Metropolitan Area', *Urban Studies*, 17, 185–92

Amato, P. W. (1970), 'A Comparison: Population Densities, Land Values and Socio-economic Class in Four Latin American Cities', *Land Economics*, 47, 447–55

——(1969), 'Population Densities, Land Values and Socio-economic Class in Bogotá, Colombia', *Land Economics*, 46, 66–73

Amis, P. (1984), 'Squatters or Tenants: the Commercialization of Unauthorised Housing in Nairobi', *World Development*, 12, 87–96

Angel, S., Archer, R. W., Tanphiphat, S. and Wegelin, E. A. (1983), *Land for Housing the Poor*, Singapore: Select Books

Arnaud, J. -C. (1972), 'Le ravitaillement de Dakar en produits maraîchers', *Annales de l'Université d'Abidjan*, Series G4, pp. 91–146

Arnillas, F. (1985) 'Política urbana de Acción Popular', *Cuadernos Ciudad y Sociedad* (Quito), 7, 30–54

Aronson, D. R. (1978), 'Capitalism and Culture in Ibadan Urban Development', *Urban Anthropology*, 7, 253–70

Ashraf, A. (1977), *Government and Politics of Big Cities: An Indian Case Study*, Delhi: Concept Publishing Co.

Asiama, S. O. (1984), 'The Land Factor in Housing for Low Income Urban Settlers: the Example of Madina, Ghana', *Third World Planning Review*, 6, 170–84

Ayeni, M. A. O. (1976), 'The Empirical Development of a Disaggregated Residential Location Model in Nigeria', *Annals of Regional Science, 10(3)*, 31–54

Bahl, R. W. (ed.) (1979), *The Taxation of Urban Property in Less Developed Countries*, Madison, Washington: University of Washington Press

—— and Miller, B. D. (1983), *Local Government Finance in the Third World*, Eastborne: Holt-Saunders (Praeger)

Bähr, J. and Mertins, G. (1981), 'A Model of the Social and Spatial Differentiation of Latin American Metropolitan Cities', *Applied Geography and Development, 19*, 22–45

Bähr, J. and Riesco, R. (1981), 'Estructura urbana de las metropolis latino americanas: El caso de la ciudad de Santiago', *Revista de Geografia Notre Grande (Chile), 8*, 27–55

Ballesteros, B. (1972), *Lima: la ciudad y sus monumentos*, Sevilla: Escuela de Estudios Hispano-Americanos de Sevilla

Ballhatchet, K. and Harrison, J. (1980), *The City in South Asia Pre-Modern and Modern*, London: Curzon Press

Barat, J. (1982), 'The Financing of Urban Development in Brazil: the Case of São Paulo Metropolitan Area', *Third World Planning Review, 4*, 128–44

Bardinet, C. (1978), 'La population des vendeurs du grande marché de N'Djamrena en 1976', *Cahiers d'Outre Mer, 31*, 225–50

Barkan, J. D. and Okumu, J. J. (1979), *Politics and Political Policy in Kenya and Tanzania*, New York: Praeger

Barkin, D. (1978), 'Confronting the Separation of Town and Country in Cuba' in W. K. Tabb and L. Sawers, *Marxism and the Metropolis — New Perspectives in Urban Political Economy*, pp. 317–33, New York: Oxford University Press

Barnes, S. T. (1979), 'Migration and Land Acquisition: the New Landowners of Lagos', *African Urban Studies, 4*, 59–70

—— (1977), 'Political Transition in Urban Africa, *Annals of the American Academy of Politics and Social Science, 432*, 26–41

—— and Peil, M. (1977), 'Voluntary Association Membership in Five West African Cities', *Urban Anthropology, 6(1)*, 65–81

Batley, R. (1983) *Power Through Bureaucracy: Urban Political Analysis in Brazil*, Aldershot: Gower

Bayly, C. A. (1983), *Rulers, Townsmen and Bazaars: North Indian Society in the Age of British Expansion 1770–1870*, Cambridge: Cambridge University Press

Beavon, K. S. O. (1982), 'Black Townships in South Africa: Terra Incognita for Urban Geographers', *South African Geographer, 64*, 1–20

Belise, F. J. and Hoy, D. R. (1979), 'The Commercial Structure of Latin American Towns: the Case Study of Sangolqui', Ecuador, *Revista Geográfica, 90*, 43–63

Berry, B. J. L. (1976), *Urbanization and Counter Urbanization 11, Urban Affairs Annual Review*, Beverly Hills: Sage Publication

—— and Spodek, H. (1971), 'Comparative Ecologies of Large Indian Cities', *Economic Geography, 47*, 266–85

—— and Rees, P. H. (1969), 'The Factorial Ecology of Calcutta', *American Sociological Review, 74*, 445–9

Bethell, L. (1984) *The Cambridge History of Latin America*, vols. 1 and 2, Cambridge: Cambridge University Press

Blake, G. H. and R. I. Lawless (1980), *The Changing Middle Eastern City*, London: Croom Helm

Bobo, B. F. (1977), 'Some Observations on Orderly Development in An Emerging city', *Annals of Regional Science*, *XI(1)*, 86–97

Bonine, M. E. (1979) 'The Morphogenesis of Iranian Cities', *Annals of the American Association of Geographers*, *69*, 208–24

—— (1977), 'From Uruk to Casablanca: Perspectives on the Urban Experience of the Middle East', *Journal of Urban History*, *3(2)*, 141–80

Bose, A. (1974), *Studies In India's Urbanization 1901–1971*, New Delhi: Tata McGraw-Hill Publishing Co.

Brand, R. R. (1972), 'The Spatial Organization of Residential Areas in Accra, Ghana', *Economic Geography*, *48*, 284–98

Bromley, R. and Gerry, C. (1979), *The Casual Poor in Third World Cities*, London: Wiley and Sons

Brookfield, H. (1975), *Interdependent Development*, London: Methuen

Brown, L. C. (1973), *From Medina to Metropolis: Heritage and Change in the Near Eastern City*, Princeton, New Jersey: Darwin Press

Brunn, S. D. and Williams, J. F. (1983), *Cities of the World*, New York: Harper and Row

Brush, J. E. (1977), 'Growth and Spatial Structure of Indian Cities' in A. G. Noble and A. K. Dutt, *Indian Urbanization and Planning: Vehicles of Modernization*, pp. 65–92, New Delhi: Tata McGraw-Hill Publishing Co.

Buck, D. D. (1984), 'Changes in Chinese Urban Planning Since 1976', *Third World Planning Review*, *6*, 5–26

Burgess, R. (1985), 'The Limits of State Self-help Housing Programmes', *Development and Change*, *16*, 271–312

—— (1982), 'The Politics of Urban Residence in Latin America', *International Journal of Urban and Regional Research*, *6(4)*, 465–80

—— (1981), 'Ideology and Residential Theory in Latin America' in D. T. Herbert and R. J. Johnston, *Geography and the Urban Environment: Progress in Research and Applications*, *IV*, 57–114, Chichester: John Wiley

Burns, L. S. (1983), 'Self-help Housing: an Evaluation of Outcomes', *Urban Studies*, *20*, 299–309

Campbell, R. W. (1974), 'Stages of Shopping Centre Development in Major Latin American Metropolitan Markets', *Land Economics*, *50(1)*, 66–70

Castells, M. (1977), *The Urban Question*, London: Edward Arnold

—— (1974), *Movimientos Sociales Urbanos*, Madrid: Siglo XXI

Cazamour D'artois, P. and Moya, L. (1984), 'Los mercados y ferias de Quito', *Documentos de Investigaciones* (CEDIG Quito), *5(5)*, 16–44

Chana, T. S. (1984), 'Nairobi: Dandora and Other Projects' in G. K. Payne, *Low-Income Housing in the Developing World*, pp. 17–36, Chichester: John Wiley & Sons

Chance, J. K. (1980), 'Recent Trends in Latin American Urban Studies', *Latin American Research Review*, *XV*, 183–8

—— (1975), 'The Colonial Latin American City: Pre-industrial or Capitalist?', *Urban Anthropologist*, *4*, 24–8

Chaudhuri, K. N. and Dewey, C. J. (1979), *Economy and Society: Essays in Indian Economic and Social History*, Delhi: Oxford University Press

Chee-Meow Seah (1980), 'Government Choices and Public Transport Operations in Singapore', *Transport Policy and Decision Making*, *1*, 231–51

Cheng, L. K. (1982), 'Fresh Food Supplies in Singapore', *GeoJournal*, Supplementary Issue 4, pp. 61–72

Christopher, A. J. (1983), 'From Flint to Soweto: Reflections on the Colonial Origins of the Apartheid City', *Area*, *15(2)*, 145–9

Clark, B. D. and Costello, V. (1973), 'The Urban System and Social Patterns in Iranian Cities', *Transactions of the Institute of British Geographers*, *59*, 99–128

Clignet, R. and Jordan, F. (1971), 'Ecological Analysis as a Prerequisite to Social Planning: the Case of Douala and Yaounde', *Cahiers d'Études Africaines*, *11*, 261–97

Clignet, R. and Sween J. (1969), 'Accra and Abidjan: A Comparative Examination of the Theory of Increase in Scale', *Urban Affairs Quarterly*, *4*, 297–324

Cohen, M., English, J. and Brookfield, H. (1977), 'Functional Diversity at the Base of the Urban System in Peninsula Malaysia', *Journal of Tropical Geography*, *45*, 12–25

Cohen, M. A. (1974), *Urban Policy and Political Conflict in Africa: A Study of the Ivory Coast*, Chicago: Chicago University Press

Conway, D. and Brown, J. (1980), 'Intra Urban Relocation and Structure: Low Income Migrants in Latin America and the Caribbean', *Latin American Research Review*, *15*, 95–125

Cooper, F. (ed.) (1983), *Struggle for the City: Migrant Labour, Capital and the State in Urban Africa*, Beverly Hills: Sage Publications

Cox, K. R. (ed.) (1978), *Urbanization and Conflict in Market Societies*, London: Methuen & Co. Ltd

Croll, E. (1983), *The Family Rice Bowl: Food and the Domestic Economy in China*, Geneva and London: UNRISD and Zed Press

Crowder, M. 'Indirect Rule French and British Style', *Africa XXXIV*, *3*, 197–205

Cullen, M. and Woolery, S. (eds) (1982), *World Congress on Land Policy 1980*, Lexington, Mass. Lexington Books

Cunningham, W. H. (1974), 'Urban Markets in Industrialized Countries: the São Paulo Experience', *Journal of Marketing*, *38(2)*, 2–12

Dakhil, F. H., Ural, O. and Tewfik, M. F., *Housing Problems in Developing Countries: Proceedings of IAHS International Conference 1978*, vol. 1, Dhahran and Chichester: University of Petroleum and Minerals, John Wiley & Sons

Dannhaeuser, N. (1977), 'Distribution and the Structure of Retail Trade in a Philippine Commercial Town Setting', *Economic Development and Cultural Change*, *25*, 471–503

Davidson, B. (1978), *Africa in Modern History: A Search For A New Society*, Penguin Books

274   *References*

Davies, R. J. (1981) 'The Spatial Formation of the South African City', *GeoJournal*, Supplementary Issue 2, pp. 59–72

Dawsey, S. B. (1979), 'Income and Residential Location in Piracicaba, São Paulo, Brazil', *Revista Geográfica*, *89*, 185

Dayal, P. and Thakur, B. (1976), 'Commercial Ribbons in Patna; Spatial Growth and Functional Structure', *National Geographical Journal of India*, *XXII(3, 4)*, 164–77

Diambra-Hauhouot, A. (1972), 'Le commerce de détail dans l'agglomération d'Abidjan', *Annales de l'Universite d'Abidjan*, Series G4, pp. 39–90

Dietz, H. A. (1982), 'National Recovery vs Individual Stagnation: Peru's Urban Poor Since 1978', Paper delivered at the 44th International Congress of Americanists, University of Manchester

—— (1980), *Poverty and Problem-solving under Military Rule: the Urban Poor in Lima, Peru*, Austin, Texas: University of Texas Press

Doebele, W. A., Grimes, O. F. and Linn, J. F. (1979), 'Participation of Beneficiaries in Financing Urban Services: Valorization Charges in Bogotá, Colombia', *Land Economics*, *55*, 73–91

Drakakis-Smith, D. (1981), *Urbanization, Housing and the Development Process*, London: Croom Helm

DucNhuan, N. (1978), 'Désurbanisation et développement régional du Vietnam (1955/77)', *International Journal of Urban and Regional Research*, *2*, 330–50

Dunkerley, H. B., *et al.* (1983), *Urban Land Policy: Issues and Opportunities*, New York: Oxford University Press

Edwards, M. (1983), 'Residential Mobility in A Changing Housing Market: the Case of Bucaramanga, Colombia', *Urban Studies*, *20(2)*, 131–43

—— (1982), 'The Political Economy of Low-income Housing: New Evidence from Urban Colombia', *Bulletin of Latin American Research*, *1(2)*, 45–61

Eichler, G. (1977), 'From Colonialism to National Independence: Algiers' Social Ecology', *GeoJournal*, *1*, 5–12

Eisenstadt, S. N. and Roniger, L. (1980) 'Patron-client Relations as A Model Structuring Social Exchange', *Comparative Studies in Society and History*, *22*, 42–77

Elvory, P. and Lavely, W. (1977), 'Rustication, Demographic Change and Development in Shanghai', *Asian Survey*, *17*, 440–55

Farmer, E. L., Hambly, G. R. G., Kopf, D., Marshall, B. K. and Taylor, R. (1977), *Comparative History of Civilizations in Asia*, vols. 1 and 2, Reading, Mass.: Addison-Wesley Publishing Inc.

Ferchiou, R. (1982), 'The Indirect Effects of New Housing Construction in Developing Countries', *Urban Studies*, *19*, 167–76

de Figueiredo Ferraz, J. C. (1976), *São Paulo e Seu Futuro*, Rio de Janeiro: Instituto Brasileiro de Administraçao Municipal

Findlay, Allan, Findlay, Anne and Paddison, R. (1984), 'Maintaining the Status Quo: An Analysis of Social Space in Post Colonial Rabat', *Urban Studies*, *21*, 41–51

Findlay, S. (1977), *Planning for Internal Migration: A Review of Issues and Policies in Developing Countries*, Washington: Bureau of the Census, US Department of Commerce

Forde, D. and Kaberry P. M. (eds) (1967), *West African Kingdoms in the 19th Century*, International African Institute, Oxford University Press

Freedman, D. S. (1975), 'Consumption of Modern Goods and Services and its Relation to Fertility: A Study of Taiwan', *Journal of Development Studies*, *12*(1), 95–117

Friedmann, J. and Wolff, R. (1976), *The Urban Transition*, London: Edward Arnold

Frishman, A. (1980), 'The Changing Revenue Base and Budget Crisis of the Kano Metropolitan Local Government', *African Urban Studies*, *8*, 11–20

Frykenberg, R. E. (ed.) (1969) *Land Control and Social Structure in Indian History*, Madison: University of Wisconsin Press

Gakenheimer, R. A. (1972), 'The Early Colonial Mining Town: Some Special Opportunities for the Study of Urban Structure' in Schaedel *et al.*, *Urbanización y Proceso Social en América*, 359–371, Lima: Instituto de Estudios Peruanos

Gale, T. S. (1981), 'Segregation in British West Africa', *Cahiers d'Etudes Africaines*, *XX*, 495–507

—— (1979), 'Lagos: the History of British Colonial Neglect of Traditional African Cities', *African Urban Studies*, *5*, 11–24

Gboyega, A. (1983), 'Local Government Reform in Nigeria' in Mawood, P. (ed.), *Local Government in the Third World: the Experience of Tropical Africa*, Chichester: John Wiley & Sons

Geertz, C. (1963), *Peddlars and Princes: Social Change and Economic Modernization in Two Indonesian Towns*, Chicago: University of Chicago Press

Germani, G. (1980), *Marginality*, New Brunswick, NJ: Transaction Books

Giese, E. (1979), 'Transformation of Islamic Cities in Soviet Middle Asia into Socialist cities' in French, R. A. and Hamilton, F.E.I. (eds),*The Socialist City: Spatial Structure and Urban Policy*, Chichester: John Wiley & Sons

Gilbert, A. G. (1984), 'Planning, Invasions and Land Speculation: the Role of the State in Venezuela', *Third World Planning Review*, *6*(3), 221–4

—— and Gugler, J. (1982), *Cities, Poverty and Development*, Oxford: Oxford University Press

Gilbert, A. G. (ed.), in association with Hardoy, J. E. and Ramirez, R. (1982), *Urbanization in Contemporary Latin America*, Chichester: John Wiley & Sons

Gilbert, A. G. and Ward, P. M. (1985), *Housing, the State and the Poor: Policy and Practice in Three Latin American Cities*, Cambridge: Cambridge University Press

—— (1984), 'Community Action by the Urban Poor: Democratic Involvement, Community Self-help or A Means of Social Control?, Community Participation in Upgrading Irregular Settlements: the Community Response', *World Development*, *12*(8), 769–82

—— (1982), 'Residential Movement Among the Poor: the Constraints on Housing Choice in Latin American Cities', *Transactions of the Institute of British Geographers*, New Series, 7(2), 129–49

Goldman, A. (1974), 'Outreach Consumers and the Modernization of Urban Food Retailing in Developing Countries', *Journal of Marketing*, 38(4), 8–17

Green, H. A. (1977), 'Urban Planning in Nigeria', *Journal of Administration Overseas*, 18, 22–33

Greenfield, M. G. (1982), 'Privatism and Urban Development in Latin America: the Case of São Paulo, Brazil', *Journal of Urban History* 8(4), 397–426

Griffin, E. and Ford, L. (1980), 'A Model of Latin American City structure', *Geographical Review*, LXX, 397–422

Grimes, O. F. (1976) *Housing for Low Income Urban Families*, Baltimore: Johns Hopkins University Press

—— and Lim, G. C. (1976), 'Employment, land values and the residential choice of low income households: the case of Bogotá, Colombia', *Land Economics*, 52, 347–354

Gugler, J. (1980), 'A minimum of urbanism and a maximum of ruralism: the Cuban experience', *International Journal of Urban and Regional Research*, 4, 516–35

—— (1978), *Urbanization and Social Change in West Africa*, Cambridge: University Press

—— and Flanagan, W. G. (1977), 'On the Political Economy of Urbanization in the Third World: the Case of West Africa', *International Journal of Urban and Regional Research*, 1, 272–92

Gwynne, R. N. (1978), 'City Size and Retail Prices in Less-developed Countries: An Insight into Primacy', *Area*, 10(2), 136–40

Haeringer, P. (1973), 'Propriété foncière et politiques urbaines à Douala', *Cahiers d'Études Africaines*, 13, 469–96

—— (1969), 'Structures foncières et création urbaine à Abidjan', *Cahiers d'Études Africaines*, 9, 219–70

Hake, A. (1977), *African Metropolis: Nairobi's Self-help City*, London: Sussex University Press

Handwerker, W. P. (1979), 'Daily Markets and Economic Development', *Human Organization*, 38 366–76

Hanten, E. W., and Ma, L. J. C. (1981), *Urban Development in Modern China*, Boulder, Colorado: Westview Press

Hardoy, J. E. (ed.) (1975), *Urbanization in Latin America: Approaches and Issues*, Garden City, NY: Anchor

—— and Satterthwaite, D. (1981), *Shelter: Need and Response*, Chichester: John Wiley & Sons

Hardoy, J. E. and Schaedel, R. P. (1969), *El Proceso de Urbanización en América desde sus Orígenes Hasta Nuestros Días*, Buenos Aires, Editorial del Instituto Torcuato di Tella

Harris, N. (1978), *Economic Development, Cities and Planning: the Case of Bombay*, Bombay: Oxford University Press

Hart, K. (1973), 'Informal Income Opportunities and Urban Employment in Ghana', *Journal of Modern African Studies*, 11, 61–89

Harvey, D. (1973), *Social Justice in the City*, London: Edward Arnold
—— (1982), *The Limits to Capital*, Oxford: Basil Blackwell
Haynes, K. E. and El-Hakim, S. M. (1979), 'Appropriate Technology and Public Policy: the Urban Waste Management System in Cairo', *Geographical Review*, LXIX, 101–08
HMSO (1908), *Imperial Gazette of India*
Home, R. K. (1983), 'Town Planning, Segregation and Indirect Rule in Colonial Nigeria', *Third World Planning Review*, 5, 165–75
—— (1976), 'Urban Growth and Urban Government: Contradictions in the Colonial Political Economy' in G. Williams, *Nigeria: Economy and Society*, 55–75, London: Rex Collings
Houyoux, J. (1973), *Budgets Ménagers, Nutrition et Mode de Vie à Kinshasa*, Kinshasa: Presses Universitaires du Zaire
Howland, M. (1975), 'Delhi's Large-scale Land Acquisition, Development and Disposal Policy: An Appraisal', *Urban and Rural Planning Thought*, *181(1)*, 23–54
Hoyle, B. S. (1979), 'African Socialism and Urban Development: the Relocation of the Tanzanian Capital', *Tijdschrift voor Economische en Sociale Geografie*, 70, 207–16
Hsu, Y. A. and Pannell, C. W. (1982), 'Urbanization and Residential Spatial Structure in Taiwan', *Pacific Viewpoint*, 23, 22–52
Hull, R. W. (1976), *African Cities and Towns before the European Conquest*, New York: W. W. Norton
Humphrey, D. H. and Oxley, H. S. (1976), 'Expenditure and Household Size Elasticities in Malawi: Urban-rural Comparisons', *Journal of Development Studies*, *12(2)*, 252–69
Hutton, J. (ed.) (1970), *Urban Challenge in East Africa*, Nairobi: East African Publishing House
Imoagene, O. (1978), 'Urban Ecology and Urban Renewal: the Case of Ibadan and Sapele' in Aschbrenner, J. and Collins, L. (eds), *The Processes of Urbanism*, 319–332, The Hague: Mouton
Ingram, G. K. (1982), 'Land in Perspective: Its Role in the Structure of Cities' in M. Cullen and S. Woolery, *World Congress on Land Policy*, 103–18, Lexington, Mass.: Lexington Books
—— and Carroll, A. (1981), 'The Spatial Structure of Latin American Cities', *Journal of Urban Economics*, 9, 257–73
Islam, N. (1982), 'Food Consumption Expenditure Pattern of Urban Households in Bangladesh', *GeoJournal*, Supplementary Issue, 4, 7–14
Jackson, J. C. (1975), 'The Chinatowns of South East Asia: Traditional Components of the City's Central Area', *Pacific Viewpoint*, *16(1)*, 47–77
Jacolin, P., Seck, F. and Ndiaye, A. (1976), 'Actors and Social Forces: Dynamics of Change in An Urban Ward of Dakar', *African Environment*, *2(1–2)*, 20–36
Johnstone, M. (1983), 'Housing Policy and the Urban Poor in Peninsular Malaysia', *Third World Planning Review*, *5(3)*, 249–71
—— (1981), 'The Evolution of Squatter Settlements in Peninsular Malaysian cities', *Journal of South East Asian Studies*, *XII(2)*, 364
—— (1979), 'Urban Squatters and Unconventional Housing in Peninsular Malaysia', *Journal of Tropical Geography*, 49, 19–33

Joshi, H., Lubell, H. and Mouly, J. (1976), *Abidjan: Urbanisation and Employment on the Ivory Coast*, Geneva: ILO

Kabagambe, D. and Moughton, C. (1983), 'Housing the Poor: A Case Study in Nairobi', *Third World Planning Review*, 5, 227–48

Kacowicz, M. (ed.) (1976), *Desenvolvimento e Política Urbana*, Rio de Janeiro: Instituto Brasileiro de Administraçao Municipal

Kanyeihamba, G. W. and McAuslan, J. P. (1978), *Urban Legal Problems in Africa*, Uppsala: Scandinavian Institute of African Studies

Kaynak, E. (1981), 'Food Distribution Systems: Evolution in Latin America and the Middle East', *Food & Policy*, 6(2), 78–90

—— (1980), 'Government and Food Distribution in LDCS: the Turkish Experience', *Food Policy*, 5(2), 132–42

Keung, J. K. (1985), 'Government Intervention and Housing Policy in Hong Kong: A Structural Analysis', *Third World Planning Review*, 7 23–44

Kicza, J. E. (1982), 'The Great Families of Mexico; Elite Maintenance and Business Practices in Late Colonial Mexico City', *Hispanic American Historical Review*, 62, 429–57

Kimani, S. M. (1979), 'Location and Functional Structure of Shopping Centres in Nairobi' in R. A. Obudho, and D. R. F. Taylor, *The Spatial Structure of Development: A Study of Kenya*, Boulder, Colorado: Westview Press

—— (1972), 'The Spatial Structure of Land Values of Nairobi, Kenya', *Tijdschrift voor Economische en Sociale Geografie*, 63, 105–14

King, A. D. (1976), *Colonial Urban Development: Culture, Social Power and Environment*, London: Routledge & Kegan Paul

Kirk, W. (1978), 'Town and Country Planning in Ancient India According to Kantilya's Arthasastra', *Scottish Geographical Magazine*, 94, 67–75

Kirkby, R. J. R. (1985), *Urbanization in China: Town and Country in a Developing Economy, 1949–2000 AD*, London: Croom Helm

Kliest, T. J. and Scheffer, M. R. (1981), 'John Turner's Theory of Intra Urban Mobility and the African Reality', *Tijdschrift voor Economische en Sociale Geografie*, 72, 259–65

Krausse, G. H. (1978), 'Intra Urban Variation in Kampung Settlements of Jakarta: A Structural Analysis', *Journal of Tropical Geography*, 46, 11–46

Kuhn, M. W. (1971), 'The Central Business Function of Sūq el Gabir, Omdurman', *African Urban Notes*, 6(2), 39–53

Kurian, G. T. (1982), *Encyclopedia of the Third World*, revised edn, 3 vols., London: Mansell

Kusnetzoff, F. (1975), 'Housing Policies or Housing Politics: An Evaluation of Chilean Experience', *Journal of Inter American Studies and World Affairs*, 17, 281–310

Lapidus, I. M. (ed.) (1969), *Middle Eastern Cities*, Berkeley and Los Angeles: University of California Press

Latif, A. (1974), 'Factor Structure and Change Analysis of Alexandria, Egypt, 1947 and 1960' in W. P. Schwirian, *Comparative Urban Structure* 332–49, Lexington: D. C. Heath

Laval, G. (1981), 'Enquête sur les "tabliers" de Niamey: dépérissement et reconquête d'une ville', *Cahiers d'Études Africaines*, XXI, 211–20

Lee, Y. and Schmidt, C. G. (1980), 'A Comparative Location Analysis of A Retail Activity: the Gasoline Service Station', *Annals of Regional Science*, *XIV*(2), 65–76

Leeming, F. (1978), *Street Studies in Hong King: Localities in a Chinese City*, Hong Kong: Oxford University Press

Lewandowski, S. J. (1980), *Migration and Ethnicity in Urban India, Kerala Migrants in the City of Madras 1870–1970*, New Delhi: Manohar

—— (1975), 'Urban Growth and Municipal Development in the Colonial City of Madras 1860–1900', *Journal of Asian Studies*, *34*, 341–60

Lewis, B. C. (1976), 'The Limitations of Group Action Among Entrepreneurs: the Market Women of Abidjan, Ivory Coast' in N. J. Hafkin and E. G. Bay, *Women in Africa*, 135–56, Stamford University Press

Lewis, O. (1966) 'The Culture of Poverty', *Scientific American*, October, 19–25

van der Linden, J. J. (1982), 'Squatting by Organised Invasion in Karachi: A New Reply to A Failing Housing Policy', *Third World Planning Review*, *4*(*4*), 400–12

—— *et al.* (eds) (1981), *Between Basti Dwellers and Bureaucrats: Lessons in Squatters Settlement Upgrading in Karachi*, Amsterdam: Vrije Univesitat

Lindert, P. V. and Verkoren, O. (1983), 'Segregación residencial y polítíca urbana en La Paz, Bolivia', *Boletín de Estudios Latinamericanos y del Caribe*, *33*, 127–38

Linn, J. F. (1983) *Cities in the Developing World*, London: Oxford University Press

—— (1981) 'Urban Finances in Developing Countries' in R. Bahl, *Urban Government Finance: Emerging Trends*, 245–83, Beverly Hills: Sage Publication

Loar, R. M. (1980), *An Analysis of Change in the Factor Structure of Three Puerto Rican Cities 1960–1970*, PhD thesis, Ohio State University

Lomnitz, L. (1978), 'Mechanisms of Articulation Between Shanty Town Settlers and the Urban System', *Urban Anthropology*, 7, 185–205

Lowder, S. (1982), 'From Lemmings to Guinea Pigs: the Role of the Urban Poor in Latin American Cities', *Bulletin of Latin American Research*, vol. 2, 113–22

—— (1978), 'The Context of Latin American Labour Migration: A Review of the Literature Post 1970', *Sage Race Relations Abstracts*, vol. 3, 1–50

—— (1973), *Aspects of Internal Migration in Peru: Two Case Studies*, PhD thesis, University of Liverpool

Lubeck, P. M. (1981), 'Islamic Networks and Urban Captialism: An Instance of Articulation from Northern Nigeria', *Cahiers d'Études Africaines*, *XXI*, 67–78

—— and Walton J. (1979), 'Urban Class Conflict in Africa and Latin America', *International Journal of Urban and Regional Research*, *III*(*1*), 3–28

Lubell, H. (1974), *Urban Develpoment and Employment: the Prospects for Calcutta*, Geneva: ILO

Lubell, H. and McCallum, D. (1978), *Bogotá: Urban Development and Employment*, Geneva: ILO

Ma, L. J. C. (1979), 'The Chinese Approach to City Planning: Policy, Administration and Action', *Asian Survey*, *19*, 838–55

Maack, S. C. (1975), 'Public Taps: the Human Dynamics of Urban Improvement', *African Environment*, *1(4)*, 93–110

Majid, R. (1970), 'The CBD of Dacca: Delimitation and Internal Structure', *Oriental Geography*, *14(1)*, 44–63

Makin, J. S. (1984), *Self-help Housing in Mexico City and the Role of the State*, PhD thesis, Heriot-Watt University

Mangin, W. (ed.) (1970), *Peasants in Cities: Readings in the Anthropology of Urbanization*, Boston: Houghton Mifflin

Mann, S. (1984), 'Urbanization and Historical Change in China', *Modern China*, *10(1)* 79–113

Massell, B. F. and Heyer, J. (1969), 'Household Expenditure in Nairobi: A Statistical Analysis of Consumer Behaviour', *Economic Development and Cultural Change*, *17*, 212–34

Mawhood, E. (1983), *Local Government on the Third World: the Experience of Tropical Africa*, Chichester: Wiley

McGee, T. G. (1976a) 'The Persistence of the Proto-proleteriat: Occupational Structures and Planning for the Future of Third World cities', *Progress in Geography*, *Vol, 9*, 3–38

—— (1976b), 'The Place of Street Vendors in the Social and Economic Structure of Asian Cities in *Hawkers In Jakarta*, Jakarta: Atma Jaya University

—— (1967), *The South East Asian City*, London: G. Bell & Sons

Meek, C. K. (1949), *Land Law and Custom in the Colonies*, London: Oxford University Press

Memon, P. A. (1982), 'The Growth of Low-income Settlements: Planning Response to the Peri-Urban Zone of Nairobi', *Third World Planning Review*, *4(2)*, 145–58

Merillat, H. C. L. (1970), *Land and the Constitution in India*, New York: Columbia University Press

Michaelson, K. L. (1979), 'Power, Patrons and Political Economy: Bombay' in M. B. Leons and F. Rothstein, *New Directions in Political Economy: An Approach from Anthropology*, 235–48, Westport, Connecticut: Greenwood Press

Miller, F. and Romsa, G. (1982), 'Residential Mobility, Vacancy Chains and Perceived Benefits from New Detached Housing in Quito, Ecuador', *Tijdschrift voor Economische en Sociale Geografie*, *73(3)*, 162–72

Mills, E. S. and Tan, J. P. (1980), 'A Comparison of Urban Population Density Function In Developed and Developing Countries', *Urban-Studies 17*, 313–21

Mills, E. S. and Song, B. N. (1979), *Urbanization and Urban Problems: Studies in the Modernization of the Republic of Korea 1945–75*, Massachusetts: Council on East Asian Studies, Harvard University

Misra, R. P. (ed.) (1978), *Million Cities of India*, Delhi: Vikas Publishing House

Mittendorf, H. J. (1978), 'The Challenge of Organizing City Food Marketing Systems in Developing Countries', *Zeitschrift fur auslandische Landwirtschaft*, *17(4)*, 323–45

Mohan, R. and Villamizar, R. (1982) 'The Evolution of Land Values in the Context of Rapid Urban Growth: a Case Study of Bogotá and Cali, Colombia in M. Cullen and S. Woolery, *World Congress on Land Policy 1980*, Lexington, Mass.: Lexington Books

Morice, A. (1981), 'Les vélos de Kaolack', *Cahier d'Études Africaines*, *XXI*, 197–210

Morris, A. S. (1978), 'Urban Growth Patterns in Latin America with Illustrations from Caracas', *Urban Studies*, *15*, 299–312

Morris, F. B. and Pyle, G. F. (1971), 'The Social Environment of Rio de Janeiro in 1960', *Economic Geography*, *47*, 286–302

Morrison, M. K. C. and Gutkind, P. C. W. (eds) (1982), *Housing the Urban Poor in Africa*, Syracuse, New York: Syracuse University, Maxwell School of Citizenship and Public Affairs

Morse, R. M. (1975), 'The Development of Urban Systems in the Americas in the 19th Century', *Journal of Inter American Studies and World Affairs*, *17*, 4–26

Moser, C. (1977), 'The Dual Economy and Marginality Debate and the Contribution of Micro-Analysis: Market Sellers in Bogotá, *Development and Change*, *8*, 465–89

Musgrove, P. (1978), *Consumer Behaviour in Latin America: Income and Spending of Families in 10 Andean Cities*, Washington: Brookings Institute

Nelson, J. M. (1979), *Access to Power: Politics and the Urban Poor in Developing Nations*, New York: Princeton University Press

Newcombe, K. (1977), 'From Hawkers to Supermarkets', *Ekistics*, *43*, 336–41

Noble, A. G. and Dutt, A. K. (1982), *India: Cultural Patterns and Processes*, Boulder, Colorado: Westview

—— (eds) (1978), *Indian Urbanization and Planning: Vehicles of Modernization*, Bombay: Tata McGraw-Hill Publishing Co.

Norton, A. and Symanski, R. (1975), 'The Internal Marketing Systems of Jamaica', *Geographical Review*, *65*, 461–75

O'Connor, A. M. (1983), *The African City*, London: Hutchinson

—— (1981), *Urbanization in Tropical Africa: An Annotated Bibliography*, Boston: G. K. Hall

Okpala, D. C. I. (1985), 'Finance for Urban Management: the Evolution and Status of Property Rate Management in Nigeria', *Third World Planning Review*, *7*, 219–40

——(1979) 'Accessibility Distribution Aspects of Public Urban Land Management: A Nigerian Case', *African Urban Studies*, *5*, 24–44

—— (1978), 'Housing Standards: A Constraint on Urban Housing Production in Nigeria', *Ekistics*, *45*, 249

—— (1978), 'Urban Ecology and Urban Residential Themes: Application in Nigeria's Socio-cult Milieu, *Socio-Economic Planning Sciences*, *12(4)*, 177–83

Onibokum, G. A. (1971), 'Housing Finance in Nigeria', *Town Planning Review*, *42*, 277–92

Onokerhoraye, A. G. (1977a), 'The Spatial Pattern of Residential Districts; Benin Nigeria', *Urban Studies*, *14*, 291–302

—— (1977b), 'The Evolution and Spatial Structure of House Types in the Traditional Nigerian City: A Benin Example', *Journal of Tropical Geography*, *45*, 34–42

—— (1977c), 'Occupational Specialization by Ethnic Groups in the Informal Sectors of the Urban Economies of Traditional Nigerian Cities: the Case of Benin', *African Studies Review*, *20(1)*, 53–70

—— (1977d), 'Public Involvement in Urban Development Planning: the Case of Environmental Sanitation in Ibadan', *Journal of Administration Overseas*, *16*, 171–7

—— (1977e), 'The Changing Pattern of Retail Outlets in West African Urban Areas: the Case of Benin Nigeria', *Geografiska Annales*, *59(b)*, 28–42

—— (1975), 'Sociocultural Factors in the Development of Residential Districts in Traditional Nigerian Cities', *African Urban Notes*, *B2(1)*, 29–37

Onyekwere, G. (1984), 'Management Problems of the Proliferation of Local Government in Nigeria', *Public Administration and Development*, *4*, 63–76

Oyebande, L. (1978), 'Urban Water Supply: Planning and Management in Nigeria', *GeoJournal*, *2*, 403–12

Pacione, M. (ed.) (1981), *Problems and Planning in Third World Cities*, London: Croom Helm

Pahl, R. (1975), Whose City?, 2nd edn, Harmondsworth: Penguin

—— (1979), 'Socio-political Factors in Resource Allocation' in D. Herbert and D. Smith (eds), *Social Problems and the City*, London: Oxford University Press

Pannell, C. W. (1976), 'Cities East and West: Comments on Theory, Form and Methodology', *Professional Geographer*, *XXVIII(3)*, 233–40

—— and Ma, L. J. C. (1983), *China: The Geography of Development and Modernization*, London: Edward Arnold

Pasteur, D. (1979), 'The Ibadan Comfort Stations Programme: A Case Study of the Community Development Approach to Environmental Health Improvement', *Journal of Administration Overseas*, *18*, 46–58

Payne, G. W. (ed.) (1984), *Low-income Housing in the Developing World: the Role of Sites and Services and Settlement Upgrading*, Chichester: John Wiley & Sons

Payne, G. K. (1977), *Urban Housing in the Third World*, London: Leonard Hill

Peattie, L. and Aldrete-Haas, J. A. (1981) 'Marginal Settlements in Developing Countries', *Annual Review of Sociology*, *7*, 157–75

Peil, M. (1981), *Cities and Suburbs — Urban Life in West Africa*, London: Africana Publishing Co./Holmes & Meier

—— (1976), 'African Squatter Settlements: A Comparative Study', *Urban Studies*, *13*, 155–66

Peil, M. with Sada, P.O. (1984), *African Urban Society*, Chichester: John Wiley & Sons

Perlman, J. (1976), *The Myth of Marginality: Urban Politics and Poverty in Rio de Janeiro*, Berkeley: University of California Press

Pradilla, E. (1976), 'La ideología burguesa y el problema de la vivienda: crítica de dos teorías', *Ideología y Sociedad*, 16, 70–107

Pryor, E. G. (1983), *Housing in Hong Kong*, 2nd edn, Hong Kong: Oxford University Press

Qadeer, M. A. (1983), *Lahore: Urban Development in the Third World*, Lahore, Pakistan: Vanguard Books Ltd

Rapoport, A. (1976), *The Mutual Interaction of People and Their Built Environment Across Cultural Perspectives*, The Hague: Mouton

Ray, T. (1969), *The Politics of the Barrios in Venezuela*, Berkley, Calif.: University of California Press

Rayfield, J. R. (1974), 'Theories of Urbanization and the Colonial City in West Africa', *Africa*, *XLIV*(2), 163–85

Rex, J. and Moore, R. (1967), *Race, Community and Conflict*, London: Oxford University Press

Rimmer, P. J. (1982), 'Theories and Techniques in Third World Settings: Trishaw Peddlars and Towkays in Georgetown, Malaysia', *Australian Geographer*, *15*(*3*), 147–58

—— and Dick, H. W. (1981), 'Improving Urban Public Transport in S.E. Asia: Reflections on the Conventional and Unconventional Wisdom', *Transport Policy and Decision Making*, *2*, 97–120

Rimmer, P. J., Drakakis-Smith, D. W. and McGee, T. G. (1978), *Food, Shelter and Transport in S.E. Asia and the Pacific*, Canberra: Australian National University, Research School of Pacific Studies

Riofrío, G. and Rodríguez, A. (1980), *De Invasores a Invadidos* (*2*): *Diez Años de Autodesarrollo en una Barriada*, Lima: DESCO

Roberts, B. (1978), *Cities of Peasants*, London: Edward Arnold

Rondinelli, D. A. (1983), *Secondary Cities in Developing Countries: Policies for Diffusing Urbanization*, Beverly Hills: Sage Publications

Rosenthal, D. B. (ed.) (1976), *The City in Indian Politics*, India: Thomson Press

Rothman, N. C. (1975), 'Urban Administration and African Organization in Colonial Central Africa: A Case Study', *African Urban Notes*, *B1*(2), 75–93

Rowat, D. C. (ed.) (1980), *International Handbook on Local Government Reorganization: Contemporary Developments*, London: Aldwych Press

Roxborough, I. (1979), *Theories of Development*, London: Macmillan

Sada, P. O. (1972), 'Residential Land Use in Lagos: An Inquiry into the Relevance of Traditional Models', *African Urban Notes*, *17*, 3–26

Safa, H. I. (ed.) (1982), *Towards a Political Economy of Urbanization in Third World Countries*, Delhi: Oxford University Press

Sánchez, A. and Calderón J. (1980), *El Laberinto de la Ciudad: Políticas Urbanas del Estado 1950–1979*, Lima: DESCO

Santos, M. (1979), *The Shared Space*, London: Methuen

—— (1976), 'Articulation of Modes of Production and the Two Circuits of Urban Economy: Wholesalers in Lima, Peru', *Pacific Viewpoint*, *17*(*1*), 23–36

Sargent, C. (1972), 'Towards A Dynamic Model of Urban Morphology', *Economic Geography*, *48*, 358–74

Sarin, M. (1982), *Urban Planning in the Third World*, London: Mansell

Saunders, P. (1981), *Social Theory and the Urban Question*, London: Hutchinson

Schaedel, R. P., Hardoy, J. E. and Kinzer, N. S. (1978), *Urbanization in the Americas from its Beginnings to the Present*, The Hague: Mouton
Schaefer, K. (1976), *São Paulo: Urban Development and Employment*, Geneva: ILO
Schlyter, A. and Schlyter, T. (1980), *George: the Development of a Squatter Settlement in Lusaka, Zambia*, Stockholm: the National Swedish Institute for Building Research
Schwerdtfeger, F. W. (1982), *Traditional Housing in African Cities: A Comparative Study of Houses in Zaria, Ibadan and Marrakech*, Chichester, John Wiley & Sons
Schwimmer, B. (1979), 'Market Structure and Social Organization in A Ghanaian Marketing System', *American Ethnologist*, 6(4), 682–701
Serjeant, R. B. (1980), *The Islamic City*, Paris: UNESCO
Sethuraman, S. V. (1976), Jakarta: Urban Development and Employment, Geneva: ILO
——— (1981), *The Urban Informal Sector in Developing Countries*, Geneva: ILO
Siddiqi, N.A. (1970), *Land Revenue Administration Under the Mughals 1700–1750*, London: Asia Publishing House, Aligarh Muslim University
Simon, D. (1984), 'Third World Colonial Cities in Context: Conceptual and Theoretical Approaches with Particular Reference to Africa', *Progress in Human Geography*, 8, 493–54
Simons, H. J., Seymour, T., Martin, R. and Miller, M.S. (1976), *Slums or Self-reliance? Urban Growth in Zambia*, Lusaka: Institute for African Studies, University of Zambia
Singh H. (1975), 'Patterns of Socio Economic Structure in Indian Cities', *Asian Profile*, 3, 283–98
Sjoberg, G. (1960), *The Pre-Industrial City*, New York: The Free Press
Skinner, G. W. (1978), 'Vegetable Supply and Marketing in Chinese Cities', *The China Quarterly*, 76, 733–93
Skinner, R. J. and Rodell, M. J. (1983), *People, Poverty and Shelter*, London: Methuen & Co. Ltd
Smith, R. H. T. (ed.) (1978), *Market Place Trade: Periodic Markets, Hawkers and Traders in Africa, Asia and Latin America*, Vancouver: University of British Columbia, Centre for Transportation Studies
Sousson, J. G. (1982), 'Urban Planning and the Community: An Example from the Third World', *Environment and Planning A*, *14*, 901–16
Southall, A. (1971), 'The Impact of Imperialism Upon Urban Development in Africa' in V. Turner, *Colonialism in Africa 1870–1960*, vol. 3, Cambridge: Cambridge University Press
de Souza, A. (1978), *The Indian City: Poverty, Ecology and Urban Development*, New Delhi: Manohar
Spodek, H. (1975), 'From "Parasite" to Generative: the Transformation of Post-colonial Cities in India', *Journal of Interdisciplinary History*, *V(3)*, 413–43
Stanley, J. M. (1980), *Migrant Settlement in West Africa: The Case of Ayija, Kumasi*, PhD thesis, University of Glasgow
Steinberg, F. (1982), 'Slum and Shanty Upgrading in Colombo: A Help

for the Urban Poor?' *International Journal of Urban and Regional Research*, 6(3), 372–92

Strassman, W. P. (1984), 'The Timing of Urban Infrastructure and Housing Improvements by Owner Occupants', *World Development 12*, 743–53

Streefland, P. (1977), 'The Absorptive Capacity of the Urban Tertiary Sector in Third World Cities', *Development and Change*, 8, 293–305

Stren, R. (1970), 'The Evolution of Housing Policy in Kenya', pp. 57–96 in J, Hutton, *Urban Challenge in East Africa*, Nairobi: East Africa Publishing House

—— (1982), 'Underdeveloped, Urban Squatting and the State Bureaucracy: A Case Study of Tanzania', *Canadian Journal of African Studies*, 16, 67–91

Stretton, H. (1978), *Urban Planning in Rich and Poor Countries*, Oxford: Oxford University Press

Suret-Canale, J. (1971), *French Colonialism in Tropical Africa*, New York: Pica Press

Swanson, M. W. (1983), 'The Asiatic Menace: Creating Segregation in Durban 1870–1900', *The International Journal of African Historical Studies*, 16(3), 401–21

Tanabe, H. (1983), 'Characteristics and Problems of Asian Port Cities', *Proceedings of the Department of Humanities, University of Tokyo LXXVIII Series of Human Geography*, 8, 19–42

Taylor, J. L. and Williams, D. G. (ed.) (1982) *Urban Planning Practice in Developing Countries*, Oxford: Pergamon Press

Temple, F. T. and Temple, N. W. (1980), 'The Politics of Public Housing in Nairobi' in M. S. Grindle, *Politics and Policy Implementation in the Third World*, Princeton, New Jersey: Princeton University Press

Thomas, R. N. and Wittick, R. I. (1981), 'Migrant Flows to La Paz, Bolivia, as Related to the Internal Structure of the City: A Methodological Treatment', *Revista Geográfica*, 94, 41–51

Thompson, I. B. (1982), 'The Commercial Centre of Oran', *Occasional Papers*, Geography Department, University of Glasgow

Tickner, V. (1978), 'New Directions in Food Marketing Policies in LDCs', *Food Policy*, 3(4), 299–307

Tinker, H. (1968), *Foundations of Local Self-Government in India, Pakistan and Burma*, London: Pall Mall Press

Tiwari, R. C. (1979), 'A Comparative Analysis of the Functional Structure of Central Business Districts in East Africa' in K. A. Obudho and D. R. F. Taylor, *The Spatial Structure of Development: A Study of Kenya*, Boulder, Colorado: Westview Press

—— (1972), 'Some Aspects of the Social Geography of Nairobi, Kenya', *African Urban Notes*, Winter, 36–61

Todaro, M. P. (1976) *Internal Migration in Developing Countries: A Review of Theory, Evidence, Methodology and Research Priorities*, Geneva: ILO

Turner, J. F. C. (1968), 'Housing Priorities, Settlement Patterns and Urban Development in Modernising Countries', *Journal of American Institute of Planners*, 34, 354–63

—— (1967), 'Barriers and Channels for Housing Development in Modernizing Countries', *Journal of American Institute of Planners*, *34*, 167–87

United Nations (1981), *The Residential Circumstances of the Urban Poor in Developing Countries*, New York: Praeger for the UN

United Nations, Department of International Economic and Social Affairs (1979), *Review of Rent Control in Developing Countries*, New York, United Nations

United Nations, Department of Economic and Social Affairs (1973), *Urban Land Policies and Land-use Control Measures*, vol. 1, *Africa*, New York: United Nations

United Nations, Economic and Social Commission for Asia and the Pacific (1980), *Policies Towards Urban Slums*, ed. by Madhu Sarin, Bangkok: Bouwcentrum International Education

Valladares, L. P. (1978), 'Working the System: Squatter Response to Resettlement in Rio de Janeiro', *International Journal of Urban and Regional Research*, *2*, 12–25

Varley, A. (1985), 'Urbanization and Agrarian Law: the Case of Mexico City', *Bulletin of Latin American Research*, *4*, 1–16

Vaughan, S. and Schwirian, K. P. (1979), 'A Longitudinal Study of Metropolitan Density Patterns in A Developing Country: Puerto Rico, 1899–1970', *Environment and Planning A*, *11*, 423–33

Vincent, J. (1976), 'Urbanisation in Africa', *Journal of Commonwealth and Comparative Politics*, *14(3)*, 286–98

Waldron, K. (1981), 'Public Land Policy and Use in Colonial Caracas', *Hispanic American Historical Review*, *61*, 258–77

Walsh, A. H. (1969), *The Urban Challenge to Government: An International Comparison of 13 Cities*, New York: Praeger

Walton, J. (1977), *Elites and Economic Development: Comparative Studies on the Political Economy of Latin American Cities*, Austin, Texas: University of Texas

Ward, P. M. (ed.) (1982), *Self-help Housing: A Critique*, London: Mansell Publishing Ltd

—— (1981), 'Financing Land Acquisition for Self-build Housing Schemes', *Third World Planning Review*, *3(1)*, 7–20

—— (1981), 'Political Pressures for Urban Services: the Response of Two Mexico City Administrations', *Development and Change*, *12(3)*, 380–407

Winters, C. (1982), 'Urban Morphogenesis in Francophone Black Africa', *Geographical Review*, *72(2)*, 139–54

Yadav, C. S. (1979), *Land Use in Big Cities: A Study of Delhi*, Delhi: Inter India Publications

Yusuf, A. B. (1975), 'Capital Formation and Management Among the Muslim Hausa Traders of Kano, Nigeria', *Africa*, *45*, 167–82

INDEX